CANTERB   LLEGE

5008

Do Fish

Drink Water.

D1100481

Do Fish Drink Water?

Puzzling and Improbable Questions and Answers

Bill McLain

Collins

A hardcover edition of this book was published by William Morrow and
Company in 1999.

First published in Great Britain 2006 by Collins
an imprint of
HarperCollins Publishers
77-85 Fulham Palace Road
London
W6 8JB

www.collins.co.uk

A CIP catalogue record for this book is available from the British Library

ISBN-13   978-0-00-724049-4
ISBN-10   0-00-724049-X

Printed and bound in Great Britain by Clays Ltd, St Ives plc

To Possum, with love

Acknowledgments

Although an author gets the credit for writing a book, there are always others who are instrumental in its creation. I would like to thank them.

First of all, I want to thank the people at Xerox, including Bob Taylor, who persuaded me to accept a position with Xerox, Mark Resch, who persuaded me to write a book, Jeff Simek and Karen Arena, who encouraged and supported me from the beginning and were always there when I needed them, and my wonderful staff, especially Christine Lamm, and Sonja-Lin Rose.

I want to thank Sonia Saruba not only for her wonderful job in editing my original draft but also for her suggestions, comments, and support.

I also want to thank the people at William Morrow, especially my editor, Zach Schisgal, whose insight and recommendations greatly enhanced the book; his assistant, Taije Silverman, who was always there with help whenever I needed it; Rich Aquan for his creativity in designing the wonderful book jacket; Virginia McRae for her excellent job on editing the final draft; and all of the other people at William Morrow who contributed their time and talents.

Finally, I want to thank the thousands of people who have sent me questions. Without them, this book could never have been written.

•

Contents

4 Food

5 Geography

6 History

7 Holidays

8 Language

9   Literature

10   The Human Body

11   Music

12   Odds and Ends

13   Off the Wall

14 Religion

15 Science

16 Sports

Transportation and Travel

18 United States

19 Weather

20 World

Animal

Kingdom

Do dolphins ever sleep? (Yes and no.)

Dolphins must be conscious to breathe. If they went into a full deep sleep, they would suffocate. In addition, they must be constantly alert to avoid danger. Yet virtually every animal needs to sleep. The dolphins have solved this problem in a unique way.

The dolphin brain has two hemispheres, just like ours. However, a dolphin's hemispheres each operate independently of the other. For eight hours, both hemispheres are awake; for the next eight hours, only the left hemisphere sleeps; and for the next eight hours, only the right hemisphere sleeps. This way the entire brain gets eight full hours of sleep, although only half is sleeping at any given time. During the time half the brain is sleeping, the dolphin remains physically active but tends to move as little as necessary.

When the dolphin is sleeping, circumstances and individual preferences determine how it continues to breathe. It may swim slowly and surface only now and then to take a breath. If in shallow water, the dolphin may rest on the bottom and occasionally rise to the surface. Or, it might simply rest at the surface and keep its blowhole exposed.

When a dolphin is underwater, it holds its breath. Just before reaching the surface, it opens the blowhole and begins to exhale. Once at the surface, it quickly takes in air and then closes the blowhole. A dolphin typically surfaces to breathe about every two minutes.

When we breathe, we exchange only about 17 percent of the air in our lungs. The efficient dolphin exchanges about 80 percent of its lungs' air with each breath.

FACTOIDS

It is believed that dolphins can live as long as 50 years.

A group of dolphins is called a "pod." Being social, they tend to congregate and spend their entire lives with fellow podmates. A pod can contain anywhere from 10 to 30,000 dolphins.

Dolphins can look forward with one eye while using the other to look to the side or behind. They see well both underwater and out of the water.

The closest land animal relatives to the dolphin are hoofed animals such as horses and cows.

Dolphins can swim at a sustained speed of 20 mph and can reach 25 mph in short bursts.

Dolphins use clicks, whistles, and other sounds as well as body language to communicate.

A dolphin's brain, in proportion to body size, is larger than a human brain. Dolphins are considered to be extremely intelligent and have developed many unique skills to aid living in their watery environment.

The dolphin produces high-pitched clicks that bounce off any object in its path, whether a fish, rock, or man-made object. By listening to the echo and estimating the time it takes to come back, the dolphin can determine the size of the object and how far away it is. Although similar to SONAR, the dolphin's method is far superior. SONAR uses a single frequency, while a dolphin emits clicks ranging from low to very high frequencies. For instance, the bottlenose dolphin can detect metal as thin as 13 thousandths of an inch.

People who train dolphins have discovered that dolphins can understand words and how the words work together. The trainer might put various objects in a pool and ask the dolphin to pick the "ball" for instance, which the dolphin will do. But if the trainer says, "Basket, ball, in," the dolphin will swim to the ball, pick it up, carry it to the basket, and then put it in the basket.

Dolphins use other skills when hunting for food. A group of dolphins might encircle a school of fish and then take turns swimming to the center for feeding while the other dolphins keep the fish from escaping. Dolphins also often use the shoreline as a barrier to prevent fish from escaping. One dolphin will vocalize a command telling the other dolphins to charge together in a coordinated assault on a school of fish.

A combination of sleek beauty, high intelligence, and an affinity for humans has made the dolphin one of our most loved ocean mammals.

Where do butterflies go in the winter?

Some butterflies live for only a few weeks during the summer. Others hibernate during the winter for up to eight months and then revive in the spring. How long a butterfly lives and whether it hibernates during the winter depends on the species and the time of year the butterfly is born, or more correctly, comes out of its cocoon.

During hibernation, butterflies cling to the boughs and trunks of trees for protection from the drying wind and freezing cold. Many die, but many more survive. As the spring sun warms them, the butterflies begin to move and spread their wings to soak up the warmth of the sun. Then they fly away to feed and mate, and eventually die.

Other butterflies, such as the monarch, migrate over thousands of miles rather than hibernate.

A meteorologist, discovering that a simple model of heat convection possesses intrinsic unpredictability, called it "the butterfly effect," suggesting that the mere flapping of a single butterfly's wings can change the weather.

FACTOIDS

A Native American legend says that to make a wish come true you must catch a butterfly, whisper your wish to it, and then set it free. Your winged messenger will then carry your wish to the Great Spirit who will grant it.

Some species of butterflies have developed a survival tactic by mimicking other butterflies. Certain butterflies are noxious and inedible by birds. Edible butterflies have taken on the same wing markings as their inedible relatives to cheat the birds out of a tasty meal.

Nineteen species of butterflies in the United States are on the endangered species list.

In Appalachia it is believed that if a new bride sees a butterfly on her wedding day it is a sign of good luck.

At one nursing home, butterflies are raised so that Alzheimer's patients can watch and enjoy them. Residents look forward to each day's display of butterflies. Some wait patiently for the transformation from caterpillar to butterfly to take place. Others spend hours just watching the butterflies flutter and then land in the cage to feed.

A growing business is that of supplying butterflies for weddings. Each guest is given an envelope with a butterfly inside. When the bride and groom leave the church, the guests tear open the envelopes to release the butterflies which soar overhead in a group, circle for a short time to create a fluttering canopy, and then fly off.

Why do cats purr? (Does any other animal purr?)

It seems that even scientists are not certain why cats purr. There are three theories. The first is that purring is caused when a cat rapidly contracts the muscles of both the larynx and diaphragm. The second theory is that purring is produced by vibrating membranes close to a cat's vocal cords. These membranes are called "false vocal cords." The third theory proposes that purring is related to the cat's circulatory system. Experts think that muscles around a vein oscillate like a fluttering flag and the noise is amplified by the bronchial tubes and sinuses.

Although most people believe that purring is a sign of content-ment, cats also purr at other times. A kitten purrs to tell its mother it is okay, doing so without interrupting its suckling. A mother cat purrs when approaching her kittens to tell them they are not in danger. Some older kittens purr to entice adults into playing with them. When playing, a dominant cat will purr when approaching a subordinate.

Purring can often mean just the opposite of contentment. A cat may purr when frightened. A sick cat unable to defend itself will purr in an effort to calm a potential aggressor. Cats have been known to purr when giving birth, when they are injured, and sometimes when they are dying. Scientists believe that when a cat purrs, calming endorphins are released. If true, this would explain why cats purr when in pain.

Tigers, leopards, jaguars, ocelots, mountain lions, and cheetahs also purr after a fashion, although experts disagree as to whether their purring is the same as in domestic cats. But after all, they are all members of the cat family.

Is purring unique to members of the cat family? Scientific studies have found that purring occurs in other species, such as black bear cubs and nursing spotted hyenas.

So why do cats purr? Well, it is a voluntary act. And any cat owner knows that a cat won't do anything at all unless it wants to.

FACTOIDS

Because it has no collarbone, a cat can squeeze through an opening that is no larger than the size of its head.

Most blue-eyed white cats are deaf.

The frequency of a cat's purr is about 26 cycles per second, the same frequency as an idling diesel truck engine.

If your cat's name ends in an "ee" sound, such as "Rocky," it will respond more readily than to any other name.

Cats are now the number one pet in the United States, and 37 percent of homes have at least one cat.

A cat can jump the height of up to five times the length of its tail.

The ancient Egyptians, the first to tame cats, used them to control pests around 3000 B.C. When the family cat died, family members shaved their eyebrows in mourning.

A domestic cat can sprint at about 30 mph for a short distance.

A typical cat spends one third of its life grooming itself.

DID YOU KNOW?

Many scientists believe that cats have a very complex language. In addition, each cat has a unique voice. Not only does pitch and loudness vary among cats, different cats even pronounce vowels differently. Although dogs can produce 10 different vocal sounds, a cat can produce almost 100 different sounds.

But to truly understand cat communication, it is easier to interpret body language, especially that of the tail. A rapidly twitching tail means irritation, a slowly moving tail means contentment, a tail between the legs signifies worry, a tail held straight out is a warning, a tail held low with hairs fluffed indicates fear, and a tail held fully erect means "I'm glad to see you."

Ears are another barometer of a cat's feelings: back when angry, flat when scared, and forward when happy or alert.

There are many other forms of cat communication, but we will probably never know them all until the independent cat decides to tell us.

Is it true that elephants are afraid of mice? (You can tell by looking in their eyes.)

There is no evidence that elephants are afraid of mice. Elephants ignore mice and other small creatures because they have poor eyesight and can't see them. An elephant relies mainly on its sense of smell and mice do not smell enough to attract an elephant's attention. The only creatures an elephant fears are humans and large cats such as tigers.

The myth about elephants fearing mice dates back to the ancient Greeks. A Greek fable told about a mouse that crawled up an elephant's trunk and drove it insane. There is no truth to the story.

Another fable tells about a village overrun with mice. The villagers brought in cats to get rid of the mice but the village was eventually overrun with cats. To control the cats, the villagers brought in dogs but soon there were too many dogs. Bulls were used to control the dogs but the town ended up with too many bulls. Finally, in desperation, the villagers brought in elephants to solve their dilemma. Unfortunately, there were soon too many elephants and the villagers brought in mice to scare the elephants away and return the village to its original condition.

FACTOIDS

Elephants are also called "pachyderms," which means thick-skinned.

Elephants are nomadic because they quickly eat up all of the food in any area where they are grazing. Each elephant eats between 300 and 500 pounds of vegetation a day.

An average elephant is from 6 to 12 feet tall at the shoulder and weighs from 5,000 to 14,000 pounds.

An elephant's trunk has over 40,000 muscles and is so sensitive that an elephant can use it to pick up a small coin.

Of all the animals living on earth, the elephant has the largest brain. It is four times the size of a human brain.

An elephant's body language is the same whether it is upset or happy. The elephant holds its tail straight out, flaps its ears, and often trumpets. The emotions of irritation, anger, and joy show only in the elephant's eyes.

Although lions or tigers might kill a baby or young elephant, the only true elephant predators are humans.

In ancient Asia white elephants were extremely rare and regarded as holy animals. It was very expensive to keep one because the elephant required special food and its owner also had to serve the numerous pilgrims that would come to worship it. If a king was displeased with one of his administrators, he would give him a white elephant as a gift. The administrator could not refuse a gift from the king but the upkeep of the elephant could financially ruin its new owner. This is the origin of the expression "white elephant."

The expression "an elephant never forgets" has no factual basis. An elephant's memory is good, but no better than the memory of a cat, dog, or human.

DID YOU KNOW?

Many people have seen films of elephants participating in a tiger hunt or working by hauling logs or other burdens. However, very few people have ever watched elephant polo.

Each December the annual tournament of the World Elephant Polo Association is held on an airstrip in Nepal, just north of the Indian border.

Elephant polo is quite similar to horse polo. Players wear traditional polo hats and use a polo ball and mallets. There are four players on each side. Any elephant, baby, young adult, or mature adult may participate in the game. The largest elephant is always given to the referee because it gives him an excellent vantage point from which to watch the game.

Because of the unique nature of the game, special rules have been instituted. Because one team trained a baby elephant to dribble the ball with its front foot, elephants are no longer allowed to touch the ball with their trunk or feet. Another team trained an elephant to lie down in front of the goal, which now draws a penalty.

The most interesting rule is "Rule 14," which states, "Sugarcane or rice balls packed with molasses and rock salt shall be given to each elephant at the end of the match and a cold beer, or soft drink, to the elephant drivers, *and not vice versa*."

It sounds like a fascinating sport to watch, if you just happen to be in Nepal in December.

On a turkey, what is the name of that red thing that hangs down over the beak? (Make a wish.)

The red fleshy growth from the base of a turkey's beak that hangs down over the beak is officially called a "wattle." However, people in the turkey industry usually use the nickname "snood."

If you remember much about World War II, you've probably heard the word "snood" before. The word originated in the Victorian era as a name for the hair nets women wore for decoration. In the 1930s, a snood came to mean a netlike bag that held the back of a woman's hair at the base of the neck. Snoods became very popular during World War II among women working in factories, to prevent their hair from being caught in the machinery.

It's not known whether the woman's netlike bag hairpiece or the turkey's growth was the first to be called a snood. However, if you look at both, you'll see a distinct resemblance.

Turkeys are native to North and Central America and have been around for approximately 10 million years. The Aztecs in Mexico domesticated the turkey centuries ago and used them for sacrifices to the Aztec gods.

After the conquistadors conquered Mexico in 1520, they took turkeys back to Spain. The turkeys rapidly spread throughout Europe and reached England about twenty years later.

No one knows for sure why they are called turkeys. One explanation is that the North American turkey was confused with the "turkey hen," a bird native to Turkey.

Another explanation is that the name mimics the noise a turkey makes when scared, which sounds like "turk, turk, turk."

Others believe that the Native American word for the bird was *firkee*, which sounds similar to turkey.

FACTOIDS

Domesticated turkeys can't fly because they have been bred to have a large amount of breast meat, which makes them too heavy to get off the ground. However, wild turkeys can fly at speeds of up to 55 mph for short distances and can run on the ground at speeds up to 25 mph.

Turkeys have excellent hearing and eyesight and see in color. However, they have a poor sense of smell.

Although a mature turkey has around 3,500 feathers, Apaches thought the bird was cowardly and refused to eat it or use its feathers on their arrows. However, Native Americans in the Southwest revered and respected the turkey.

Only male turkeys gobble; female turkeys make a clicking sound. Males gobble in the spring and fall to attract females. They also gobble whenever they hear a loud noise.

The first meal that astronauts Neil Armstrong and Buzz Aldrin ate on the moon was roast turkey in foil packets.

In the early 1900s, there were only about 30,000 wild turkeys left in the United States. Wildlife preservation efforts have been so successful that there are now more than 4 million wild turkeys in this country.

Although we've all tried to win the game of breaking a turkey's wishbone so that our wish will come true, few people know how this custom originated.

The Etruscans started it in 322 B.C. In those days, anyone who wanted an egg would wait for a hen to "cluck" and an egg soon followed. This gave the Etruscans the idea that a hen could foretell the future.

If an Etruscan needed an answer to an important question, he or she would draw a circle on the ground and divide it into 24 sections, one for each letter of the alphabet (that's the right number, Etruscans had a shorter alphabet than we do). A kernel of corn was then placed in each section and a hen was placed in the center. The first kernel the hen ate indicated the answer. For example, if an Etruscan was seeking a spouse, the first kernel eaten would indicate the first letter of the future spouse's name.

After the hen ate the kernel, it was sacrificed to a god and its collarbone was saved and dried. The person who had drawn the circle was allowed to make a wish on the bone. Two other people were then allowed to break the bone in the same way we do. The person who got the longer part got his or her wish.

This tradition carried down through Roman times. When the Romans conquered England, the wishbone custom came with them. We got the custom from the English.

We know that people have been breaking wishbones for well over 2,000 years, but we have no idea how many wishes came true.

Is there a land animal that has a body the color of purple grape juice? (A horse of a different color.)

The animal that is usually mentioned as being the color of purple grape juice is the South African blesbok, a type of antelope. The blesbok is actually bright brown in color but because its fur has a purple sheen, the animal looks purple.

Blesboks are medium-sized antelopes but with stronger bodies than similar-size springboks or impalas. They live primarily in Namibia in herds of about 30 animals. The main enemy of the blesbok is the cheetah. One cheetah can completely destroy an entire herd over a period of time. Man is also an enemy of the blesbok and has hunted the animal to near extinction.

Colored animals not only appear in fiction – such as pink elephants, calico cats, Paul Bunyan's blue ox, and Barney the purple dinosaur – but also appear in real life. There are red foxes, orange tigers, and even pink walruses. If you ever see a walrus that appears to be blushing all over, it's only an indication that the animal is warm. When a walrus is warm, its skin turns pink.

Cattle can be red or blue, such as the Estonian Red and the Belgian Blue. Horses have always come in a variety of colors: white, black, gray, chestnut, bay, cremello, buckskin, and palomino.

When a white animal is born to a species that normally does not produce white animals, it is called an albino. This condition occurs if the animal does not have the pigment melanin in its body. Albinos are pure white and usually have pink eyes.

FACTOIDS

The only white koala bear in captivity was born at the San Diego Zoo in California. The koala has white fur, a pink nose, and pink eyes. He is called Onya-Birri, which means "ghost boy" in the language of the Australian aborigines.

There are white alligators with blue or black eyes and dark blotches on their skin but true albino alligators are extremely rare. The only known collection of albino alligators with white skin and pink eyes is at Alligator Adventure in South Carolina.

DID YOU KNOW?

When buffalo roamed the plains of the United States in enormous herds, the odds of a white buffalo being born were 1 in 10 million.

Because the buffalo herds were hunted to near extinction in the late 1800s and only 500 were left in the early 1900s, scientists believed that the white gene was lost and there would never be another white buffalo.

In August 1994, a white female buffalo was born on a farm south of Janesville, Wisconsin. The buffalo, named Miracle, was not an albino. Over time, the fur changed color until it became almost black.

A Native American myth explains that White Buffalo Calf woman came to them during a great famine and brought the buffalos, which provided food and shelter. The legend also says that White Buffalo Calf woman would return someday and unite the nations of the four colors: black, red, yellow, and white.

Another Native American myth says that when the earth was created the four colors of man were given the job of caring for the world's life forces. Africans were to care for fire, Europeans were to take care of the air, Asians were to care for the water, and the people of America were to protect the land.

Is a pinto a breed of horse or just a color? (That's a horse of a different color.)

The pinto, traditionally associated with Native Americans, is a color rather than a breed. Pintos were among the horses that the Spanish explorer Cortés took to South America in the early 1500s. The name comes from *pintado*, which is the Spanish word for "painted."

Pinto coloring falls into two types, predominately white with patches of any other color (called "tobiano"); and a dark color, such as black, with white patches (called "overo"). Another horse that is a color rather than a breed is the palomino.

Some horses look exactly like pintos but are called "paints" rather than pintos. If the horse is a quarter horse or an Arabian horse it is called a paint. Horses of all other breeds are pintos. Pintos are typically used as cow ponies as well as for pleasure riding, showing, racing, and trail riding.

Each pinto or paint horse has a unique pattern and color combination that makes it look unlike any other horse.

Some of the pintos introduced by Cortés escaped and their descendants eventually produced large herds of wild horses that roamed the Great Plains of the Midwest. These horses were popular with Native Americans because they were tough and their coloring was good camouflage when the horses were part of a war party. Over time these hardy horses were also sought by cowboys.

FACTOIDS

Over 50 million years ago the ancestor of the modern horse was only 10 to 14 inches tall.

In Asia and the Middle East horseshoes were actually reed or grass sandals. These were used until the nineteenth century.

An ancient Arabian king entered a battle with his soldiers riding black horses while enemy troops rode white and gray horses. After losing the battle, he reasoned that it was because black horses grew weak in the heat. He ordered all his black horses killed and persuaded other Arab tribes to do the same. As a result, true black Arabian horses are extremely rare, even today.

The brass trim on many draft horse harnesses was originally intended to protect the horse from evil spirits.

The record for horse longevity goes to Old Billy. Born in 1769, he worked as a towing horse until his retirement in 1819. He died three years later at the age of fifty-three.

Horseshoes have been considered lucky for centuries. Although most people hang a horseshoe over a doorway open side up so the luck won't run out, some hang it open side down so that the luck spills over all who enter the house.

Many amazing tales are associated with man's involvement with horses. Once such tale recounts the story of the ancient Greek "dancing horses."

The Greek citizens of Sybaris devised a form of riding in which their horses performed to music. Although spectators loved the performance, the dancing horses caused the downfall of the city.

The legend says that a neighboring town, Crotona, was planning to engage the Sybarites in battle. The Crotona general had a brilliant plan. In addition to his troops, he entered the battle with a group of musicians. As the battle raged, the musicians played tunes familiar to the Sybarites' horses. Suddenly, the entire Sybarite army was in disarray because all the horses had started dancing. As a result, the Crotona general won the battle.

However, Sybaris was not destroyed forever. The Greek town still exists today.

Is it true you can't teach an old dog new tricks? (Every dog has its day.)

Most experts believe that this old saying is completely false. In fact, some say that an older dog might be easier to teach than a puppy because a mature dog has a longer attention span. However, it's best to teach a dog to socialize when it's a puppy. A number of books tell you how to teach an old dog new tricks.

A factor often overlooked in teaching a dog new tricks is the breed of the dog. For example, some of the brightest dogs are the Border collie, poodle, German shepherd, golden retriever, and Doberman pinscher. They usually can understand a new command with five repetitions or less and, once they have learned it, will obey it the first time 95 percent of the time.

On the other hand, dogs with the lowest intelligence are the basset hound, bulldog, bloodhound, chow chow, and Pekingese. It usually takes 80 to 100 repetitions or more before they learn a new command. Once they have learned it, they will obey the command the first time less than 25 percent of the time.

Whether a dog, old or otherwise, learns a new trick really depends on the owner. It is the owner's responsibility to educate the dog and learn to communicate with it. Whenever the owner interacts with the dog, the dog learns something. If the owner is not teaching proper behavior, the dog is learning the wrong behavior.

FACTOIDS

At birth a dalmatian is always pure white. The spots appear later as the dog grows.

The haircut typically seen on poodles is a carryover from when the dog was used as a retriever. Hair pompoms were left on the joints to keep the dog warm and help it swim better.

The "apso" in the Lhasa apso dog from Tibet is a Tibetan word meaning "goatlike." The dog was named after the city of Lhasa in Tibet.

Queen Victoria was the first person in England to ever own a dachshund. Dachshunds were actually bred to fight badgers in their lairs.

The Irish wolfhound is the largest breed of dog and the Chihuahua is the smallest. The Saint Bernard is the heaviest breed.

According to the American Kennel Club, the five most popular breeds of dog, in order, are: Labrador retriever, rottweiler, German shepherd, golden retriever, and poodle – all in the top ten list of most intelligent dog breeds.

DID YOU KNOW?

Although people talk about "training a dog," the truth is that the owner must be trained first. A good dog trainer's prime job is to teach you how to become the trainer for your own dog.

Unlike humans, dogs do not believe in equality. Dogs classify everything as either "leader" or "follower." If you do not become the "leader" the dog will learn nothing. If you start reacting to the dog's behavior, then it is training you!

There are many factors that enter into proper training of an animal. However, the two most important things when dealing with any living creature are quite simple: love and patience.

Do fish drink water? ("Water, water, every where, Nor any drop to drink.")

Although fish do drink water, their primary method of obtaining fresh water is through osmosis. The water seeps into their body through tiny holes in their skin.

Osmosis is simply the movement of a solution (such as salt and water) through a semiporous membrane (such as a fish's skin) until the concentration of the solution becomes equal on both sides of the membrane.

When a fish lives in salt water, the ocean water contains more salt than does the liquid in the fish. Thus, osmosis draws water out of the fish and the fish needs continually to drink water to replenish the liquid being drawn out of its body.

When a fish lives in fresh water, the water has less salt than does the liquid in the fish and water is drawn through the fish's skin into its body. Therefore, freshwater fish do not need to drink water. However, they swallow some water when they open their mouths to eat.

FACTOIDS

Some very small reef fishes live only a few weeks or months, but sturgeons can live to be more than 50 years old. Rougheye rockfish can live to be 150 years old.

The ocean sunfish is so heavy that it is difficult to catch and weigh. All species of this fish are from 7 to 10 feet long. One sunfish tipped the scales at just over 3,100 pounds.

The largest fish is the whale shark, which can be more than 50 feet long and can weigh about 2 tons. The smallest fish is the goby, which is rarely longer than a half inch when it's fully grown.

Although it's estimated that there are 20,000 different species of fish (some scientists believe there may be as many as 40,000 species), the most common fish in the ocean is the cyclothone. It is a deepwater fish about the size of a small minnow and lives in all the oceans of the world at depths of 1,500 feet or more.

DID YOU KNOW?

One of the most fascinating fishes is the seahorse, which is a true fish. These small creatures, which look like miniature horses, have some fascinating habits.

Seahorses are monogamous and stay with one partner for their entire lives. Every morning they perform a greeting dance to reaffirm their pledge to each other. If a partner dies, it is a long time before the seahorse will search for a new partner.

The male seahorse becomes pregnant and nourishes the young until they are born. Once the young are born, parental care ends and the baby seahorses must fend for themselves. A baby seahorse faces many dangers. It must protect itself from predators, and if it mistakenly eats a small air bubble thinking it's food, it will die.

Seahorses are not very agile and rely on camouflage for protection. They can rapidly change the color of their bodies to blend into whatever background they are in at the time.

Unfortunately these wonderful little horselike fishes are becoming an endangered species. Asian countries use them for food, medicine, and aphrodisiacs, and the curio and aquarium market is also steadily growing. China alone consumes over 6 million seahorses a year. There are at least 36 countries engaged in buying and selling seahorses.

A seahorse rarely lives more than three years, but with its popularity as a food and medicine, not many will live even that long.

More questions?
Try these websites.

A VIRTUAL ZOO

http://www.sandiegozoo.org/apps/animals/

This site provides both pictures and descriptions of animals. Click on Mammals, Birds, or Reptiles. Then click on the name of the animal you'd like to see. For other zoo sections, use the Available Main Sections pull-down menus on this page.

LIVESTOCK

http://www.ansi.okstate.edu/

Everything you want to know about livestock: horses, cattle, goats, sheep, pigs – even buffalo and camels. First click on Breeds of Livestock, then click on the category you want to see, such as Horses. Scroll down the left column and select the breed of horse, such as Appaloosa. The page will display a photograph of the horse as well as its history and other interesting information.

CATS

http://noahspets.com/catbreed1.html

This site is very easy to use. Just click on the breed of cat you want to see, such as Siamese. You'll see a photograph of the cat and a very thorough description, including tips on purchasing the cat, related websites, cat care, news, and shows.

2

Clothing
and Apparel

**When and where were the first eyeglasses
made? (Seeing is believing.)**

Although Nero used emerald-colored lenses to view the
gladiator games in A.D. 60, it's questionable whether he could
actually see better. The first "reading glass" was developed around
A.D. 1000 but was more of a magnifying glass than an eyeglass. Most
historians believe the first eyeglasses were invented in 1284 or 1285.
No one knows if the inventor was a monk, a scientist, or a craftsman,
but all agree that the inventor was Italian.

In the 1300s eyeglasses were a luxury used by the rich as a symbol of their wealth and power. However, when Gutenberg invented the printing press in 1456, the history of eyeglasses changed forever. Because of the widespread availability of books, the use of reading glasses gradually filtered down to the common people and became an important part of everyday life.

However, eyeglasses still had a long way to go. Finding a pair that helped the wearer see better was a time-consuming process of trying on one pair after another until sight improved. In the seventeenth century the Spanish invented the first graded lenses, which solved the problem of the trial-and-error fitting of eyeglasses.

Until the eighteenth century, eyeglasses either balanced precariously on the nose or were held by the rim with one hand. Finally, an optician in Paris added short arms that extended to the temples, and an optician in England carried the idea further by extending the arms to the ears. This became the world standard for eyeglass frames.

FACTOIDS

Although many people have heard that Benjamin Franklin invented the first bifocals, they were actually invented by an English optician almost ten years before Franklin.

Approximately 70 percent of the U.S. population wears eyeglasses or contact lenses.

The first eyeglasses were quartz lenses set into bone or metal mountings. The frames looked as if two magnifying glass handles were riveted together to form an inverted V over the wearer's nose.

Leonardo da Vinci had an idea for contact lenses in 1508. In 1845 John Herschel had the same idea but it was almost another 50 years before the first contact lens appeared. A German who made glass eyes blew a lens to cover the eyeball of a man whose eyelid had been destroyed by cancer. The patient wore the lens until his death 20 years later. He never lost his vision.

Perhaps the reason that the patron saint of eyeglass makers is not popular is that it's difficult to remember his name: Sofronius Eusebius Hieronymus.

Where did the idea for underwear come from? (Not from Jockeys.)

U nderwear is one of the earliest known types of clothing; its use was recorded as far back as 3000 B.C. It started as a narrow band around the waist from which both decorative and magical pendants were hung. The Egyptians wore woven material wrapped around the body several times and then tied in front.

Loincloths were worn in Crete around 2000 B.C. They were usually decorated, often with intricate patterns. Even today, loincloths are worn in many tropical and semitropical regions of the world.

Between 2105 B.C. and 1240 B.C., men in Babylonia and Mesopotamia wore loincloths as undergarments and women wore short skirts as undergarments.

Around A.D. 200 the Romans wore undergarments. Both men and women wore a loincloth similar to our modern briefs. The women also wore a breast band called a "mammillare."

In 1850 Amelia Jenks Bloomer advocated a costume for women made up of a short jacket, a skirt extending below the knee, and loose "Turkish" trousers, which were later referred to as "bloomers." This fashion never caught on, but the term "bloomers" stuck and eventually became the name for loose, baggy underwear worn by women.

The term "underwear" did not come into use until 1879.

FACTOIDS

During World War II, Americans stationed in Europe had a hard time finding men's underwear. At that time most Europeans considered underwear to be "optional." Even today American underwear is extremely popular in Europe.

The word "negligee" comes from the French word meaning "careless" or "neglected." The garment was a soft, loose-fitting gown in contrast to the fashion of tightly corseted and laced clothing.

In the 1900s both men and women wore corsets. Men wore them during sports such as horseback riding.

DID YOU KNOW?

No one knows for sure who started manufacturing underwear in the United States. Some claim it was the Union Underwear Company in Indiana. Others say it was BVD (Bradley, Voorhees, and Day were the three founders of the company). Still others say that the first underwear in the United States was imported from Stanfields in Nova Scotia.

Although there is still debate about who first manufactured underwear in the United States, there is no debate about the product itself. Underwear was made of wool and the itching could drive a person crazy. Relief came when the garment was taken off for the night. It wasn't until the 1920s that the process of carbonizing wool to remove burrs created a softer fabric. Eventually cotton became the industry standard for underwear.

Although it rarely happens, cotton underwear can fall apart during washing. Because of this, some people actually take their underwear to the dry cleaners.

But with all the available underwear, one debate still rages on. Which is better for a man to wear, briefs or boxer shorts? Despite many compelling arguments on either side, there is still no answer.

Are denim, jeans, and Levi's the same thing? (Not just for cowboys anymore.)

Denim, jeans, and Levi's are three completely different items. Denim is a very durable cotton fabric that is usually light blue because it is woven with one colored thread and one white thread. However, the origin of denim is still hotly debated by historians, designers, and writers. Most believe that the origin of the word comes from the French *serge de Nîmes*, a serge fabric made in the French town of Nîmes before the seventeenth century. However, serge de Nîmes was a silk and wool fabric while denim is always made of cotton. Some think that denim or serge de Nîmes referred to any fabric with a twill weave that resembled the serge made in Nîmes.

In the sixteenth century a fabric called "jean" became quite popular. It was originally a blend of cotton, linen, and/or wool but by the eighteenth century was made completely of cotton. The name is derived from Genoa, the town in Italy where it was first made. The French called the cloth from Genoa "*gênes*" after the name of that Italian city. Jean cloth was prized because it remained durable even after many washings. Unlike denim, jean cloth is woven from two blue threads rather than a white thread and a blue thread.

Levi Strauss was a wholesale dry goods merchant. After coming to San Francisco in 1853, Strauss earned a reputation for selling quality goods. A tailor who had been making metal-riveted pants for the California gold rush miners needed money for a patent application and asked Strauss to be his partner. The two obtained a patent and began making copper-riveted overalls out of brown cotton duck and blue denim. Denim was a much sturdier fabric than jean cloth.

The company founded by Levi Strauss flourished after his death and the garments produced by the factory were named "Levi's" after Levi Strauss. By the 1920s Levi's had become a synonym for the waist overalls which were the most popular men's work pants in the western United States.

FACTOIDS

Levi Strauss & Company did not start selling its products nationally until the 1950s. Prior to that time people in the Midwest and East could buy products by other manufacturers, but not the true "Levi's jeans."

Approximately 2.5 billion yards of denim are produced throughout the world each year.

Over 515 million pairs of jeans are sold in the United States every year.

Today the word "jeans" refers to any pair of pants with two

pockets in the front, two in the back, and a small change pocket inside the right front pocket. The pants can be made from any fabric, including corduroy, twill, canvas, or denim.

A pair of 1950s Levi's jeans that had never been washed was sold to a collector for $91,000.

Most employees of Levi Strauss & Company wear Levi's jeans to work.

The oldest pair of Levi's jeans in the world were found in an abandoned silver mine in the California Mojave Desert. They had been made in 1890, and the woman who found them patched them up and wore them for some time before selling them back to Levi Strauss & Company. They are known today as the "Calico Mine Pants."

DID YOU KNOW?

It took jeans (or denims or Levi's) many years to climb the ladder of social acceptance.

They were first worn as work clothes because of their durability and were always associated with laborers. In the 1930s the West captured the imagination of people in the United States. Real cowboys as well as stars in Western films wore jeans, and western clothing became a symbol of independence and individualism.

In the late 1940s jeans became more fashionable for leisure activities, but even in the 1950s jeans were associated with juvenile delinquents and could not be worn in most schools. It didn't help that in the 1960s college protesters wore jeans – once more jeans earned a bad reputation.

Attitudes changed in the 1980s and jeans were finally accepted and could be worn almost anywhere, including places where they had previously been banned, such as fine restaurants.

Today jeans have become a symbol of life in the United States and will probably be popular for many decades to come.

What is the origin of the neckties that men wear? (Bow or bola?)

It is possible that neckties date back to prehistoric times, although it cannot be proven. Prehistoric humans may have often puffed and pounded their chests to show authority, and the rank of a male in a prehistoric culture often probably depended on his chest ornaments.

The earliest form of a necktie appears in ancient Rome. Roman public speakers wore a neck cloth to protect their throats and keep them warm. Later on, Roman soldiers wore a neck cloth as did ancient Chinese warriors. It is believed that these were not worn as adornments but were used to pad and support the armor the soldiers wore. However, these neck cloths disappeared completely during the Middle Ages.

Most historians believe that the necktie originated in the 1660s during the reign of Louis XIV of France. A regiment of crack Croatian mercenaries who were celebrating their victory over the Turks visited France and were presented as heroes to King Louis. The king, known for his fondness for fashion, noticed that the Croatian officers wore brightly colored silk handkerchiefs around their necks. The king was so enthralled with these that he made them a royal insignia and created his own regiment of royal "Cravattes." "Cravat" comes from the word "Croat," referring to the Croatians. When today's U.S. soldiers wear their dress uniforms, they also wear colored neck cloths representing their unit (blue for infantry, red for artillery, yellow for armored, and so on).

This new fashion quickly spread to other countries. English gentlemen always wore some type of cloth around their necks, the more elegant the better. Cravats were fashioned from plaid, embroidered linen, and other fabrics. They were often decorated with ribbon bows, lace, and tasseled strings. Some were so high a man couldn't turn his head, while others were so thick they could stop a sword thrust.

In the United States, colonists wore colorful bandannas around their necks rather than cravats. Eventually the cravat shrunk in size and evolved into the modern necktie.

Although most men cannot tie all the common necktie knots, it could be worse. In the 1800s there were 32 different ways to tie a cravat.

FACTOIDS

Until the Civil War, virtually all neckties were imported from Europe except for the "bola" tie that was popular in the Southwest.

When Napoleon wore black silk handkerchiefs around his neck during a battle, he always won. At Waterloo, he wore a white cravat and lost the battle and his kingdom.

The name for the common "four-in-hand" knot comes from English coach drivers who used the knot to handle the reins of a four-horse team.

In 1917 Dr. Walter G. Walford wrote a discourse, "Danger in Neckwear," which claimed that tight collars and ties made people ill by retarding blood flow to the brain.

DID YOU KNOW?

In addition to the standard tie we are familiar with, there is also the bola tie, which is usually a braided leather cord with silver tips at the end. The center of the tie is a brooch, often handcrafted from silver and turquoise, that holds the cords together. The bola tie is so popular in the Southwest that it is Arizona's official state emblem.

The name comes from the leather "bolas" used by the gauchos in Argentina. A bola has three leather straps, each wrapped around a large stone. The gauchos use bolas for hunting rheas and ostriches. When thrown properly, the weighted cords wrap themselves around the bird's legs so it cannot move. (We didn't have the heart to say that the bola constricts or ties the bird's legs.)

More questions?
Try these websites.

FASHION IN THE 1900S

http://www.vintagevixen.com/html/fashionhistory.html

This fascinating site covers lady's fashions in the first seven decades of the twentieth century, including the Gibson girl, flappers, and hippies. Detailed descriptions of the fashions of each decade are included.

CLOTHES IN THE 1800S

http://womenshistory.about.com/od/history18th

Interesting Web pages that describe lady's fashions in the 1800s, including drawings of what a Victorian lady wore and a brief mention of Amelia Jenks Bloomer (creator of the bloomers).

ALL ABOUT SHOES

http://www.designershoes.com

Covers many aspects of shoes, including tips on shoe care, hints for a proper fit, a footwear glossary, and interesting facts and quotes. There are also links to other sites, including footwear of the Middle Ages and a history of Viking footwear.

3

Finance

Does the government still print two-dollar bills? (They're so unlucky that no one uses them anymore.)

In spite of what many people think, the Treasury Department still prints two-dollar bills. However, when a new bill is created it often takes quite some time for people to adjust to it. For some reason, the two-dollar bill has never become popular. Many people consider it unlucky, while others still believe it is not valid currency.

Although the government can create and print new types of bills, it cannot force banks, businesses, or individuals to use them.

If bank customers request a denomination in sufficient quantity, the government will quickly supply the bills needed to stock the bank vaults.

U.S. bills are currently available in denominations of $1, $2, $5, $10, $20, $50, and $100. Up until 1969 the government also produced bills in denominations of $500, $1,000, $5,000, and $10,000. These bills were used primarily for transferring funds between banks. With the electronic transfers used today these larger bills are no longer needed. However, they are still legal tender and may occassionally be found in circulation even today.

The largest bill ever printed was a $100,000 gold certificate issued in 1934. These bills were used only for official transactions and were never placed in circulation.

Although U.S. bills, which are sometimes referred to as "notes," were printed and backed by the government, these are no longer printed. In 1913 Congress passed the Federal Reserve Act, which authorized Federal Reserve Banks to issue bills. These are the only bills being printed today.

FACTOIDS

The Bureau of Engraving and Printing prints approximately 22 million paper bills daily. About 95 percent of these bills replace the soiled and worn bills taken out of circulation, while the remaining 5 percent are used to increase the money supply.

The Lincoln Memorial was dedicated in 1922 with the names of the then 48 states engraved on it. However, if you look at the back of a 5-dollar bill, you will see the Lincoln Memorial and only 26 names.

If you have a bill that has been partially destroyed, you can exchange it for a new bill at any bank, provided you have more than half of the original bill.

You can order uncut sheets of bills through the mail by contacting the mail-order division of the Bureau of Engraving and Printing.

Shredded bills can be recycled into useful products such as

roofing shingles or insulation. They can also be used in novelty items such as pens or jewelry, provided they are in sealed containers. However, shredded bills are sold only to companies that can buy all the shredded bills produced in one year.

All bills are printed on paper that has red and blue fibers embedded in it. It is against the law for any person or firm other than companies authorized by the U.S. government to make this type of paper.

DID YOU KNOW?

Because color copiers are so popular today, U.S. bills are now printed with a number of features to deter counterfeiting.

A clear polyester thread is imbedded vertically to the left of the seal in all bills except the one-dollar bill. The denomination of the bill is printed along the length of this thread and can be read from either the front or the back of the bill by holding it up to the light.

A line of microprinting will eventually be printed on the rim of the portrait on a bill. To the naked eye, it will appear as a solid line, but under a magnifying glass the words "The United States of America" will be visible.

Neither the thread nor the microprinting can be duplicated by today's copiers.

If you suspect a bill is not genuine, you can ask your banker or local police department to examine it for you.

To avoid run-ins with the law, it is strongly suggested that you do not try to copy bills on your office copy machine. To do so is a felony and can result in a fine, prison, or both. People who copy paper money with a color copier are almost always apprehended.

What does the information on a U.S. penny represent? (A penny saved is a penny earned.)

The front side of today's penny, unchanged since 1959, shows the head of President Abraham Lincoln, the sixteenth president of the United States.

Above the image is the phrase "In God We Trust," with the word "Liberty" to the left. The Coinage Act of 1792 decreed that each U.S. coin must have "an impression emblematic of Liberty," a mythical female figure that appeared as the symbol of the United States during colonial times.

The date the coin was minted also appears on the front of the penny. A single letter beneath the date indicates the U.S. mint that produced it. If no letter appears beneath the date, it means it was minted at the Philadelphia mint. A "D" indicates Denver, Colorado; "S" indicates San Francisco, California; and "CC" indicates Carson City, Nevada. However, today pennies are minted only in Denver and Philadelphia.

The reverse side of the penny shows the Lincoln Memorial. Above the image is the phrase "E Pluribus Unum," which means "one out of many" or, more literally, "from many, one." This Latin phrase, attributed to the Roman poet Virgil, is on the Great Seal of the United States and on all U.S. coins. The phrase was chosen by the Continental Congress and adopted in 1782 despite the objections of Benjamin Franklin, who wanted the motto "Rebellion to Tyrants Is Obedience to God."

FACTOIDS

During World War II, copper was needed for bullets and cartridges. In 1943 pennies were made from zinc-coated steel and were referred to as "war pennies."

Because the mint was losing money making pennies from pure copper, the last copper penny was minted in 1981. Since then, all pennies have been made from copper-coated zinc. Older pennies are 95 percent copper; modern pennies are 2.4 percent copper.

The first coin with the words "United States of America" was a penny coined in 1727. It also had the simple motto "Mind Your Own Business."

The penny accounts for two thirds of all coins minted in the United States.

Since its inception, the U.S. Mint has produced so many pennies that, when lined up edge to edge, they would circle the earth 137 times.

The penny was the first U.S. coin with an image of a historic figure, President Abraham Lincoln, who has been on the penny since 1909, the one hundredth anniversary of his birth.

DID YOU KNOW?

In colonial America, it was quite common to find coins in circulation from Great Britain, Portugal, Spain, France, and Germany. Items such as livestock and local crops were also used as trade items. This variety of trade goods not only led to confusion, but slowed trade and economic growth.

As early as 1776, Thomas Jefferson became a strong advocate for a unified system of coins, but it wasn't until 16 years later that the Mint Act was authored by Treasury Secretary Alexander Hamilton. This act also authorized construction of the first mint in Philadelphia.

Where are all the billions of pennies that have been minted for the past 215 years and the 136 billion that are currently in circulation?

With 75 percent of the population admitting they save coins at home, chances are that there are thousands of jars full of shiny pennies gracing the shelves of many a home in the United States. You may have a few yourself.

How much gold does the United States store in Fort Knox? (All that glitters is not gold.)

Founded in 1918, Fort Knox, known as the home of mounted warfare, is a military base, which in 1940 became a training center for tank warfare. Most people equate Fort Knox with the U.S. Bullion Depository, which houses the gold reserves of the United States, but it is famous for its training of armored personnel. The depository contains approximately 315 million troy ounces of gold. At the official government price of $42.222 per troy ounce, the gold in the vault is worth $13 billion. At a market price of $300 an ounce, the gold would be worth $94.5 billion.

The U.S. Treasury Department started construction of the Bullion Depository at Fort Knox in 1936 and opened it in 1937. Designed to hold the bulk of the country's gold, it was built for maximum security. The depository is a solid, square, bomb-proof structure with mechanical and electronic protective devices.

During World War II the depository was used to safeguard such priceless items as the English crown jewels and the Magna Carta. The original Constitution, Bill of Rights, Declaration of Independence, and the draft of Lincoln's Gettysburg Address were also kept there during the war. These documents were removed in 1944 and put on public display in the Library of Congress.

The fort was named after Major General Henry Knox, who was artillery chief for the Continental Army during the American Revolution. He was also the first U.S. Secretary of War.

FACTOIDS

If all the gold in the entire world were compressed into a single cube it could easily be placed under the Eiffel Tower. It would form a cube about 20 yards on each side.

It is rarer to find a one-ounce gold nugget than a five-carat diamond.

Although ancient cultures such as the Aztecs and Egyptians were known for their gold artifacts, over 90 percent of the world's gold was discovered after the California gold rush in 1849.

It is easier to find gold than to win a state lottery.

About three tons of ore must be mined and processed to produce a single ounce of gold.

One cubic foot of gold weighs about 1,000 pounds.

Gold is extremely malleable and can be hammered into sheets so thin that a one-inch stack of sheets would require 200,000 sheets of gold. A single ounce of gold can be hammered into a sheet covering 100 square feet.

Gold will not tarnish, corrode, or rust. Gold-leafed church towers hundreds of years old still shine as if they were new. The mask of the Egyptian pharaoh Tutankhamen was still bright and shiny when it was found even though it was about 4,000 years old.

DID YOU KNOW?

What is true or pure gold? Pure gold is too soft to be used for jewelry so it is usually alloyed with copper, silver, nickel, or some other metal to give it strength and durability. Adding these metals to gold can give the gold a rose, green, or white hue.

Gold is measured in "karat" weights. Some typical karats are:

24 karat 100 percent gold

18 karat 75 percent gold

14 karat 58.5 percent gold

10 karat 41.6 percent gold

The higher the karat weight, the more valuable the jewelry. In the United States, jewelry must be at least 10 karats to be called gold.

According to U.S. law, all gold jewelry must be marked with the karat weight. This mark is usually on the inside of rings and on the clasps of necklaces or bracelets.

A word of warning. Other countries use different standards for gold. For example, in Mexico it is legal to call an item gold if it is at least 8 karats.

Why are gasoline prices listed to three decimal places, such as $1.479 per gallon? (Pumping up prices at the pump?)

Many years ago gasoline taxes were less than a cent per gallon. The oil companies simply added the required tax to the current price per gallon. For example, if the tax was nine tenths of a cent, or $0.009 and the price of gasoline was $0.25 per gallon, then the two added together became $0.259. Over a period of time this practice became a custom.

The price of gasoline is determined by the price of crude oil, refining costs, transportation and storage costs, and taxes. Taxes are often 40 percent of the cost per gallon.

Because many people feel that "gasoline is gasoline," they wonder why some gasoline stations have lower prices than others. Actually, gasoline sold by different stations is different. Although each manufacturer must adhere to strict government regulations, many manufacturers add antioxidants, metal deactivators, corrosion inhibitors, and other elements to the gasoline. Each manufacturer has its own "package of additives." Higher-priced gasolines have many additives, cheaper gasolines have few if any.

FACTOIDS

The first station designed to service automobiles was opened in St. Louis, Missouri, in 1907. Today there are over 196,000 service stations in the United States.

The United States produces over half of all the oil used in the country. Of the imported oil, 51 percent comes from countries in the Western Hemisphere, about 20 percent from the Middle East, 18 percent from Africa, and 11 percent from other countries.

Two gallons of recycled engine oil can generate enough electricity to run an average house for a day or run a television set for 180 hours.

It is estimated that undiscovered oil in the United States alone may exceed 200 billion barrels, which could fill the country's needs for about 70 years at the current rate of consumption.

A new automobile in the 1960s produced almost 20 times as much pollution as a new automobile today.

In the early 1900s there was an increased search for a gasoline additive that would reduce engine "knock." Almost every known chemical, including such substances as melted butter, were tested. Iodine seemed to be the best antiknock additive, but in 1919 aniline was found to be superior. In 1922 lead was introduced as an antiknock gasoline additive and remained the preferred additive until the 1980s.

Although there has been much talk about running out of oil, new estimates indicate that there is enough oil left in the world to supply world demands for the next 60 to 95 years.

DID YOU KNOW?

Crude oil is also referred to as petroleum, which means "liquid rock." Petroleum can be refined to produce a number of different products.

We've all heard of gasoline refineries that convert crude oil into gasoline. Although they look impressive and complex, the basic process of refining is quite simple. It's similar to the process used to create distilled water in which steam from heated water is collected and cooled, turning the steam back into water without any impurities.

In an oil refinery, crude oil is first heated and the resulting vapors are transferred to a "fractionating tower" that breaks down the crude oil into different parts, or fractions. The lightest vapors rise to the top of the tower while the heavier ones stay near the bottom.

When the lightest vapors from the fractionating tower are condensed, gasoline is produced. Medium-weight vapors are condensed to produce kerosene, diesel fuel, and heating oil. The heaviest vapors are condensed to produce lubricating oil. The heavy sludge remaining at the bottom of the tower is used to make asphalt.

In addition to gasoline, the vapors at the top of the fractionating tower are also used to produce petrochemicals. Chemists have used these petrochemicals to create thousands of products we use every day. Products such as clothes, toothpaste, fertilizers, bandages, food additives, lipstick, shampoo, compact disks, vitamin capsules, shampoo, candles, and sunglasses, to name just a few.

What caused the Great Depression of 1929? (The whole world had the blues.)

A severe economic depression is never caused by one single factor. Many complex elements contributed to the Great Depression of 1929. However, most economists believe that the two main causes of the Depression were the immensely uneven distribution of wealth during the previous decade and the extensive speculation in stock that took place in the latter half of the decade.

The decade preceding the Depression was a time of tremendous prosperity and became known as the "Roaring Twenties." However, prosperity was not for everyone. The number of wealthy people in the country was less than a tenth of a percent of the total population yet they controlled most of the money in the country.

In a well-functioning economy, demand must equal supply. But in 1929 wealth was so unevenly distributed that the supply of products far exceeded the demand for them. People may have wanted the products at the time but they couldn't afford them. If supplies keep building and demand lessens, the economy can collapse. One way to balance the equation is to allow people to buy products over time. By the end of the Roaring Twenties, over 60 percent of all automobiles and 80 percent of all radios had been purchased on credit. With this new influx of money into the market, the economy was booming at the end of the 1920s.

Stock speculation became rampant. Profits as high as 3,400 percent could be made in less than a year and people could buy on margin. In other words, they only had to put down 10 percent cash when buying a stock. Because of this, everyone was buying stocks. The poor were equal players with the rich. This buying spree pushed the market to new highs. In 1928 alone the Dow Jones Industrial Average rose from 191 to 300.

There were warning signs as minor recessions occurred in the spring of 1929. Investors became nervous. In October people started selling their shares of stock. As the market started dropping, more and more people sold stock, margins were called, and by October 1929 there was panic selling. Stock prices dropped so fast that many rich people became poor in a matter of hours.

FACTOIDS

In 1929 the average U.S. citizen earned $750 per year while farmers earned an average of $273 a year. Henry Ford earned $14 million that year.

By 1932 over 13 million people in the United States had lost their jobs, 10,000 banks had failed, and stocks had lost 80 percent of their value.

The Depression was worldwide; the first country to fully recover was Sweden.

Of all the countries affected by the Depression, Germany was the hardest hit.

More questions?
Try these websites.

INTERESTED IN STOCK PRICES?
http://www.stockmaster.com/

Simply enter the symbol for a stock and click on Go to display the current price of the stock and a chart showing the stock's performance over the past year. You can click on the name of a stock to go to the website for that company, if available. If you don't know the stock symbol, click on Alphabetical List under Stocks, then click on a letter of the alphabet to see a list of company names that begin with that letter and their associated stock symbols.

Stockmaster also has information on most active stocks, currency rates, and reference material. You can create your own portfolio and view the current prices of all your stocks with one mouse click.

CURRENCY CONVERTER
http://www.oanda.com/converter/classic

This site lets you quickly find the value of a foreign currency. Simply select the currency you have, enter an amount, select the currency you want to convert to, and click on Convert Now! For example, if you want to know how much 800 Mexican pesos is worth in U.S. dollars, select Mexican Peso in the left-hand menu, enter 800, select U.S. Dollar in the right-hand menu, then click on Convert Now! to see the result. In this example, 800 Mexican pesos is worth $87. Note that this is only an example, as currency rates of exchange change daily.

ANECDOTE: A RARE DISEASE LEADS TO A WEDDING

Although I never answer medical questions because I'm not a doctor, I will on occasion provide information if it comes from a recognized medical source. For instance, I would answer the question "What is diabetes?" but would never answer a question asking how to treat or prevent it.

One day I received a message from a person who said he had a rare nervous disorder and would like to find out more about it. (I won't mention the name of the disease because I respect the privacy of the person who sent the message.) I sent him the information he had requested. I thought that was the end of it, but it was only the beginning.

I next received a message of apology, explaining that the first message was a prank. The sender was a premed student and he and his fellow students were trying to stump me. As the person later said, "I received an in-depth answer within 24 hours and it was 100 percent consistent with what we had learned in medical school. Myself and my fellow students were greatly impressed." He finished the message by thanking me and then asking, rather sheepishly, if I could help him with a problem he was having. I replied, "Of course."

He responded by describing his problem. It seems that he had fallen in love with a girl he had known in high school but she was just coming off a three-year relationship and didn't want to get involved with anyone. He wanted very much to show her how much he cared for her. On the other hand, he was afraid of not giving her space and of becoming too pushy. He was in a quandary and didn't know how to find the right balance between showing affection and pushing her away.

I'm certainly not a counselor or psychologist, but I have been around for many years, so I gave him some initial advice. (I sometimes give personal advice about relationships. If I'm wrong and someone gets a broken heart it will be sad but I won't be sued for impersonating a doctor.)

A few weeks later he contacted me and told me what I had suggested was working. Now he wanted more advice, which I gave him.

We corresponded for the next 15 months. I gave him advice, and he always did what I suggested. The messages asking for advice were interspersed with various questions about food and travel, which I also dutifully answered.

Then one day I received the message I had hoped for. The two of them were in a wonderful relationship and were planning to get married. He wanted me to know that I would be invited to the wedding.

They'll be getting married in a state about 2,000 miles from where I live. I'll try to make the wedding, but if I can't, my heart will definitely be there with them on that day.

Food

4

Where did pizza originate?

Although it is believed that pizza dates back to the Stone Age, the earliest record occurs around 1000 B.C. when the word *pizziare*, meaning "to pinch" or "to pluck," was first used. It is believed that the word referred to plucking the hot pie from an oven.

Although some experts believe that pizza evolved from Egyptian flatbread, most agree that Italian pizza actually evolved from concepts introduced by the Etruscans to the north and the Greeks to the south.

Etruscans made a crude bread baked under heated stones. Once cooked, it was flavored with numerous toppings. It served as both plate and utensil because it was used to sop up gravies or broth. The idea of a flavored bread eventually evolved into the Italian focaccia.

The Greeks used this edible plate in a different manner than the Etruscans. Instead of flavoring the bread after cooking, they baked flavorings directly on the bread, which became the main course.

The Romans took both concepts and created a number of similar dishes. The idea spread throughout Italy and today there are hundreds of pizza variations from region to region and town to town.

Today, most people agree that pizza was invented by the Italians. In fact, the Roman statesman Cato talked about "flat rounds of dough dressed with olive oil, herbs, and honey and baked on stones."

FACTOIDS

Americans eat the equivalent of 100 acres of pizza each day, or about 350 slices each second.

There are over 61,000 pizzerias in the United States.

Marie Antoinette's sister had ovens built in the forest so she could enjoy pizza while the royal hunting party feasted on wild game.

In the United States, the favorite topping is pepperoni and the least popular is anchovies.

Some shops excavated in Pompeii appear to have been pizzerias.

In 1987 Lorenzo Amato and Louis Piancone made the world's largest pizza, which was 10,000 square feet and measured 140 feet in diameter. This 44,000-pound monster was cut into over 94,000 slices and eaten by 30,000 spectators.

Children between the ages of 3 and 11 have voted pizza as the number one preferred food for lunch and dinner.

Pizza as we know it today would not have been possible if Old World Europeans had not overcome a basic fear of a New World fruit native to Peru and Ecuador. This yellow or red fruit (eventually called the tomato) was thought to be poisonous. It wasn't until the late 1600s that Europeans began eating tomatoes. In Spain, tomatoes were still considered poisonous until the middle of the eighteenth century.

Modern pizza was born in 1889 when a tavern owner was asked to prepare a special dish in honor of the English queen's visit to Naples. He created a pizza with ingredients that represented the red, white, and green colors of the Italian flag: tomatoes, mozzarella cheese, and basil.

What is the difference between lager and pilsner beer? (Isn't a beer just a beer?)

Lager beer is produced by slow bottom fermentation and aged under refrigeration for several months. In German *lagern* means "to store" or "storehouse."

Pilsner beer is a light lager beer with a strong flavor of hops. It originated in Pilsen (Plzeň), a city in the Czech Republic, in 1877. Being a delicate and golden lager, it was a dramatic departure from the dark, sweet beers that were common at the time.

Pilsner beer gets its flavor from pale malts, soft water, German or Czech hops, and lager yeast. These pale malts are dried for shorter periods of time and at lower temperatures than darker malt. The result is a beer with a golden color. Pilsner is the most widely copied beer and is the world's most popular beer.

All beers can be defined as either lager or ale. The difference is in the brewing. Whether a beer is a lager or an ale depends on the yeast used and the temperature of the fermentation process.

Lager ferments more slowly and at colder temperatures than ale. Because the yeast settles to the bottom of the tank, it is called "bottom-fermented" beer.

Ale tends to ferment rapidly and is referred to as "top-fermented." Ale tends to have a higher alcohol content and to be heartier and darker than lager.

Malt liquor is a beer that has too high an alcohol content by law to be labeled lager or ale. Malt liquor is 5 to 6 percent alcohol, ale is 4 to 5 percent alcohol, and lager is 3.5 percent alcohol.

When most of the alcohol is removed from an ale, it is called "near beer" and has an alcohol content of one half of a percent.

In America, 90 percent of all malt beverages produced are lager beer.

FACTOIDS

An ancient Babylonian clay document indicates that beer making dates back to around 6000 B.C. Hops were first used around 3000 B.C.

Ancient Greeks believed that drinking beer would cause leprosy.

When visiting Dortmund, Germany's King William IV of Prussia drank a 10-year-old strong ale and was unconscious for over twenty-four hours.

In the eighteenth century, ale was brewed very strong so that it could survive the six-month voyage from England to the British troops in India.

Beer cans were not produced until 1935.

American pale lager beer has fewer calories than an equivalent amount of 2 percent milk or apple juice.

DID YOU KNOW?

Early beer makers left their brews in open vessels exposed to airborne yeasts. They didn't realize that the foam on top of the fermenting brew consisted of millions of yeast cells. However, they always scooped off the foam to use it as a starter for the next batch. Without realizing it, they were breeding top-fermenting yeasts.

Later, Benedictine monks took up beer brewing. Monks carved beer cellars into the rocks beneath the monastery and packed them with ice from frozen rivers and lakes so that beer brewed in the fall could be saved for later use in the summer. Stored in such cold temperatures, the beer became more stable and the yeast sank to the bottom. This was the origin of bottom-fermenting yeasts.

Yeast is one of the most important ingredients in brewing and is jealously guarded by brewmasters, sometimes unsuccessfully. Once the son of a Bavarian brewmaster and an Austrian friend journeyed to England and, with the aid of a metal tube with a hidden valve, stole yeast samples from the British.

As more and more scientific methods were applied to the brewing process, both the quality and types of beer improved. Today there are over 25 different types of beer.

How many colors of M&M's are there? (Color me blue.)

A typical bag of M&M's includes six colors: red, orange, yellow, green, blue, and brown. However, there are actually 21 different colors available.

Around certain holidays, for example, you may see M&M bags with different colors or color combinations. At Christmastime you may find M&M bags with red and green M&M's only. During Easter, you may find bags with pastel-colored M&M's.

Large customers, such as retail stores, can special-order bags with the colors they like.

Individuals can also order M&M's of up to four different colors, but they have to buy a ten-pound bag of each color and then mix the colors in any way they choose. The minimum order is forty pounds.

The 21 colors are black, blue, light blue, dark blue, brown, cream, gold, gray, green, aqua green, teal green, dark green, maroon, orange, pink, dark pink, purple, light purple, red, white, and yellow.

M&M's are the nation's top-selling candy and the only sweets offered on *Air Force One* (probably supplanting former President Reagan's jelly beans).

In 1995, after an election that drew 10 million votes, the company added blue and dropped the tan color, prompting a backlash. Some people alleged that the blue M&M's murdered the tan M&M's.

It is rumored that M&M's were originally developed so that soldiers could eat candy without getting their fingers sticky.

Various colors have created a "mystique" of their own:

Green M&M's are widely considered aphrodisiacs.

Orange M&M's are thought to augment breast size.

Brown M&M's were written into Van Halen's standard contract. If the rock group members saw them anywhere in the area, the show was canceled.

Many Americans still refuse to eat the red M&M's because of the Red No. 2 scare in 1976 (M&M's never contained the dye).

DID YOU KNOW?

Some elementary school math classes use M&M's to help students learn mathematical calculations. In one class, students were asked to calculate the percentage of different-colored M&M's in a bag.

The students first discovered that brown, red, and yellow M&M's were most prevalent in the small bags they studied. These three colors accounted for 81 percent of the total, while the other three colors (blue, orange, and green) accounted for only 19 percent.

The students then compared percentages between small bags and large one-pound bags. To their surprise, there was a significant difference. For example, 25 percent of the M&M's were yellow in the small bags, while only 10 percent were yellow in the large bags.

The study was not repeated, as the students ate all the M&M's.

What is the difference between caffe latte and cappuccino? (You can blame it on the priests but not on the Pope.)

Both caffe latte and cappuccino are made from espresso. Espresso is coffee brewed by forcing steam through finely ground darkly roasted coffee beans. When espresso is mixed with steamed milk, it is called caffe latte. When espresso is mixed with frothed hot milk or cream and flavored with cinnamon, it is called cappuccino.

The actual proportions of the ingredients depend on the person making the drink. For instance a cappuccino is usually a shot of espresso with the rest of the drink consisting of 50 percent steamed milk and 50 percent frothed milk. However, it is sometimes made with equal parts espresso, steamed milk, and frothed milk. Sometimes caffe latte is topped with frothed milk.

There are many variations of these drinks such as mocha latte, which contains chocolate syrup, granita latte, which is frozen espresso topped with whipped cream, and flavored lattes such as raspberry latte.

FACTOIDS

Gourmet coffees account for 30 percent of all coffee sold in the United States.

A single coffee tree produces only about a pound of coffee beans per year.

All the world's coffee is grown within 1,000 miles of the equator.

Coffee cherries are red and are a delicious fruit that cannot be sold because it spoils quickly after picking. It's the only fruit that is discarded while the seed (the coffee bean) is used.

Coffee is the second largest internationally traded commodity in the world, right behind oil.

Hawaii is the only state in the United States that grows coffee.

Coffee was usually roasted at home up until the 1870s. The coffee beans were put in a frying pan and roasted over a charcoal fire.

DID YOU KNOW?

Although the first coffee plants were found in Ethiopia, they soon spread to Arabia and other parts of the world. Some legends trace the discovery of coffee to the third century, but most authorities believed it was discovered around A.D. 900 or 1000 by Arabs who used it for medicinal or religious purposes.

Coffee was part of the Arab culture for hundreds of years but it was virtually unknown in Europe. Venetian ships sailed the known world trading in spices, silks, and perfumes they had procured in the East. This is how coffee eventually reached Rome. Roman priests, however, believed that coffee was invented by Satan as a substitute for the wine that Muslims were not allowed to drink, and forbade the consumption of coffee.

Finally, in the late 1500s, Pope Clement VIII asked that coffee be brought to him. He was intrigued by the aroma, sipped the brew, and said it was delicious. He blessed the coffee. With the Pope's blessing, imports of coffee came flooding into the Western world. It was not until 150 years later that coffee was introduced in England and North America.

It took another hundred years before coffee drinking became popular in the United States. When King George of England levied a tax on tea, the American colonists not only staged the Boston Tea Party but also started drinking coffee instead of tea. Later, during the Mexican War and the Civil War, U.S. soldiers considered coffee beans to be their most precious ration.

Today the United States consumes one third of the world's coffee, or over 4 billion cups of coffee each day. Slightly more than 50 percent of coffee is drunk at breakfast. Perhaps we Americans just have trouble waking up in the morning.

What makes peppers so hot? (Add a little spice to your life.)

Not all peppers are hot. For example, paprika, pimiento, and bell peppers are not hot. However, peppers such as chili, jalapeño, and habanero are very hot. These peppers contain capsaicin, which stimulates the nerve endings in the mouth and makes the brain believe it is experiencing true heat. Eating a hot pepper can also make the eyes water and the nose run, and can induce perspiration.

To counteract the pain, the brain releases morphinelike endorphins that create a mild euphoria, similar to a "runner's high." Because of this, peppers can be slightly addictive.

Pure capsaicin is so hot that if you dilute a single drop in 100,000 drops of water and then sip the water, it will blister your tongue.

Another interesting trait of capsaicin is that, unlike ginger or mustard, it can desensitize one to pain if small amounts are eaten repeatedly or if a large amount is eaten all at once. This is why chili lovers can eat progressively hotter peppers and foods.

When you burn your mouth by eating a hot pepper, the typical reaction is to drink water or milk. This won't help at all. Capsaicin will not dissolve in water and drinking a liquid only spreads the capsaicin more until your whole mouth is burning.

To alleviate the burning, many people recommend sour cream or yogurt because the casein in these products breaks down the bond between the capsaicin and the pain receptors in your mouth. The most effective method we've found to relieve the burning sensation is to take a level spoonful of sugar, moisten it with some water, and then roll it around in your mouth for a half minute or so.

In 1912, Wilber Scoville devised a method of measuring the "hotness" of peppers. Although much more modern methods are used today to actually measure the capsaicin in a pepper, the relative hotness is still measured in "Scoville Units."

Here are some measurements of a few typical hot peppers:

Scoville Units	Pepper	Comment
100,000 to 350,000	Habanero	Blistering
50,000 to 100,000	Chiltepin, Thai	Scorching
30,000 to 50,000	Cayenne, Tabasco	Fiery
15,000 to 30,000	Chile de Arbol	Super hot
5,000 to 15,000	Serrano	Very hot
2,500 to 5,000	Jalapeño	Hot to very hot
1,500 to 2,500	Cascabel	Hot
1,000 to 1,500	Poblano (Ancho when dried)	Warm
500 to 1,000	Anaheim, New Mexico	Mild to warm
100 to 500	Cherry pepper	Sweet to warm
0 to 100	Bell pepper, pimiento	Sweet

FACTOIDS

The hottest pepper ever tested was a Red Savin habanero grown in 1994. It was an amazing 577,000 Scoville Units, almost double that of a typical habanero.

Next to salt, peppers are the most popular seasoning in the world.

Cancer patients often suffer painful mouth sores when undergoing chemotherapy. Researchers at the Yale University School of Medicine have found that a candy made of hot peppers and taffy relieves the pain.

The capsaicin found in peppers has been found to be an anticoagulant. Anticoagulants tend to reduce the risk of heart attacks and strokes caused by blood clots.

Peppers are a rich source of vitamin C. Green bell peppers have twice as much vitamin C as citrus. A hot pepper contains 3.5 times as much vitamin C as an orange.

Residents of the U.S. Territory of Guam consume more Tabasco sauce per capita than any other group of people in the world.

Capsaicin is not evenly distributed throughout a pepper so it's quite likely that one part of the pepper might be hotter than another part.

Peppers have probably been around for hundreds of thousands of years, if not more. Archeologists have found pepper seed remains in prehistoric caves in Peru.

Although peppers were in common use in pre-Columbian Central and South America, they were unknown in Europe until introduced by Columbus. Columbus was looking for more efficient spice trade routes when he bumped into Haiti and the Dominican Republic (then known as the island of Hispaniola). He noticed that the natives grew a vegetable that had a sharp taste that reminded him of black pepper from the East Indies. Thinking he had discovered a new type of black pepper, Columbus named the new vegetable "pepper" and it's been called that ever since.

When Columbus brought peppers back to Spain they were an instant hit, and their popularity soon spread throughout Europe. Early colonists brought pepper seeds with them and introduced the new vegetable in New England. Peppers have enjoyed worldwide popularity for some time and are now steadily gaining popularity in the United States.

People still argue whether it is spelled "chile" or "chili" but either way it's a tasty food.

What is the difference between apple juice and apple cider? (Where does applejack fit in?)

Typically apple juice is simply the juice of apples, while cider is fermented apple juice. Cider is often made sparkling by carbonation or by fermentation in a sealed container.

In the United States apple juice can also be called apple cider, hence the confusion between the two. In Europe the name "cider" is reserved for fermented juice. In the United States apple juice is generally called "sweet cider," while apple juice that has been allowed to ferment is called "hard cider."

When apples are crushed (or "pressed") and allowed to ferment, the wild yeast on their skins converts the sugars in the juice into alcohol. At some point in history, someone discovered that drinking this fermented juice produced a soothing warmth and had a pleasant effect on the disposition.

Hard cider can be distilled to produce an alcoholic beverage called applejack. Applejack is a brandy made by first freezing hard cider and then siphoning off the concentrated liquor.

True cider can have an alcohol content ranging from 2 percent to 12 percent. Apple wine is a fermented apple drink to which sugars have been added. The alcohol content of apple wine exceeds 12 percent.

FACTOIDS

Throughout the centuries, over 350 varieties of apples have been grown expressly for cider making.

During the eighteenth century, farm workers were given cider as part of their wages.

In England juice for cider is often made from imported apple concentrate and is full of sweeteners and preservatives. For those who want real cider made from nothing but fermented apple juice, the Apple and Pear Produce Liaison Executive (APPLE) publishes a guide listing the pubs in England that serve real cider.

All apples are one of three colors: red, green, or yellow.

Although cider was probably the most popular drink in the United States in colonial times and later, it all but disappeared by the late 1800s. In fact, most people in the United States have never tasted hard cider and for some time only expensive English imports were available in this country. However, cider is now making a strong comeback.

Although it is believed that apples were eaten around 750,000 years ago because of remnants found in prehistoric caves, and were planted extensively in the Nile River Delta in 1300 B.C., the earliest known cider didn't appear until around 55 B.C. At that time two of Julius Caesar's legions arrived in England and discovered that alcoholic cider was a common drink. Some historians believe that the Romans later introduced cider into France.

Early presidents, such as George Washington, John Adams, and Thomas Jefferson, were cider drinkers. Later, William Henry Harrison used a barrel of cider as his logo during the 1840 presidential campaign. He said that on election day his party would serve cider to everyone who voted for him. He won the election.

For some reason, cider was an accepted drink and didn't carry the stigma of whiskey and ale. Clergy and deacons who would never dream of drinking whiskey had no qualms about drinking cider.

What is the difference between jelly, jam, preserves, and marmalade? (Don't get in a jam with this very sticky question.)

The difference between jelly, jam, preserves, and marmalade is primarily the proportion of whole fruit that remains after processing.

Jelly has no fruit pieces. The fruit is pureed, sweetened, boiled, and then strained to separate the fruit from the juice. The juice jells when it cools to produce a smooth, clear, brightly colored jelly. Pectin or gelatin is often used to aid congealing. The word "jelly" comes from the French word *gelé* meaning "frozen," or "congealed."

Although fruit jellies are the most common, jellies can also be made from cooked peppers, tomatoes, mint, and other produce. These are traditionally used to complement meat dishes such as lamb, which is typically served with mint jelly.

Jam has crushed fruit pieces. The fruit is finely chopped or pureed and then mixed with sugar and boiled. Unlike jelly, which is only the juice, jam contains both the juice and the pulp of the pureed fruit.

Jams and jellies are typically eaten on toast, scones, English muffins, or some similar type of breakfast bread. They are also one half of the famous peanut butter and jelly sandwich team.

Preserves have large pieces of fruit. Preserves are basically jellies containing large pieces of fruit and are much chunkier than jelly or jam.

Marmalade, almost always made from citrus fruit, is actually a clear jelly that has pieces of both the fruit and rind suspended in it. Although we tend to think of marmalade as "orange," other fruits such as lemons and quinces are also used.

FACTOIDS

Centuries ago Arabs in southern Spain called oranges "sours" and grew them primarily because they believed the skin had medicinal qualities.

The main reason for making jellies, jams, and preserves was to find a use for blemished, bruised, or inferior fruit that was not suitable for eating fresh.

The pectin that causes jelly, jam, preserves, and marmalade to thicken is found primarily in the peels of citrus fruits and to a lesser degree in apple pomace (the pulp left after apples have been pressed to obtain the juice). Pectin is also used commercially in the candy, pharmaceutical, and textile industries.

Some jellies are made from seaweed (agar-agar) extract and are noted for their clarity and body. These jellies are often used to coat candy centers or candied fruit slices.

DID YOU KNOW?

For those of us who have a sweet tooth, the word "jelly" reminds us of jelly bean, which is not really a bean at all.

A candy known as "Turkish delight" originated in biblical times.

Most experts today believe that the jelly center of the jelly bean is a descendant of that candy. Turkish delight consists of rose water and sugar which is jelled and then cut into cubes. Turkish delight was well known in ancient Rome.

The coating on the outside of the jelly bean is put on the jelly center by a process called "panning," which was invented in seventeenth-century France to coat almonds. Almonds, sugar, and syrup were put into a shallow pan, which was rocked until the almonds were coated with a candy shell. Panning today is done with large rotating pans. The jelly center consists of sugar, syrup, and various grain starches. It is patterned after the Turkish delight; it was eventually combined with this panning process to coat it and the jelly bean was born.

The jelly bean made its first appearance in the United States in 1861 when William Schrafft of Boston suggested sending jelly beans to the Union soldiers during the Civil War. The late 1800s saw a "penny candy" craze with candy makers using the panning process to produce gumdrops, jelly beans, and jawbreakers. Although popular as "penny candy," jelly beans did not become a part of the Easter tradition until the 1930s.

For many years only the jelly bean coating was flavored, not the center. In 1976 the "Jelly Belly" jelly bean was introduced with natural flavors blended into the center of the bean. These beans were also smaller and had a deeper color than traditional jelly beans.

When Ronald Reagan became governor of California in 1967 he started eating jelly beans to help him break the habit of smoking a pipe. When he became president of the United States, three and one-half tons of beans were shipped to the White House for the inauguration celebrations. The blueberry-flavored bean was invented in honor of Reagan's inauguration. Along with existing flavors, the president now had red, white, and blue jelly beans for the festivities.

More questions?
Try these websites.

THE KITCHEN LINK

http://www.kitchenlink.com/companies.html

If you want to know about a particular food product, this site lists all the food products and companies that have websites. Over 193 products are included, ranging from A.1. steak sauce to Welch's grape products. Just click on the name of a company to automatically go to that website.

In the upper left-hand corner is a pull-down menu called TKL Hot Spots. Simply select a subject, such as Healthy Cooking, Cookbooks, Recipe Archives, or Grocery Coupons, and click on Go to enter that site.

If you go to the Grocery Coupons area and enter your zip code, you'll see a list of supermarkets in your area. Click on the supermarket you like, and follow the instructions to print out a page of coupons that you can redeem at that supermarket.

EVERYTHING YOU WANT TO KNOW ABOUT FRENCH FRIES

http://www.select-ware.com/fries/

A wonderful site dedicated to one of our favorite foods. It has a wealth of french fry information, including a history of the french fry, answers to questions, interesting facts, how to make your own french fries, and information on french fries around the world.

THE INCREDIBLE EDIBLE EGG

http://www.aeb.org/

This site has just about anything you'd like to know about eggs, from basic egg facts to an eggcyclopedia. You can even fill out a form to receive a free copy of the "Most Loved Morning Meals" pamphlet, compliments of the American Egg Board.

OVER 30 RECIPES FOR BUFFALO WINGS

http://www.bababooey.com/monkey/wings.html

For those of you hooked on Buffalo wings, here are over 30 different recipes you can try.

5

Geography

What is the lowest point on earth? (How low can you get?)

The lowest point on land is the shoreline of the Dead Sea in Israel, which is 1,310 feet below sea level. The southern shore of the Dead Sea has salt caves purported to be in the area where the biblical cities of Sodom and Gomorrah were once located.

The salt water of the Dead Sea has a higher concentration of minerals than other bodies of water and contains more than 25 minerals. The water has been recognized for its therapeutic value since ancient times. In addition, the air is pure and dry and has the richest oxygen content in the world. It is claimed that Aristotle and Cleopatra, among others, went there to be cured. Even today people go to the Dead Sea to relieve arthritis, rheumatism, psoriasis, eczema, foot aches, and other maladies. Various Dead Sea products are sold in local pharmacies.

The rocky cliffs that rise steeply 400 feet above the Dead Sea hold the remnants of Massada, the impregnable fortress built by King Herod. During the rebellion against Rome, Jewish zealots took over the fortress. When the two-year Roman siege ended, the Jewish defenders chose to kill themselves and their families rather than become Roman slaves.

FACTOIDS

Israel has only two major exports, potash and magnesium. Both come from the Dead Sea.

The salt content of the world's oceans is around 3 percent, while the salt content of the Dead Sea is 39 percent.

The area around the Dead Sea has over 300 days of sun per year but rarely more than 2 inches of rain annually.

The water level of the Dead Sea drops almost 6 feet a year due to evaporation, which often creates a thick mist over the water.

DID YOU KNOW?

When talking about the Dead Sea, it's not unusual to think of the mysterious Dead Sea Scrolls, considered to be one of the greatest manuscript discoveries of all time.

In 1947 two young Arabs tending their goats in the Judean desert discovered ancient manuscripts in nearby caves. The manuscripts were fashioned from leather, papyrus, and copper. Because the scrolls were found in a cave on the northwest shore of the Dead Sea they were immediately named the "Dead Sea Scrolls." Over the next 20 years other documents were discovered in adjacent areas and were also called "Dead Sea Scrolls."

Most of the documents found were composed during the first century B.C. and the first century A.D., making them almost 2,000 years old. At one site archeologists found legal documents hidden in a cave by Samaritans who were later massacred by the soldiers of Alexander the Great. These documents date from 375 B.C. and are the oldest found in the area.

The Dead Sea Scrolls have been studied by a number of scholars and theologians. They are of both theological and historical importance. They confirm the antiquity of the Hebrew Bible and clarify the relationship between Jewish and Christian communities during the time of Christ. They also reveal many facts about the little-known period of history before the birth of Christ.

Perhaps the lowest point on earth has led to the high point of historical discovery in this century.

How did each of the seven continents get its name? (Did you know that all the continents except Europe begin with the letter "A"?)

Although no one knows for sure how Africa, Asia, and Europe got their names, most historians agree with the following explanations.

Africa   Some say the name comes from the Latin word *aprica*, meaning "sunny," or the Greek word *aphrike*, meaning "without cold." Others believe that it came from the Romans who ruled the North African coast at one time and referred to everything south of them as "Afriga" or "Land of the Afrigs." The Afrigs were a Berber colony south of Carthage.

Americas   The Americas consist of two continents, North America and South America. Amerigo Vespucci was an Italian explorer and friend of Christopher Columbus. He wrote about his travels in letters to his friends and in 1504 (long after Columbus's discovery of the New World in 1492) one of his letters was read by

Martin Waldseemuller, a German mapmaker. Waldseemuller wrote a book in which he said that another part of the world had been discovered by Amerigo Vespucci and should be called America in his honor.

Antarctica This name comes from the Greek word *antarktikos*, which means "opposite from the bear." Arktos, or the bear, refers to the Great Bear constellation above the North Pole. We usually call this constellation either Ursa Major (Latin for "big bear") or the Big Dipper. Antarktikos, or "opposite the bear," refers to an area opposite the north pole, or the south pole. A Polynesian legend tells the story of a traveler from Raratonga who "sailed south to a place of bitter cold where rocklike forms grew out of a frozen sea." If the legend is true, that Polynesian was the first human to see Antarctica.

Asia Because this is an ancient name, there is no historical source of its origin. Some authorities believe that Greeks used the name to describe lands to the east. Others believe it came from *asu*, an Assyrian word meaning "east."

Australia The ancient Greeks believed that because the earth was a sphere, there had to be a large southern mass of land to balance the northern part of the known world. They called this the "unknown land to the south." Later mapmakers used the Latin name *Terra Australis Incognita* and the continent eventually became known simply as Australia.

Europe Once again the ancient Greeks had a hand in naming a continent, in this case Europa. While it was once generally thought that Europa meant "sunset," it is now believed that the term meant "mainland" and referred to the unknown lands north of Greece.

FACTOIDS

Africa Africa has the shortest coastline of all the continents even though it is almost an island with the only connection to other land being the small Sinai Peninsula. The various cultures, including both the shortest (Pygmy) and tallest (Watusi) people in the world, speak over 1,000 different languages.

Antarctica This is the driest, coldest, windiest, and highest continent on earth. Antarctica's rainfall is similar to that of the world's hottest deserts. The lowest temperature ever recorded (of minus 129 degrees Fahrenheit) was in Antarctica. Wind speeds of up to 198 mph have also been recorded. The average elevation is one and a half miles above sea level, and the highest mountain is three miles high.

Asia   The site of the Indus Valley civilization that thrived in 5000 B.C. is located in northwest India and Pakistan. This ancient civilization boasted complex cities, civil engineering, advanced social structures, and sophisticated agricultural techniques. The writing of this ancient culture has not yet been deciphered.

Australia   The smallest continent, Australia is completely isolated from other land masses, which accounts for its unique vegetation and animal life. Native animals such as the kangaroo, duck-billed platypus, and koala bear are found nowhere else on earth.

Is it true that at one time the entire world consisted of a single continent? (If that were true today, you could drive all the way around the world in your car.)

S cientists believe that millions of years ago the earth's entire land mass was concentrated in one supercontinent called Pangea, a Greek word that means "all earth."

About 200 million years ago Pangea broke into two continents, Gondwanaland and Laurasia. These two continents eventually broke up into smaller pieces that drifted to different parts of the world around 50 million years ago to form the continents we see today.

Some continents seem "pointed," such as Africa and South America, while others do not. A good analogy is what happens when you drop a plate on the floor and break it. Some broken pieces are definitely pointed while others are more square.

Over the years countless people, including many scientists, have noticed that if you take a paper map and cut out all the continents, they almost fit together like pieces of a jigsaw puzzle. Although the French scientist Antonio Snider-Pelligrini studied the idea in depth in 1858, it wasn't until the 1960s that scientists developed the theory of "plate tectonics." Simply put, this theory states that the outer shell of the earth consists of a number of rigid plates that are always moving. A plate can underlie both continents and oceans.

The theory of the supercontinent of Pangea and plate tectonics is accepted by most of today's geologists because there is scientific evidence to back it up. However, some scientists theorize that continents break apart and recombine in a never-ending cycle, similar to clumps of soap bubbles in the dishwater. Although this theory is lacking in evidence and not widely held, you may also hear the names scientists have given these billion-year-old supercontinents that existed before Pangea. For example, the continents of Ur and Rodinia.

FACTOIDS

The ancient supercontinent of Gondwanaland included the areas we now know as Africa, Arabia, India, Ceylon, Australia, New Zealand, South America, and Antarctica.

Most continents are more or less triangular in shape and are located in the Northern Hemisphere.

Although the theory of drifting continents was proposed in the early 1900s, lack of geological evidence prevented it from becoming accepted at that time.

Is there really a north pole?
(Yes, Virginia, there are two of them.)

Scientists call the northernmost point on earth the north pole. However, for those of us who still believe in fantasy, the north pole is where Santa Claus lives.

There is an actual town called North Pole. It's in Alaska, was incorporated in 1953, and has fewer than 2,000 residents. The town is about 17 miles east of Fairbanks, Alaska. North Pole sits between two mountain ranges and has a semiarid climate. The summers are hot, the temperature often reaching into the nineties, but winters are cold. Sometimes the temperature drops to minus 70 degrees Fahrenheit in the winter. However, there is no wind because North Pole is protected by the surrounding mountains.

North Pole claims to be the real home of Santa Claus. You can write to him at:

Santa Claus
North Pole, AK 99705

With all the work he has to do every year, Santa Claus uses as many modern conveniences as possible. Because most of the people and the children in North Pole are on the Internet, Santa Claus decided to get a computer. If you don't want to write him, you can e-mail him at:

npole@alaska.net

Although situated in the magnificent Alaskan wilderness, North Pole has all the amenities of most cities, including police and fire departments, restaurants, schools, and stores. It can be a very lovely place to live, especially around Christmastime.

FACTOIDS

North Pole radio and television station KJNP not only broadcasts world and local news, it also forwards messages to people in the outlying "bush" areas and, on occasion, relays birthday greetings, emergency messages, or a personal message.

Although North Pole has a large grocery store, some restaurants, and a few gas stations, there is only one traffic signal in the entire town.

Private airplanes are a common method of traveling in Alaska.

It's not unusual to see a small aircraft in the driveway next to the family car. Dog sleds are also quite common.

North Pole is only 3,675 miles away from our nation's capital of Washington, D.C.

A summer day in North Pole can have up to 22 hours of daylight, but a winter day may have only 4 hours of daylight.

If you live in North Pole, on a clear day you can see Mount McKinley, the tallest mountain peak in North America. It is 20,320 feet high. The Native Americans call the mountain Denali, which means "The Great One."

DID YOU KNOW?

For many years, explorers from around the world wanted to be the first to find the "other" north pole, and for years there was a debate about who finally discovered it.

Frederick Albert Cook was an American physician and explorer who claimed he had discovered the north pole in 1908. Another American explorer, Robert E. Peary, claimed to have found the north pole a year later and denounced Cook's claim as fraudulent.

Native American Alaskans, called Inuits, who were part of Cook's expedition later alleged that Cook had stopped hundreds of miles south of the pole. The controversy between Cook and Peary lasted until 1917. By then, most people believed that Peary had discovered the north pole and that Cook was no more than a con man.

The public opinion of Cook was proved to be true in 1923 when Cook was convicted of using the U.S. mail for fraud and was sent to prison. He was paroled in 1929. President Franklin D. Roosevelt granted him a pardon in 1940.

Six men first reached the north pole: Robert Peary, four Inuits, and Peary's black companion, Matthew Alexander Henson. Henson was an orphan who went to sea as a cabin boy at the age of 12. When Henson was 22, Peary hired him for an expedition to Nicaragua. Peary was so impressed with Henson's ability that he hired him on seven expeditions to the Arctic. Although Henson received a congressional medal, which was given to all members of Peary's expedition, not many people knew that Peary did not discover the north pole by himself. It was discovered by him, Henson, and the four Inuits.

More questions?
Try these websites.

GEOGRAPHY GUIDE
http://geography.about.com/

This is a wonderful geography site and is a gold mine of information. I've corresponded with its creator, Matt Rosenberg, who is eminently qualified in geography, and I have nothing but praise for this site. However, it is so full of information, you need to spend some time exploring it. I suggest starting out by looking at what's available under Net Links in the right-hand column. If you want to know more about Matt or want to e-mail him, click on Guide Bio in the left-hand column.

HOW FAR IS IT?
http://www.indo.com/distance/

If you'd like to know how far it is from one place to another, this site is for you. Just enter the two locations to find the distance between them. For instance, if you enter Palo Alto, California, and Bangalore, India, you'll see that the distance between the two cities is 8,690 miles.

LIST OF MAPS
http://www.cgrer.uiowa.edu/servers/serversreferences.html

If you love maps as I do, you'll love this site. It has hundreds of maps, all on-line. There are two ways to use this site. You can scroll down the entire page, which will take some time. An easier way is to select a category at the top of the page, such as United States – City. You'll then see a list of available maps. Just click on a city, such as Map of San Antonio, Texas, to display the map.

MAP WEBSITES
http://www.lib.utexas.edu/maps/

If you like historical maps, weather maps, or just about any other type of map, this site is for you. Start by selecting a category at the top of the page, such as Weather Map Sites. Then just click on the name of the map you want to see.

CIA FACT BOOK
http://www.odci.gov/cia/publications/factbook/docs/profile guide.html

Who better knows what's going on in our world than the U.S. Central Intelligence Agency? Simply look at the list of countries on the left-hand side of the page and then select the country you're interested in. Once the page opens, be sure to scroll down the entire page to find out a great deal of information about that country, including geography, population statistics, government, economy, communications, transportation, and military.

6

History

**How did the ship that landed at Plymouth
harbor get the name *Mayflower*?
(Pilgrims, Plymouth, and poets.)**

*M*ayflower was a very common ship name and many other
ships with the same name made trips to New England. The
most famous, however, was the ship that brought the Pilgrims to
America.

The exact dimensions of the *Mayflower* are not known but
specifications can be determined based on designs of other
merchant ships of that time. It was probably a three-masted sailing
vessel weighing around 180 tons. Scholars disagree on the exact

dimensions, but it was probably between 90 and 100 feet long and about 26 feet wide.

The ship was dirty, cramped, and old. During the voyage, her main beam cracked, dislodging the main mast. Three years after returning from the New World, the ship was in ruins. It was later sold and, because wood was scarce in England at that time, reputedly dismantled to make a barn.

During the voyage, the *Mayflower* carried 102 passengers and a crew of 30. There were 18 women, and the rest were men. Many of the women were forced to leave some of their children behind and hoped to send for them at a later date.

FACTOIDS

Two people died on the voyage and two children were born on the ship.

Historians disagree on why the *Mayflower* did not land at its intended spot. Some say it was because of rough seas and storms, while others say it was because the captain threatened to put the passengers ashore wherever the ship happened to be at the time.

The *Mayflower* remained at Plymouth during the terrible winter of 1620. Half of the colonists died. Only 4 of the 18 women survived.

In 1992 a replica of the *Mayflower* led a procession of tall ships through Cape Cod Canal. It set sail again in 1995 to commemorate the 375th anniversary of the original *Mayflower's* arrival in the New World.

Miles Standish was a professional soldier hired by the Pilgrims as military adviser. He and John Alden, one of the Pilgrim Fathers, were made famous in Longfellow's poem "The Courtship of Miles Standish."

DID YOU KNOW?

Separatist Puritans, fleeing religious persecution in England, had settled in Holland. However, 44 of these separatists thought the Dutch way of life was too frivolous and decided to move to the New World.

They made a deal with a London stock company to finance a pilgrimage to America. In return, the company was to receive free labor from the settlers for seven years. The other passengers on the *Mayflower* were non-Separatists hired to protect the interests of the company.

The Dutch Separatists called themselves "Saints" and referred to the other passengers as "Strangers." During the trip, the Saints and Strangers had many disagreements. After a 66-day voyage, land was sighted and the two groups held a meeting to try to reach an accord. The resulting agreement, the famous "Mayflower Compact," guaranteed equality for all. The two groups then united and called themselves "Pilgrims."

Although Governor William Bradford referred to the Saints who had left Holland to come to the New World as "pilgrimes," the term was rarely used until two hundred years later.

These first settlers were originally called the "Old Comers." Much later, they were referred to as "the Forefathers." During a bicentennial celebration in 1820, the famous orator Daniel Webster referred to these first settlers as the "Pilgrim Fathers" and the term has been used ever since.

Did Napoleon lose the battle of Waterloo because of hemorrhoids? (That's not where the English caused him pain.)

Although Napoleon was very sick when the battle of Waterloo began and there were signs his military ability had deteriorated, there is no record of his having had hemorrhoids. He did, however, suffer from poor health for many years, including frequent bladder stone attacks.

A 1970 movie may have led to this myth. In the film, Napoleon is watching the battle when he becomes ill and has to retreat to his tent. His commanders then launch an attack on the British but send in foot soldiers without cavalry protection. The foot soldiers are routed and the French forces never recover. But there is no actual record of this happening.

Napoleon's defeat was the result of a number of conditions, not the least of which was the fact that he was outnumbered. At Waterloo the French had about 70,000 men. Although the British had only 60,000 men, the Prussian army, which came to their aid, also had 70,000 men. This combined force was almost double that of Napoleon's army.

FACTOIDS

Although most people think Napoleon was short, he was actually five feet six inches tall, an average height for a Frenchman in those days. He was often seen in the presence of taller men, which may have led to the myth that he was short.

During the entire Napoleonic wars, over five million people died.

Napoleon took 14,000 French decrees and simplified them into a unified set of 7 laws. This was the first time in modern history that a nation's laws applied equally to all citizens. Even today Napoleon's 7 laws are so impressive that by 1960 over 70 governments had patterned their own laws after them or used them verbatim.

People wonder why Napoleon is usually shown with his hand inside his coat. Some of the many theories are that he had a skin disease, he had a deformed hand, he was afraid of being shot, or he was winding his watch. The simple explanation is that the pose was common at that time for men of stature and was almost always used when a portrait was painted.

During Napoleon's conquest of Egypt his soldiers discovered the Rosetta stone, which had the same text inscribed in three different languages, including Egyptian hieroglyphics. This was the stone that unlocked the secret of the hieroglyphs and enabled scholars to translate the vast amounts of ancient Egyptian writing.

When Napoleon conquered Spain he outlawed the Inquisition, calling it "A wrong upon the masses."

The commanders of the English and Prussian armies that defeated Napoleon met at a village called La Belle Alliance. The Prussian commander wanted to name the battle after the village. But Wellington, the British commander, refused because he always named his battles after the place he had stayed the night before the battle. Thus, the battle became known as "the battle of Waterloo."

DID YOU KNOW?

The battle of Waterloo was a complex affair with many nations providing troops to support both the French and the English.

The battle began with four French attacks against the British army. The intent was to weaken the center so the French could break through. The attacks failed because there was no coordination between the French infantry and cavalry.

Eventually the French launched a coordinated attack with infantry, cavalry, and artillery, capturing a farmhouse in the middle of the British line. Artillery then started blasting holes in the center of the British defenses.

Had the French intensified the attack, the British would have been vulnerable. Napoleon refused to send reinforcements, however, because he was busy fighting the Prussians attacking his flank. By the time he did send additional troops, it was too late to press the advantage because the British had reorganized their defenses.

The British began a concentrated advance while the Prussians attacked the French elsewhere. The attack panicked the French and they retreated in disarray. Napoleon saw 25,000 of his men killed and 9,000 captured. Four days later he abdicated.

Although Napoleon is usually portrayed as a power-hungry conqueror, his other achievements are often ignored. In the states that he created, he instituted constitutions, abolished slavery, introduced uniform laws for all people, created efficient governments, and fostered both science and the arts.

Whatever Napoleon was, he was definitely not a small man.

Is it true that in ancient Greece 300 soldiers held off 200,000 Persian elite troops for 3 days? (A Spartan stand against overwhelming odds.)

In 480 B.C. Xerxes, the son of the King of Persia, prepared to invade Greece. Leonidas, a Spartan king, agreed to help stop the invading Persians to give the rest of Greece time to mobilize its army. He decided that the best defensive position was Thermopylae, where a 4-mile-long pass narrowed to 60 feet or less. Xerxes would have to cross this pass to reach the rest of Greece.

Leonidas picked up 7,000 troops in addition to his own 300 on his way to Thermopylae but these did not believe in the Spartan phrase "stand and die" and most fled or surrendered once the fighting began. It was up to Leonidas and his 300 Spartan soldiers to hold back the force of 200,000 battle-trained Persians.

The battle initially went as planned. The Persian advantage of numbers was minimized because only a few soldiers could go through the narrow pass at a time. The Persians used short javelin-type spears and wicker shields that were superior in an open field but no match for the Greeks' long thrusting spears, heavy shields, and body armor, so effective in close quarters.

The Spartans held off the Persians, even beating back the crack 10,000 Persian troops known as the Immortals. For two days the Persians suffered heavy losses. But on the third day, a Greek traitor offered to show the Persians a way to reach the rear of the Spartan force. Xerxes sent his Immortals to encircle the Spartans. Knowing that every minute they fought would provide more time for the rest of Greece to prepare, the Spartans fought to the death. Every man died.

The Persians finally won at Thermopylae and conquered central Greece. However, they suffered considerable losses and, because of the holding action of Leonidas and the brave Spartans, most of the

Greek troops and ships escaped to the Isthmus of Corinth. Beaten badly in later battles, the Persians retreated to Asia.

The battle at Thermopylae is celebrated as an example of heroic resistance against overwhelming odds.

FACTOIDS

Thermopylae has been the scene of three other famous battles. In ancient battles, the Greeks fought the Gauls and the Romans defeated the Syrians. In 1941, brave New Zealanders fought a holding action against the Germans.

In every famous battle at Thermopylae, the defenders failed to hold the pass. This was usually because the attacking force took another route and came up from behind to surprise them.

An oracle said that Sparta would be destroyed unless one of its kings was killed. Scholars still debate whether King Leonidas refused to surrender because he feared the oracle's prophecy or because he simply wanted to hold off the Persians as long as possible.

DID YOU KNOW?

There have been many battles where a superior force was held at bay by relatively few defenders. The Texans did just that at the battle of the Alamo.

Another lesser-known battle took place in South Africa during the Zulu Wars in 1879. A small English military encampment at Rorke's Drift had just over 120 men. These men were attacked by 20,000 Zulu warriors. Even the hospitalized British soldiers took up arms.

This small contingent of soldiers fended off wave after wave of Zulu warriors and suffered only minimal losses. Their heroism was recognized by their government. More Victoria Crosses (similar to our Congressional Medal of Honor) were awarded to that group than to any other group in the history of the British Army.

What does "flying the hump" mean?
(Have you ever seen a tiger fly?)

Japan and China had been at war for some time before the United States entered World War II. When the Japanese conquered Hong Kong in 1941, China lost its air link to the rest of the world. By spring of 1942 the Japanese had conquered most of Burma, and China was completely cut off. There were no land, sea, or existing air routes that could be used to send supplies to the ill-equipped Chinese army. The only way to help the beleaguered Chinese was to fly cargo from Assam, India, to Kunming in southwest China. Because pilots had to fly over the Himalayas, they said they were flying over the "hump." These men flew through the world's worst weather over the world's highest mountains.

The United States and Britain knew the Japanese were planning to advance southward to conquer and occupy Indochina, Thailand, British Malaya, and the Dutch East Indies. If they accomplished their mission, they would be at Australia's door. Although the United States had lent China $500 million and Great Britain had lent it $50 million, the money would have been of little use if the Chinese could not receive the arms they purchased.

The airlift over the hump was successful but costly. U.S. cargo planes flew the hump day and night for three and a half years. This air route was so dangerous that it was nicknamed "the aluminum trail" because of the more than 600 transport planes that were lost.

FACTOIDS

Supplies flown over the hump first traveled 12,000 miles by ship from the United States, then traveled 1,500 miles by rail to the Indian airstrip. After making the 500-mile flight over the hump, the supplies were delivered by trucks and donkey carts to the Chinese forward bases 400 to 700 miles away.

Most casualties among pilots were caused not by bullets but by disease. Malaria, jaundice, dysentery, and other diseases were common. Worse still, none of the bases had a flight surgeon.

Paper was so scarce that combat logs and other records were kept on the backs of envelopes or letters and even on matchbook covers.

In addition to flying the dangerous hump, pilots often helped maintain and repair the planes. With no hangars and exposed to the weather, they still worked from dawn to dusk.

DID YOU KNOW?

Before the United States formally entered World War II, a group of U.S. civilian pilots volunteered to fight the Japanese in Burma and China.

Although facing a superior force in both size and strength, these volunteer pilots scored victory after victory, managed to protect the Chinese capital, and inflicted considerable damage to the Japanese air and ground forces.

Flying beat-up planes and always facing shortages of parts, fuel, and pilots, this volunteer air force continued to win battles against the Japanese. They were successful because they used the element of surprise, were capable of precision flying, and adopted highly unorthodox military tactics.

The pilots flew the famous Curtiss P-40 fighter, which had a top speed of almost 380 mph and a range of about 100 miles. They painted eyes and large teeth on the conical nose to make it look very much like a tiger shark, hence the name "Flying Tigers." After every few missions the planes were repainted with different numbers and insignia. The planes were also continually moved from one small airstrip to another so the Japanese never knew where they would come from next. Both strategies made the pilots appear to have numerous airfields and aircraft, many more than they really did.

Once the United States entered the war, these civilian pilots were allowed to join the U.S. Air Force and became the nucleus of the

China Air Task Force. Only this time, they had newer planes and no longer faced the shortages that had plagued them before. As U.S. Army Air Force pilots, the intrepid volunteers continued to rack up victories in the air.

The Flying Tigers are still active today and are known as the "23d Fighter Group." They are headquartered at Pope Air Force Base in North Carolina.

Has a U.S. vice president ever been assassinated? (It's much safer to be vice president than president.)

No vice president of the United States has ever been assassinated. However, four presidents have been assassinated and another four have died while in office. Those assassinated were Abraham Lincoln, James A. Garfield, William McKinley, and John F. Kennedy. Those who died in office were William Henry Harrison, Zachary Taylor, Warren Harding, and Franklin Delano Roosevelt. In addition, unsuccessful assassination attempts were made on Harry Truman and Ronald Reagan.

President Lincoln was at Ford's Theater in Washington, D.C., watching the melodrama *Our American Cousin* when the actor John Wilkes Booth shot him.

President McKinley was shot twice at point-blank range while visiting the Pan-American Exposition in Buffalo, New York. His assailant was the anarchist Leon Czolgosz. McKinley rarely exercised. Doctors said that if he had been in better shape he might have survived.

President Garfield was entering a Washington, D.C., railroad station when a disappointed office seeker shot him. However, the bullet did not kill him. Doctors kept probing for the bullet with unsterilized instruments, resulting in the blood poisoning that eventually killed him.

President Kennedy was shot while traveling in a motorcade in Dallas, Texas. Many believe that the assassin was Lee Harvey Oswald, but others still believe there was a conspiracy. The debate goes on.

FACTOIDS

McKinley holds the record for presidential handshaking at 2,500 handshakes per hour.

Garfield was the first left-handed president.

Lincoln's son Robert was at the scene of his father's assassination as well as at the scene of both Garfield's and McKinley's assassinations.

Kennedy was the youngest elected president (43) and the youngest to die in office (46). William Jefferson Clinton was 46 when he became president.

Lincoln was awarded a patent for a device that lifted boats over shoals. He is the only president ever to receive a patent.

The only president to win a Pulitzer Prize was Kennedy, who won it for his biography, *Profiles in Courage*.

Most presidents have nicknames. The nicknames of those who were targets of assassins are "Honest Abe" (Lincoln), "Idol of Ohio" (McKinley), "JFK" (Kennedy), "Give 'Em Hell Harry" (Truman), and "the Gipper" (Reagan). Garfield did not have a nickname.

DID YOU KNOW?

President Warren G. Harding died in office under extremely suspicious circumstances.

Harding seemed to be a friendly and kindly man. His marriage was a stormy one and because he was quite handsome women found him attractive, which led him into numerous affairs.

One of these affairs may have cost him his life. At one point there was a rumor in Washington, D.C., that he had fathered an illegitimate child by a woman 30 years his junior. Harding's wife hired an investigator from the Bureau of Investigation (which later became the F.B.I.) to investigate the rumor and prove it false. Unfortunately, upon delving into the case the investigator proved just the opposite: the rumor was true.

Sometime later Mrs. Harding told the investigator that she had heard of a "little white powder" that could be slipped into a person's food or drink and would cause death. She demanded that the investigator tell her where to get this powder but he refused.

When returning from an Alaskan vacation the president's party stopped in Vancouver. The president became quite ill from what was thought to be food poisoning. Continuing the journey, the party stopped in San Francisco. The president and his wife checked into a hotel where the president suddenly died.

No one else in the party came down with food poisoning even though they had all eaten the same food.

The official cause of Harding's death was a stroke, but some doctors believed he had a heart attack or might have even been poisoned. These rumors intensified when Mrs. Harding refused to allow an autopsy or a death mask to be made.

Is it possible that the first lady, Florence Harding, had found some of that "little white powder" after all?

How many people died in the Civil War? (Can any war truly be civil?)

More Americans perished in the Civil War than in all the worldwide conflicts in United States history combined. At the beginning it was called a "90-day war" because most northerners believed it would be over by then. No one at that time had the faintest idea that it would last for four bloody years. The war produced 700,000 fatalities and nearly tore the nation apart. The number of Americans killed was more than double the number killed in World War II and accounted for 2 percent of the country's population.

The Union forces lost 23 percent of their troops and the Confederate forces lost about 24 percent. Not all died from bullets; disease was a major killer during that time. Almost two out of every three deaths were due to disease rather than battle wounds.

Even the soldiers who survived did not have an easy time of it. For example, it is estimated that every Confederate soldier was either wounded or fell ill from some sickness about six times during the course of the war.

Arlington National Cemetery is the final resting place for 18,000 Civil War soldiers. Another 15,000 soldiers who survived the war but later died of natural causes or accidents are also buried there. General Robert E. Lee is buried in a crypt on the campus of Washington and Lee University in Virginia and General Ulysses S. Grant is buried, where else, in Grant's Tomb in New York City.

One member of the Union Army was a large, reddish, white-faced water spaniel called Curly. During battles he would run between the skirmish lines barking. A badge around his neck proclaimed "I am Company A's dog. Whose dog are you?" Curly had a number of close calls, including being shot in the neck and breaking a leg. After the war, Curly attended all of his comrades' reunions for a number of years. He finally was sent to the National Soldier's Home in Dayton, Ohio, where he lived a luxurious life with his army companions until he died at the age of 12. He was buried on the grounds of the National Soldier's Home.

FACTOIDS

The youngest soldier killed in the Civil War was 12 years old.

Soldiers on both sides came from all walks of life and fought side by side. They were rich and poor, U.S.-born and immigrants, and as young as 10 and as old as 73 years old.

The bloodiest battle of the war was the 3-day battle of Gettysburg, which produced 51,116 casualties. Lincoln wrote his famous Gettysburg Address to honor those who had fallen in this battle.

Some women disguised themselves as men, enlisted in the army, and fought in the battles alongside the men.

There were 186,000 African Americans in the Union Army; many died as heroes.

Is it true that a former king of England had blue urine? (Does blue urine make you go crazy?)

It's almost true, but the color's a shade off. The king's urine was actually a deep purple. The king was George III, who ruled England and Ireland from 1760 to 1820. Experts believe that he suffered from porphyria, a hereditary disease that causes an overproduction of porphyrins, the reddish components of the portion of the red blood cell that carries oxygen through the body. Overproduction of porphyrins can cause the skin to turn red or blister in sunlight, can stain teeth to a reddish brown, and can cause the urine to vary in color from light pink to deep purple, depending on the severity of the disease and how long a person has had it.

Porphyria was just one of the king's problems. George III was also known as "Mad King George." Although some may have called him mad because he was arrogant, belligerent, and often irrational, history refers to him as mad because he was pronounced insane in 1811 and remained so the rest of his life, with only occasional lapses into reality. Some authorities believe that porphyria caused his madness, while others believe he was suffering from mental illness in addition to his physical afflictions. He was the first and only British king to lose his sanity.

Mad King George issued the Stamp Act, which permitted colonists in the Americas to be taxed without being represented in Parliament. This act was one of the factors precipitating the American Revolution, and led to George's being known as "the king who lost the American Colonies."

Napoleon was defeated at Waterloo during the reign of King George III but the king never knew it. By 1815 he was completely insane and the Prince of Wales (the future George IV) reigned over England.

History will always remember George III as Mad King George.

Many royal families have suffered maladies often brought about by intermarriage intended to "keep the royal lineage pure."

Members of the Hapsburg family of Spain often suffered from hemophilia, a condition in which even a small cut would cause uncontrolled bleeding. Many male descendants of England's Queen Victoria also suffered from hemophilia.

Charles II of Spain, also a member of the Hapsburg line, was known as "Charles the Mad."

"Mad King Ludwig" of Bavaria was a great admirer of Richard Wagner, the German composer. King Ludwig had a passion for building castles in the Bavarian mountains. His most famous castle, Neuschwanstein, was a fairytale castle perched on a rocky crag and decorated with scenes from Wagner's operas.

DID YOU KNOW?

In one case a disease of the royal family indirectly caused the downfall of an empire. Alexis, the only son of Nicholas II, the last czar of Russia, was a hemophiliac and the only heir to the Russian throne.

In 1908, Alexis started bleeding uncontrollably and the royal family summoned Rasputin, a self-proclaimed holy man with a reputation for miraculous cures. Rasputin somehow managed to stop the boy's bleeding. His mother, Alexandra, believed that God had sent this holy man to protect her son.

With Alexandra believing in his holy powers, Rasputin steadily gained more influence over the royal family. When the czar left to command the Russian armies fighting Germany during World War I, the running of the country was left to Alexandra or, as most believed, to Rasputin.

In 1916 a group of aristocrats, fearing Rasputin's growing power and influence over the czarina, decided to assassinate Rasputin and return control to the czar. They fed him poisoned cake, poisoned wine, and shot him at point-blank range. Rasputin did not die. He was then shot twice more, bludgeoned, kicked in the temples, wrapped with heavy chains, and thrown into an icy river. A later autopsy indicated that Rasputin was still alive when thrown into the river.

The conspirators did not take into account the fact that the Russian people saw Rasputin as a "man of the people." Within three months of Rasputin's death, the Bolshevik revolution brought down the Russian monarchy.

Who were the Knights Templar? (Did they find the Ark of the Covenant?)

The Knights Templar might be called soldier-monks. In 1118, almost twenty years after the First Crusade ended and the Holy City of Jerusalem was reclaimed for Christianity, nine knights from France came to Jerusalem and asked the king of Jerusalem, Baldwin II, for permission to form a new order. The purpose of the order was to keep the roads and highways safe for the incredible number of pilgrims making the perilous journey from Europe to Jerusalem. The crusaders had few strongholds in the Holy Land and traveling pilgrims were in danger of attack by roving bands of Muslims.

The king was so impressed with the devoted knights that he gave them an entire wing of his palace for their quarters. Because the wing was built on the foundations of the ancient Temple of Solomon, the knights became known as the "Poor Fellow Knights of Christ and the Temple of Solomon," soon shortened to the "Knights Templar."

The knights vowed to live a monastic life and took oaths of poverty, chastity, and obedience, the same oaths taken by monks. No new knights joined the order for nine years until Pope Honorius recognized the order in 1128. Within two years, 300 knights had joined the order.

Many believed that the Knights Templar formed the order primarily to find the Ark of the Covenant and the gold rumored to have been buried beneath the temple by the Jewish people when the Romans put down a rebellion in A.D. 70.

Within two centuries of their founding, the Knights Templar had become so powerful that no one could defy them except the Pope.

Because of their vast wealth and military power, they set up a network of storehouses and transported bullion to and from the Holy Land and Europe. They basically invented banking as we know it today.

Because the Knights Templar were feared as warriors and envied for their wealth and power, it became clear that it would be only a matter of time until their enemies destroyed them.

In 1307 King Philip IV of France had all of the Knights Templar in France arrested and then pressured Pope Clement V, also a Frenchman, to have the Knights Templar in all countries arrested.

The arrested knights were accused of many heinous crimes, including heresy, and were tortured or executed. In 1314 Jacques de Molay, the last grand master of the Knights Templar, was burned at the stake.

FACTOIDS

In spite of handling massive amounts of funds, the Knights Templar were scrupulously honest. Any type of fraud or theft was punishable by death.

At its height the order of the Knights Templar had up to 20,000 members, but only about 2,000 were actual knights.

Some scholars believe that the famed Shroud of Turin is actually the image of the last Grand Master of the Knights Templar, Jacques de Molay.

Although many dispute the theory that Freemasonry grew out of the order of the Knights Templar, most agree that it was influenced by the Knights Templar. A good example is the modern Demolay organization (named after Jacques de Molay) for young men, which is part of Freemasonry.

DID YOU KNOW?

In 1894 a group of British Army officers set out to map the vaults below the ruins of Herod's Temple. They discovered centuries-old tunnels, many of which were vaulted with keystone arches (the

Knights Templar were known for their proficiency as architects and masons). They also found a Templar sword, a spur, part of a lance, and a small Templar cross, artifacts that had been discarded 740 years before.

Did the Knights Templar find the most holy treasure of all, the Ark of the Covenant? If they did, where is it today?

Whether it still exists today or not, the search for the lost Ark of the Covenant is still discussed in today's movies, books, and historical works.

More questions? Try these websites.

ANY DAY IN HISTORY

http://www.scopesys.com/anyday/

Simply select a month and day and click on Show Events to find out everything that occurred on that day throughout history. Listed first are famous birthdays, from centuries past to the present time, followed by a list of famous people who died on that date in this century. Finally, you'll see a list of events for that day throughout history.

For example, if you select August 17, you'll see hundreds of events such as:

Davy Crockett was born in 1786

Vivian Vance, who played Ethel Mertz on "I Love Lucy," died at age 72

Pope Leo II was selected in 682

Robert Fulton's steamboat made its first trip on the Hudson River in 1807

WORLD HISTORY

http://www.hartford-hwp.com/gateway/index.html

This is an excellent site with well-organized links to just about anything you'd like to know about history. I suggest starting at World History Archives and then selecting the region you are interested in.

ANECDOTE: PUSHING A VAN AROUND AN ISLAND

Diego Garcia is a small horseshoe-shaped island in the Indian Ocean that was once a coconut plantation. Today, a major portion of the 7-square mile island is taken up by a runway large enough for the space shuttle to land in an emergency. It is a British-owned island but has a U.S. naval base on it.

I received an e-mail from Dave Burdges, who is the manager of the Navy Federal Credit Union. The credit union had an old van that suffered from a faulty transmission. It ran fine as long as it was driven forward. However, to drive in reverse was impossible. Dave and his co-workers had to get out of the van and push it. They were tired of pushing the van all over the island. After writing to the manufacturer's dealerships throughout the United States and not receiving any help, Dave was desperate and asked if I could help.

Dave included the model year and serial number of the van in his message. I called a number of dealers in the United States and gave them the van's serial number. The dealers just gasped and informed me that there was no way they could help. It turns out that the van had been built in Japan.

There seemed to be a problem with the information about the van so I asked Dave to verify it. Dave's friend Jim Flaherty put the van on a rack but could not find a single additional tag or label. However, Jim persisted and eventually found some old records and sent me the updated information.

I then asked where they had purchased the van. Dave told me they had bought it in the Philippines. This made things more difficult. I had to try and find a transmission for a 12-year-old van that was built in Japan, purchased in the Philippines, and then shipped to a tiny remote island in the Indian Ocean.

It took some time but I finally found a dealer in Manila in the Philippines who was willing to help. He sold Dave a used transmission for under $300.

When the transmission finally arrived on the island, they had no trouble installing it. It worked perfectly. The last I heard, Dave and his co-workers were happily driving around the island both forward and backward.

Holidays

Why are eggs associated with the Easter bunny? (Don't chickens lay eggs?)

In the spring, most cultures have festivals to celebrate fertility and new life. Rabbits are known for producing a great deal of young, particularly in the spring. Bird eggs are also laid in great numbers in the spring. In many cultures, rabbits, eggs, and spring, the time that new life is born, are symbols of fertility.

In early Anglo-Saxon times, the goddess of spring was called Eostre (sometimes she was known as Ostara). One particularly harsh winter, the wings of a bird became frozen. Eostre saved the bird by turning it into a hare. Not just any hare, but a magical hare that could lay eggs.

The Easter bunny as we know it originated in Germany in the 1500s. In fact, the first edible Easter bunnies were made in Germany during the early 1800s. They were made of pastry and sugar.

German settlers in Pennsylvania Dutch country introduced the Easter bunny, or "Oschter Haws," to America in the 1700s. Children believed that if they were good, the Oschter Haws would lay a nest of colored eggs. Boys would use their caps and girls would use their bonnets to make a nest in the house, barn, or garden hoping to find them full of colored eggs the next day. From this simple tradition, the use of elaborate Easter baskets eventually evolved.

Eggs were originally painted with bright colors to represent the spring sunlight. They were given as gifts.

FACTOIDS

The most famous Easter eggs are the fabulously decorated *pysanky* from Ukraine.

In Poland, a priest blesses the Easter eggs before they are given to family and friends. Romania and other countries also have this custom.

One Easter custom is for a person to tap the end of an egg against someone else's egg. The person who cracks the other's egg first is guaranteed good luck.

Many Christians dye eggs red to signify the blood of the risen Christ.

Wooden eggs are used in the annual White House Easter egg roll. The eggs, which have a unique design each year, can be bought by the general public at a modest cost.

On Easter in 1722, Admiral Roggeveen discovered an island filled with huge, mysterious stone heads. He named it Easter Island.

Easter is derived from three different traditions: pagan, Hebrew, and Christian.

In pagan times Eostre, the goddess of spring, was venerated in the spring, the traditional time of celebrating Easter. She also had the month of April dedicated to her. It was called "Eostur-monath."

Many names for Easter are derived from the root *pasch*, which comes from the Hebrew word *pesach* (Passover). Passover celebrates the night in Egypt when the angel of death "passed over" the homes of the Israelites and spared their firstborn. Jewish Pesach is celebrated during Nisan, the night of the first full moon of the first month of spring.

The first Christians continued to observe Jewish festivals, but with a new slant. During the Jewish celebration of Passover, the Christians added the concept of Christ as the true Paschal lamb and the first fruits from the dead (the winter-to-spring, death-to-life theme). It eventually became the Christian Easter.

The lighting of the Paschal candle is also from the Jewish celebration of Passover. Before the candle was lit, a new fire was started to symbolize driving away the powers of darkness and death.

What is the origin and meaning of Valentine's Day? (A mad emperor started it all.)

In A.D. 270 the mad emperor Claudius II decided that married men made poor soldiers because they did not want to leave their families to go to war. Because the Roman Empire needed soldiers, he issued a proclamation forbidding marriage. As a result, lovers secretly went to Valentine, a Christian bishop, who would marry them. When Claudius heard of this, he brought the bishop before him and attempted to convert him to Roman paganism. Valentine, in turn, unwisely tried to convert Claudius to Christianity and was sentenced to death for his impudence.

While in prison, Valentine fell in love with the blind daughter of the jailer. He left her a farewell love note and signed it "Your Valentine." He was executed on February 14. Some years later the Catholic Church proclaimed him a saint. Thus we celebrate Saint Valentine's Day, or Valentine's Day, on February 14 and dedicate the day to lovers.

In the ancient Roman Empire, February 14 was a holiday to honor Juno, the Queen of Roman gods and goddesses. This was also the eve of the feast of Lupercalia when the names of Roman maidens were written on slips of paper and dropped into jars. Each young man would draw a girl's name from a jar and the two would be partners for the festival, and often for an entire year.

The Christian Church felt this was an obscene custom and later replaced the feast of Lupercalia with Saint Valentine's Day. Either way, the day is a symbol of love and of lovers choosing one another.

FACTOIDS

More cards are sent on Valentine's Day than on any other holiday except Christmas.

Young men and women during the Middle Ages drew a name from a bowl to see who their valentine would be and wore the name on their sleeve for a week. This gave rise to the expression to "wear your heart on your sleeve," meaning to openly show other people your feelings.

Teachers receive the most valentines, followed by children, mothers, wives, and sweethearts.

The oldest known Valentine's Day card dates from 1415 when Charles, the Duke of Orleans, smuggled a love note to his wife while he was imprisoned in the Tower of London. It can be seen today in the British Museum.

During Prohibition, members of mobster Al Capone's gang disguised themselves as policemen, entered a garage run by the Bugs Moran gang, lined up their enemies against a wall, and machine-gunned them in cold blood. Because the shootout occurred on February 14, it became known as "the Saint Valentine's Day massacre."

Symbols of Valentine's Day include the heart, rose, lace, rings, doves, and Cupid.

In ancient times, people believed that all emotions such as love, happiness, anger, fear, jealousy, and hatred were found in the heart. In more recent times, only the emotion of love was thought to reside in the heart. Today, the heart is still a symbol of love.

Venus, the Roman goddess of love, favored the rose above all other flowers. Because the color red represents strong feelings, the red rose is now a flower of love.

Fine threads are woven together to make beautiful lace. Hundreds of years ago, women were required to be coy. If a woman saw a man that interested her, she would drop her lace handkerchief in the hopes he would pick it up, return it to her, and engage in conversation. People soon began to associate lace with romance. Even today, paper lace decorates candy boxes and valentine cards.

Venus' favorite birds were doves because they remain with the same mates for their entire lives. Doves have become Valentine's Day symbols of loyalty and love.

Where did the custom of kissing under the mistletoe originate? (We come in peace.)

Mistletoe has long been associated with peace. However, no one completely agrees on the origin of kissing under the mistletoe.

Ancient Romans believed that mistletoe had the magic power of peace. If opposing soldiers met under a mistletoe-covered tree, they would temporarily put down their weapons and declare peace for the day. In later times, in both England and Scandinavia, it was customary to hang mistletoe over doorways. Anyone who passed under supposedly came in peace and was greeted in a friendly manner, perhaps with a kiss. This probably accounts for the current custom of kissing under the mistletoe.

There are many legends about mistletoe. One Scandinavian legend states that Loki, the god of destruction, killed Baldur, the god of peace, by shooting him with an arrow made from mistletoe. Other gods and goddesses were saddened by Baldur's death and asked that his life be restored, which it was. In appreciation, his mother Frigga hung up the mistletoe and promised to kiss all who passed under it. Because of this, mistletoe became the symbol of both forgiveness and love.

In England's Victorian era, it became stylish to kiss under the mistletoe. Many homes used a "kissing bow" made of two loops decorated with apples, oranges, mistletoe, and other greenery.

FACTOIDS

It was once believed that mistletoe came from bird dung because it often appeared on branches covered with bird droppings. Because of this, the Anglo-Saxon words *mistel* for "dung" and *toe* for "twig" were combined to form *mistletoe*, which means "dung on a twig."

In certain parts of England, mistletoe is burned on the Twelfth Night. If not burned, the belief is that all who kissed under it will never get married.

During the Middle Ages, mistletoe was hung from ceilings and over doors to ward off evil spirits and prevent witches from entering.

The ancient Celts called mistletoe *uile*, which means "all healer." They believed it could cure anything, including epilepsy. Modern science has shown that mistletoe contains the drug phoratoxin, used to improve blood circulation and slow the heart rate.

There is an old superstition that if you place a twig of mistletoe under your pillow you will not have nightmares.

Mistletoe is a partial parasite. Like a true parasite, it grows on trees and sends out roots that penetrate the tree and suck out the nutrients. However, it can also grow by itself just as any other plant.

DID YOU KNOW?

Ancient Druids gathered mistletoe during the winter solstice. Because it had no roots in the earth, they believed it was of divine origin or was created by lightning. Druids also believed that the oak tree was sacred to the gods and mistletoe growing on an oak tree was especially magical.

When gathering mistletoe, the Druid high priest would climb the tree to cut the mistletoe with a golden knife. The mistletoe was not allowed to touch the ground and was dropped into a white linen cloth. It was then taken to a temple and placed beneath the altar stone for three days. On the fourth day, the priests chopped the mistletoe into pieces and gave it to their followers. The priests kept the white berries to use in healing diseases.

Because this solemn ceremony took place when we now celebrate Christmas, mistletoe eventually became associated with that holiday.

What is the origin of celebrating New Year's Eve? (Ringing out the old, ringing in the new, giants beware!)

Celebrating the new year is probably the oldest holiday in the world. Virtually every culture from the beginning of time has had some custom to signify the coming of the new year.

Over 4,000 years ago the ancient Babylonians celebrated the coming of the new year around the end of March. This is a logical time for the celebration because it is the time of year when spring begins and new crops are planted. Like us the Babylonians made New Year's resolutions. However, rather than resolving to lose weight or quit smoking, their most popular resolution was to return farm equipment they had borrowed.

During the Roman Empire, the calendar eventually went out of synchronization with the moon. To put things back in order, Caesar let one year last for 445 days. In 153 B.C. the Roman senate declared that January first would be the beginning of the new year. Although this arbitrary date has neither astronomical nor agricultural significance, today we still consider it to be the start of a new year.

The Romans continued to celebrate the new year but the early church condemned the holiday as pagan and continued to oppose the festivities throughout the Middle Ages. As a result, the New Year's Day holiday has only been celebrated by Western nations for the past 400 years.

FACTOIDS

Using a baby to signify the new year started in Greece around 600 B.C. The baby was carried in a basket to represent the rebirth of Dionysus, the god of fertility. The image of a baby with a New Year's banner was brought to the United States by the Germans, who had used this symbol since the fourteenth century.

To celebrate the new year in Tibet Buddhist monks create sculptures made from yak butter, some reaching as high as 30 feet.

Many New Year's traditions include pigs. For example, in Austria each new year starts with a dinner of roast suckling pig. In most parts of the world the pig symbolizes moving forward into the new year. A pig moves forward with its snout to the ground.

In Crete nothing is thrown away on New Year's Day, not even waste. It is believed that throwing something away that day will decrease the wealth of the family during the coming year.

In most Muslim societies New Year's Day is observed by wearing new clothes. In Southeast Asia birds and turtles are released for good luck during the coming year. In India, Hindus place shrines next to their beds so they will see beautiful objects when they open their eyes at the start of a new year.

DID YOU KNOW?

The Chinese celebrate the New Year holiday a month or so later than we do. There are 12 animals in Chinese astrology and each year is named after one of them. Thus, it might be the "year of the dragon" or the "year of the snake." The cycle repeats every 12 years.

Firecrackers are always associated with the Chinese New Year holiday, stemming from an ancient Chinese legend. This legend tells the story of a foul-smelling giant who lived on the western side of a village. If someone offended the giant, he would inflict malaria on them. One of the villagers suggested that they might scare the giant away if they created a great deal of noise. So the people of the village made a huge pile of bamboo stems and set them on fire. As the stems burned, they exploded and frightened the giant so badly that he ran away and never returned.

So the next time you see firecrackers at the Chinese New Year celebration, you can be sure that no foul-smelling giants will be lurking nearby.

How did the custom of trick-or-treating on Halloween begin? (Have you ever carved a face into a turnip?)

There are a number of plausible theories about the origin of trick-or-treating. Most date back to around 800 B.C. when Britain was occupied by the Celts. At the end of summer, near our month of October, the Celts held a festival called Samhain, meaning "summer's end." To celebrate the festival, the Celts gave food offerings to the gods and often went from house to house asking for food donations to present to the gods. Younger Celts would ask residents for gifts of kindling to keep the Samhain bonfire burning throughout the festival.

Other authorities believe that in 370 B.C. the Celts, who were a farming people, had a "night of mischief" around the time of the Samhain festival. During that night, after a rendezvous at some predetermined spot, groups of boys would rush toward farmhouses, racing to see who would be first to open the kitchen door latch. The people in the house would hand them white bread or money as a levy through half-opened doors.

Another theory is that during medieval times costumed celebrants would sing and dance as they paraded through the streets, stopping at each house to ask for drink and food to reward them for their performance.

Whether the custom of trick-or-treating originated in 800 B.C. or in medieval times, it is certainly an ancient custom and one that shows no signs of disappearing today.

FACTOIDS

In the eighth century there were so many saints that there were not enough days in the year to give each saint a unique day. So Pope Gregory III dedicated a chapel to honor all saints and in 837 Pope Gregory IV ordered that All Saints' Day would be observed to honor all the saints. All Hallow Even was the evening before All Saints' Day (*hallow* means "saint" or "holy" in Old English). All Saints' Day was originally called "Hallowmas." The name Hallow Even was eventually shortened to Hallowe'en and finally to Halloween.

Halloween is usually celebrated only in North America. The customs built upon ancient Celtic traditions were brought to this country by Irish immigrants who left Ireland because of the potato famine.

Because pumpkins never grew in Europe, the original jack-o'-lantern was a turnip. The turnip is a favorite vegetable among Europeans.

Apples are also an ancient Halloween tradition. It was believed that if you peeled an apple in front of a mirror lit by candlelight you would see an image of your future spouse. The longer the unbroken peel, the longer your life was to be.

Because the Celts had to rekindle their home fires from an ember taken from the Samhain bonfire, they had to walk home in the dark. Being afraid of evil spirits on this night, they dressed in costumes and carved grotesque faces in their ember holders to frighten the evil spirits. This is the origin of wearing frightening costumes on Halloween.

In the fall, the migrating monarch butterflies return to Mexico. The ancient Aztecs and many Mexicans of today believe that each butterfly carries the spirit of a dead ancestor. These spirits are honored during "the Days of the Dead" (*Los Dias de los Muertos*), which are celebrated during Halloween, All Saints' Day, and All Souls' Day (October 31 through November 2).

DID YOU KNOW?

The term "jack-o'-lantern" is derived from an Irish folk tale prevalent in the eighteenth century. Jack tricked the Devil into climbing an apple tree and then trapped the Devil in the tree's branches by quickly carving the symbol of a cross in the trunk. It took a long time for the Devil to escape. When Jack died he was not allowed into heaven because of the mean and stingy life he had led. The Devil remembered how Jack had tricked him and refused to let him into Hell. So Jack was destined to walk the earth for eternity. The Devil felt somewhat sorry for him and gave him a burning coal to light his path. Jack had been eating a turnip and put the coal inside the turnip. Now, we place a candle in a pumpkin for our "jack-o'-lantern."

What is the origin of the Christmas tree? (Did a tree help make our country free?)

No one knows for sure exactly what started the custom of decorating a Christmas tree.

One legend claims that Saint Boniface started the custom in Germany in the eighth century. Saint Boniface found a group of pagans worshipping an oak tree and became so angry that he cut it down. Almost instantly a small fir tree sprang up from the center of the oak stump and reached the sky. Saint Boniface told the onlookers that this would be their holy tree because it was evergreen, a symbol of everlasting life.

Many authorities believe that the origin of the Christmas tree is based on more ancient customs. On December 21, the shortest day of the year, ancient Egyptians decorated their homes with green palm branches to symbolize life's triumph over death. Romans used evergreens to decorate their homes during the winter festival of Saturnalia, which honored Saturnus, the god of farming. Ancient Druids placed evergreen branches over doors to frighten away evil spirits.

Some think that the custom of decorating Christmas trees was started by Martin Luther. In 1500, Martin Luther was walking through snowy woods, enthralled with the stars, the landscape, and the branches of the snow-covered evergreen trees that shimmered in the moonlight. When he got home, he placed a small tree in the house and decorated it with candles in an attempt to show his children the majesty surrounding Christ's birth.

Aside from the myths and legends, the modern Christmas tree originated in Germany and the first written reference comes from the sixteenth century. The tree started out as a prop in a play about Adam and Eve, was adorned with apples, and was called a paradise tree. Because December 24 was the feast of Adam and Eve, people began setting up paradise trees in their homes on that day. At first they hung apples on the tree but later they added wafers, symbolizing the host. Eventually the wafers were replaced with cookies.

Although popular among German Lutherans, it was not until 200 years later that the Christmas tree became a custom throughout Germany. German mercenaries who were hired by the British to fight the American colonists during the American Revolution brought this custom with them to the Colonies and by the nineteenth century the custom had spread throughout the United States.

FACTOIDS

In 1851, the first Christmas trees in the country were sold by Mark Carr, who lived in upstate New York. Carr cut down trees in the Catskill Mountains, hauled them to New York City, set up a stall, and quickly sold them all. A small tree sold for five or ten cents, a 20-foot tree cost a quarter. The Carr family continued the business for the next 47 years.

A Christmas tree might have been instrumental in our winning the American Revolution. While General George Washington was crossing the Delaware River on a bitterly cold Christmas Eve, the German mercenaries had left their guard posts to celebrate around a candlelit evergreen tree that reminded them of home. General Washington was thus able to surprise the British forces and defeat them.

During the Depression, few people could afford landscaping and nurseries could not sell their evergreen trees. They cut them down and sold them as Christmas trees. Because the trees were more evenly shaped than wild trees, customers preferred them and Christmas tree farms started springing up around the country.

Puritans banned Christmas trees in New England, and as late as 1870 schools in Boston held classes on Christmas Day.

In 1890, A.F.W. Woolworth introduced the first glass Christmas tree ornaments from small cottage glass-blowing shops in Europe.

DID YOU KNOW?

At Christmas we often hear the story of the three kings and their gifts of gold, frankincense, and myrrh. We all know what gold is, but many people have no idea what frankincense and myrrh are.

Frankincense and myrrh are similar. Each is the sap or resin from a tree that grows in the Middle East. To speed up sap gathering, large cuts are made in the tree trunks and the desert sun quickly dries the oozing sap to form hard, knobby clumps of sap called tears.

Frankincense was burned as incense and produced a strong aromatic odor. It was also used as a cosmetic by the Egyptians. Myrrh was used for diverse medicinal purposes. The Egyptians used myrrh as part of the embalming process.

Frankincense and myrrh are believed to have great therapeutic qualities and can still be purchased today, usually as incense or oils. Most of these products are imported from Somalia, but some still come from Middle Eastern countries such as Oman.

More questions?
Try these websites.

CHRISTMAS

http://wilster.com/xmas/

A comprehensive Christmas site covering the origins of Christmas and Santa Claus. It lists a number of countries around the world, tells you how to say "Merry Christmas" in the language of that country, and describes how Christmas is celebrated in that country.

SANTA CLAUS

http://www.santaclaus.com/

Features Christmas around the world and frequently asked questions about Santa Claus, holiday stories, recipes, games, and more.

ADVENT CALENDAR

http://www.rooneydesign.com/main.html

Click on XMAS at the top of the page to see the Advent calendar. Every day click on the appropriate number to see the animated feature for that day.

SAINT PATRICK'S DAY

http://www.st-patricks-day.com/

Read about the legend of Saint Patrick's Day and the legend of the shamrock. This site also has a list of Saint Patrick's Day parades around the world, as well as a variety of sites related to Ireland. You can see a list of Irish clans or discover your Irish roots. There are also two links to children's pages.

8

Language

What is Zulu time?
(It has nothing to do with Africa.)

The world is divided into 24 time zones. To make communication easier, each time zone has been given a letter of the alphabet (the letters "I" and "O" are not used).

For military, maritime, and other activities that cross time zones, the international reference of time is the clock at Greenwich, England. The letter designation for this clock is "Z." In the phonetic alphabet, Zulu is used for the letter Z. Thus, the Greenwich, England, time zone is known as "Zulu time."

Times are usually written in a 24-hour (military) format followed by the letter designating the time zone. For instance, 1830Z would be 6:30 P.M. in Zulu time.

Zulu time is formally known as Greenwich Mean Time (GMT). The official name today is Coordinated Universal Time (CUT). Actually, GMT, CUT, and Zulu time all refer to the same thing.

FACTOIDS

Time based on the earth's rotation is irregular. Only four days in the year actually have exactly 24 hours in them (around December 25, April 15, June 14, and August 31).

In ancient times people believed that the earth was influenced by the sun, moon, and the five planets known at that time. Each of these objects was associated with a god and each god was given a day in his honor. This is the origin of the seven-day week.

At one time ancient Egyptians had a 10-day week and Romans had an 8-day week. Both eventually adopted the 7-day week used by most of the ancient world.

Although most of us are familiar with the sundial, few are aware of the night-clock that was centered on the pole star and whose arms rotated to line up with the stars in the handle of the Big Dipper.

In spite of the extreme accuracy of atomic clocks, earth time still takes precedence. If the atomic clock and the "natural" clock do not coincide, scientists add or subtract "leap seconds" on the last day of June and December.

The day of two noons occurred in 1883 when an association of railroad executives devised a system of standard time zones across the United States. Prior to that, there were 100 different time zones in the United States. The new time was telegraphed to cities and towns throughout the country. In some areas, it was already past noon when they received the new time, which was before noon. Thus, those areas had two noons on the same day.

Throughout the ages, people have striven to find better ways of keeping track of time.

In the Middle Ages hourglasses were rarely used and sundials were inadequate when skies were cloudy. Strange methods were used to circumvent these problems. England's King Alfred the Great, for example, carried a supply of candles of equal lengths. He lit each in turn to mark the passage of the hours.

The invention of the mechanical clock was influenced by monks who lived in monasteries that were the epitome of order and routine. They had to keep accurate time so that monastery bells could be rung at regular intervals to announce the seven hours of the day reserved for prayer.

Early clocks were nothing more than a weight tied to a rope wrapped around a revolving drum. Time was determined by watching the length of the weighted rope.

The discovery of the pendulum in the seventeenth century led to a proliferation of clocks and enormous public clocks.

Eventually, keeping time turned into serving time and rationing time. People started to follow the mechanical time of clocks rather than their natural body time. They ate at meal time, rather than when they were hungry, and went to bed when it was time, rather than when they were sleepy. Even periodicals and fashions became "yearly." The world had become orderly. A common expression was "regular as clockwork."

Even today, our society is preoccupied with time. We all have numerous clocks, watches, and calendars. Perhaps it's not all bad. As an anonymous author said, "Time is God's way of keeping everything from happening at once."

What does "mind your p's and q's" mean? (How about a beer?)

One of the more popular theories is that hundreds of years ago, patrons of English pubs would often run up a bar tab. To keep track of how much a patron owed, the bartender would keep a tally of the pints (p's) and quarts (q's) of beer the patron had consumed. If the bill got too high, the bartender would tell the patron "Mind your p's and q's." In other words, "Pay up!"

FACTOIDS

In Tudor England, selected innkeepers were required by a royal act to maintain stables. Some innkeepers acted as unofficial postmasters and even issued unofficial coins, which they guaranteed to redeem in the realm's currency.

Early inns or taverns were identified by simple signs, such as lions, dolphins, or black swans. Many had colorful names such as the Bag o' Nails, the Goat and Compass, and the Elephant and Castle.

Britons today are finding other ways to spend their leisure time such as visiting gyms or having a healthy meal at a restaurant. Pubs holding to tradition are expected to slowly die out over time. It is estimated that there will be 5,000 fewer pubs by the end of the century than there were at the beginning.

Although Americans savor the taste of a cold beer, Englishmen prefer their beer served at room temperature.

Some 200 of the old coaching and posting inns, including a few that date back over 400 years, are still operating in England and Wales today.

DID YOU KNOW?

Patrons of pubs certainly know the popularity of darts. Throwing feathered darts at a circular board with numbered spaces became popular in English inns and taverns in the nineteenth century and increasingly so in the twentieth century. In fact, a form of darts was a training game for English archers in the Middle Ages.

In its modern form in Britain, the game is ordinarily played in the public house (pub or tavern), or in a club, rather than in the home.

There are actually more darts players in the United States than in England. It's estimated that there are over 17 million in the United States, but only 5 million in England.

Why do people say "Gesundheit" or "God bless you" when you sneeze? (Are you plagued with sneezing?)

The expression "Gesundheit" (German for "God bless you") began in the Middle Ages when the bubonic plague was ravaging Europe. In the final stages of the disease, the afflicted had fits of sneezing. When others heard someone sneeze, they knew the person was about to die so they said, "God bless you."

The familiar nursery rhyme "Ring Around the Rosey" also dates from the time of the bubonic plague. Because the plague often caused red discolorations on the body, that person was sometimes called a "rosey." To prevent the plague from spreading to other towns, the villagers had to make sure the plague carrier did not leave. They symbolized this by saying "Ring around the rosey," which meant to hold hands and form a ring around the rosey to keep the sick person from leaving the village.

The next line in the rhyme, "A pocket full of posies," has two meanings. Some authorities say that people thought "posies" would ward off the plague. Others say it refers to the funeral wreath.

The last line, "Ashes, ashes, all fall down," refers to death. "Ashes to ashes and dust to dust" is a phrase often used in funeral ceremonies. "All fall down" meant that everyone in the village would probably die because the plague had entered their town.

Few people reciting this nursery rhyme realize its poignant meaning.

FACTOIDS

Symptoms of the bubonic plague include swelling of the lymph glands in the neck, armpits, and groin. The blackish color of these swellings gave the disease its name, the "Black Death."

An epidemic outbreak of the plague in Europe that began in 1346 killed 25 million people, one third of Europe's population, in just five years. The plague lasted for almost 300 years.

During the 1980s, there were about 18 plague cases each year in the United States, of which more than half occurred in persons under 20 years of age.

DID YOU KNOW?

There have been three major bubonic plague epidemics in history.

The first was in A.D. 542 and in just two years killed 70,000 people in the city of Constantinople alone. At its peak, 10,000 people died each week. The plague followed the trade routes to France and Italy and additional smaller outbreaks continued for 52 years.

The second epidemic was the most devastating. It began in A.D. 1346 and spread across Europe and Asia, eventually reaching Russia. In just 4 years it caused more deaths than the first outbreak had caused in 50 years. People became preoccupied with death and the afterlife. They were angry that God had not answered their prayers, and moved away from the Roman Catholic Church toward mysticism and other spiritual movements. Jews were blamed for the plague and were massacred. In England alone, over 1,000 villages became void of human life.

The third major outbreak occurred in Manchuria in 1890 and reached San Francisco in 1900. By the time it was over, more than 12 million people had died, mostly in India and Asia.

The plague still occurs. In 1992, cases were reported in Brazil, China, Madagascar, Mongolia, Myanmar, Peru, the United States,

Vietnam, and Zaire. Major outbreaks in India have occurred as recently as 1994.

Where did the term "dark horse" come from? (You can bet on it.)

The expression originated in England in 1831 in a book by Benjamin Disraeli. He said, "A dark horse, which had never been thought of, rushed past the grand stand in sweeping triumph."

A more interesting fable concerns Sam Flyn and his horse Dusky Pete. Although Dusky Pete was a swift racehorse, he was very dark and looked like a worn-out nag. Sam went from town to town, entering his horse in each local race. It was easy to take bets against the horse because no one believed that such a worn-out nag could possibly win. But Dusky Pete won every race, and Sam Flyn made a great deal of money.

Either Disraeli's story or the legend of Sam Flyn could have led to our use of the term "dark horse" to indicate someone who is expected to lose but wins.

In American politics, when a candidate is either unknown or wins unexpectedly, he is called a "dark horse" candidate. In 1844, the Democratic convention produced the first political dark horse in James Polk, who later became president. There are also dark horses in racing. A somewhat awkward chestnut horse by the name of Exterminator was used by his owner to stay behind the owner's best horse to urge it to run faster. Just prior to the Kentucky Derby, the owner's favorite horse was hurt in a workout and the only horse he had left to enter was Exterminator. He thought the horse didn't stand a chance but entered him anyway.

It rained heavily during the day of the Derby and the odds against Exterminator were 30 to 1. He was at the back of the pack as the horses neared the last turn. Exterminator picked up the pace, passing one horse after another, never giving up until he had crossed the finish line. Exterminator, the dark horse, won the Kentucky Derby by a length.

One of the all-time great racehorses and the greatest money-winning Thoroughbreds in history was Man o'War. He set three world records, two New American records, and two track records. Some of his records stood for 17 years. He was equally good at any distance and on any track: fast, good, or sloppy.

The fastest speed recorded for a racehorse was over 43 mph when Big Racket ran $\frac{1}{4}$ mile in Mexico City in 1945. In 1989 Hawkster ran $1\frac{1}{2}$ miles at a speed of almost 38 mph.

A typical Thoroughbred racehorse can run only about $\frac{1}{4}$ mile at top speed. The role of the jockey is to determine the best time to release this burst of speed.

Forego was older when he was entered in the Marlboro Cup. He was forced to carry 18 pounds more than the top horse in the race. A sloppy track made it tough for a come-from-behind horse like Forego. Although it appeared hopeless, Forego drove hard down the final stretch, relentlessly closing the gap between him and the leader. Just as he reached the finish line, he pushed his head forward to win the race. It was considered one of the greatest finishes of the decade.

DID YOU KNOW?

Horse racing is one of the most ancient sports, originating in Central Asia among prehistoric nomadic tribesmen around 4500 B.C.

When humans began keeping written records, horse racing was already an organized sport throughout the world. Chariot and mounted horse racing were not only popular in the Greek Olympics almost 700 years before Christ, but also became an obsession in the Roman Empire.

When the Crusades were over in the twelfth century, many returning English knights rode fast Arabian horses. For the next 400 years, more and more Arabian stallions were imported and bred with English mares to produce horses that had both speed and stamina. The nobility enjoyed wagering on two-horse races.

During Queen Anne's reign in the early 1700s, more horses were used in races and the spectators were allowed to bet on the outcome. Racecourses proliferated all over England and large purses were offered to attract the best horses.

The sport expanded so rapidly that in 1750 the Jockey Club was formed to govern the races. To this day, the Jockey Club has complete control over horse racing in England.

How did grapefruit get its name? (It's a lot bigger than a grape.)

A grapefruit tree is 15 to 20 feet tall with dark-green, glossy leaves. The grapefruit got its name because the fruit hangs in clusters on the tree, just like grapes.

The ancestor of the grapefruit was called a "pomelo." This subtropical evergreen was brought to Barbados from the Malay archipelago by a Captain Shaddock. The fruit was also sometimes called a "shaddock." It was also called the "forbidden fruit" because of an ancient Barbados myth that tells the story of how the shaddock and sweet orange came from across the sea and mated to produce the grapefruit. It eventually became known as grapefruit.

The West Indies pomelo was probably crossed with an orange to produce the modern grapefruit, introduced in Florida in 1840. Fifty years later a seedless fruit was found and propagated to create a seedless grapefruit.

Over half of the world's grapefruit is produced in the United States, primarily in Florida and Texas. A single mature tree can produce up to 1,490 pounds of grapefruit per season.

The two main categories of grapefruit are seeded and seedless. Grapefruit can also be white or red, both equally sweet. Only oranges and lemons have more vitamin C than grapefruit.

As with all citrus, ripened fruit may have a tinge of green but it does not affect the quality. The green occurs when extra chlorophyll is produced for the new spring blossoms.

FACTOIDS

Lemons have more sugar than strawberries.

President Lyndon Johnson liked the grapefruit-flavored soda Fresca so much that he had a fountain installed in the Oval Office from which he could dispense the beverage by pushing a button on his desk chair.

California fruit growers started growing lemons to satisfy the demand of Gold Rush miners who were willing to pay high prices for lemons and oranges because they prevented scurvy.

Some people believe that bathing in grapefruit oil or inhaling its vapors will alleviate depression, resentment, and gallstones.

Kumquat means "golden orange" in Chinese. Because kumquat rinds are sweet and thin, this is the only citrus fruit that can be eaten in its entirety, skin and all.

Mongols invented lemonade in the thirteenth century.

Why do people yell "Geronimo" when they jump off something? (Especially symbolic when jumping out of an Apache aircraft.)

Geronimo was a Chiricahua Apache war chief. There is a legend that Geronimo was being pursued by the U.S. Cavalry at Medicine Bluffs, Oklahoma. His path was cut off by a steep cliff bordering a river. The only chance he had of escaping was to jump off the cliff on horseback into the river below. As he made the daring leap, he cried out his name in defiance of the troopers. Geronimo survived and escaped.

During World War II the name "Geronimo" was adopted as a battle cry of U.S. paratroopers as they jumped out of their planes. The first paratrooper unit to use the cry was the 82d Airborne at Fort Bragg, North Carolina.

Geronimo was captured in 1885 but escaped with a small

band of warriors. Over 5,000 soldiers and 500 Indian auxiliaries attempted to capture Geronimo's band. After traveling 1,645 miles for over five months, the soldiers finally found Geronimo's band, which had eluded them for so long. The band had only 35 warriors along with 8 children and 101 women. Geronimo had been outnumbered by over 150 to 1, yet managed to hold the army at bay for almost half a year.

Geronimo later escaped but was captured once again. Although President Grover Cleveland believed all the lurid newspaper stories about Geronimo's terrible acts of evil and wanted him hanged, more sensible men prevailed and Geronimo was sent to Fort Marion, Florida. The Apaches had lived in high, dry country and could not tolerate the hot and humid climate of Florida. When Geronimo arrived in Florida, he found his comrades dying – over one hundred had died from consumption alone.

Finally, Geronimo's old enemies, the Kiowas and Comanches, offered him a part of their reservation at Fort Sill, Oklahoma. Geronimo went to Fort Sill in 1894 and remained there as prisoner of war until his death in 1909. Although he was buried in the Apache cemetery, legend says that shortly afterward his remains were secretly stolen and buried somewhere in the Southwest. No one has ever found Geronimo's bones.

FACTOIDS

Apache is actually a Zuni Indian word meaning "enemy."

Of the three major groups of Apaches (Jicarilla, Mescalero, and Chiricahua), the Chiricahua were the most nomadic and warlike.

The last U.S. census showed only slightly more than 53,000 Apache Native Americans, accounting for only 2.8 percent of the total Native American population in the United States.

Unlike other Native Americans, the Apaches had no tribal organization and lived in small autonomous bands. In 1874, the U.S. government forcibly moved 4,000 Apaches to a barren reservation in Arizona where they were deprived of all rights and lacked proper food and shelter. They turned to Geronimo and asked him to lead them to freedom. This is how he became a leader of such a large group of Apaches.

Geronimo's Apache name was Goyathlay, which means "one who yawns."

One of the first statements of the U.S. Congress under the new Constitution was from a declaration issued in 1787, which said, in part, "The utmost good faith shall always be observed toward the Indians, their lands and property shall never be taken from them without their consent ..."

DID YOU KNOW?

The Native Americans have contributed greatly to our culture. Many of the foods that are common today were unheard of in Europe. It was the Native Americans who taught the colonists how to gather and use this food.

The list of Native American food is long, but here are just a few items to give you an idea of what we owe to the Native Americans: corn, squash, pumpkins, beans, chili peppers, pecans, sassafras, cranberries, and maple syrup. By the end of the twentieth century, over one third of all food produced in the United States came from crops of Native American origin.

Much of our language comes from Native American words, including moose, caribou, raccoon, opossum, chipmunk, skunk, hickory, squash, avocado, bayou, savanna, tomato, potato, toboggan, dory, and caucus. Over 2,200 words in our language have been taken directly from Native American languages.

So much of what we take for granted today comes directly from Native Americans. Perhaps we should learn how to say the Apache word for "thank you."

What is the origin of the word "jazz"? (Does the lady sing the blues near a maple tree?)

No one knows for sure how the word "jazz" originated. There are almost as many different explanations as there are people writing about jazz. Three theories, each relating to someone's name, are widely accepted.

Some think the word came from Mr. Razz, a band conductor in New Orleans around 1904.

Others believe the word was coined around 1895 and was derived from the name of a Mississippi drummer named Charles Washington, whom everyone called Chaz.

The third theory holds that the word "jazz" was derived from the name of Charles Alexander, who made the song *Alexander's Ragtime Band* famous. Because his name was always abbreviated on programs as "Chas.," people pronounced it Chazz. When the band's music became exceedingly lively or "hot," fans would yell out "Come on, Chazz," which later became "Jazz," and eventually referred to music of that type.

Some scholars have tried to trace the word "jazz" to the following cultures but have not as yet been able to prove their theories:

- Arabic "chasse" (a dance step)

- Arabic "jazib" (one who allures)

- African "jaiza" (sound of distant drums)

- Hindu "jasba" (ardent desire)

To add to the confusion, jazz was at one time a verb for sexual intercourse and still is so used in some of today's slang.

It is believed that jazz had its embryonic beginnings in plantation brass bands around 1835 and developed a more formal structure when ragtime music was introduced. Ragtime music takes its syncopated rhythm from march music and is generally considered to be the forerunner of jazz. Scott Joplin was the "King of Ragtime."

In the 1920s some of the famous jazz groups were the New Orleans Rhythm Kings and bands led by Jelly Roll Morton, King Oliver, and Louis Armstrong. The music of these groups included improvised solos and later led to the Chicago style of jazz.

FACTOIDS

Ragtime composer Scott Joplin's best-known piece is the *Maple Leaf Rag*. Although no one knows how it got there, a large maple tree is growing at his gravesite.

Green Dolphin Street is a standard jazz tune. It is also the name of one of Chicago's largest jazz nightclubs, the name of a fictitious street in London in the 1800s, the title of a novel by Elizabeth Goudge, and the title of a 1947 movie made from her novel.

Jelly Roll Morton was a professional piano player in the bordellos of New Orleans. Although he was one of the first ragtime piano players, he was ridiculed for later claiming he had "invented" jazz in 1902.

DID YOU KNOW?

One can't talk about jazz without mentioning the greatest female jazz singer of all time, Billie Holiday.

On the darker side, Billie Holiday was self-destructive, an alcoholic and a heroin addict who was drawn to violent men who exploited her.

On her professional side, she was one of the most remarkable singers of the century. Although she had no training, she had a vivid musical style that created intricate musical effects. Most of all she was noted for the intensity of her singing. She lived every word she sang. Whether she was singing of love or pain, it seemed as if she was experiencing it right then and there. People believed her and often cried when she performed. Her voice would envelop whoever heard her in such a way that no listener was ever the same again. As Billie herself once said, "What comes out is what I feel."

She came from an impoverished family and her father abandoned the family when she was young. After school she scrubbed floors until she was exhausted just to earn enough money for her and her mother to survive. She grew up alone and felt unloved.

Her unhappy life did not improve as she got older. Her years as a singer had their highs and lows. She had years of fame with occasional days of happiness. But her sadness created some of the greatest songs of our time.

Billie Holiday died in 1959 when she was only 44 years old.

What is the origin of the phrase "It's not over until the fat lady sings"? (It's difficult to sing when you've just been stabbed to death.)

In many operas, the final scene ends with an aria sung by a lady singer, so the opera isn't over until she completes her last song. For many years female opera singers tended to be large. Therefore, you could say that the opera isn't over until the fat lady is done singing. Today the expression means that you should never assume something is finished until you're sure. Sometimes, a situation that appears to be completed is only going through a temporary pause.

Some opera haters find it amusing that in a final operatic scene, the heroine is killed and with her dying breath belts out a lengthy solo that can be heard throughout the entire opera house.

FACTOIDS

The oldest performing opera singer was Victor Han, a Russian, who sang onstage in Moscow at the age of 90.

Rossini wrote *The Barber of Seville* in just 11 days. A good copyist would take 20 days just to copy the score that Rossini wrote.

In the opera *Don Giovanni*, one scene calls for an actor to descend into hell. One portly singer got stuck in the stage trapdoor used for his descent. No matter how hard he pushed or pulled, the singer remained stuck. Finally, a voice from the audience yelled out, "Don't worry, hell is already full!"

When the opera *Carmen* premiered, critics said it was immoral, obscene, and had no artistic value. Hardly anyone attended the next few performances. The composer, Georges Bizet, died three months later. Since his death, *Carmen* has become one of the most popular operas of all time.

In 1871 there were 3,000 theaters in Italy where an opera could be performed. By 1992 the number had dwindled to 840, of which only 36 were theaters used primarily for opera.

A fan once wrote to Giuseppe Verdi and asked to be reimbursed for all of his expenses because Verdi's opera *Aida* didn't arouse any emotions in him. Verdi paid the expenses but only after the fan signed an agreement that he would never again listen to any of Verdi's operas.

During an argument between conductor Arturo Toscanini and singer Geraldine Farrar, Miss Farrar said, "Remember, the audience pays to see my face, not your backside."

DID YOU KNOW?

Opera has a long and rich history. However, if you're not an opera fan, you might have difficulty understanding the difference between an opera and a musical.

An opera is basically a drama set to music. Performers sing melodious songs (called "arias") or recite lines in a form of sung speech (called "recitative"). Operas tend to be tragedies. If an opera is not tragic, it is called a "comic opera." There are many famous and popular operas, including *Aida, Carmen, Madama Butterfly,* and *Rigoletto*. The play and film *Evita* may be considered a modern opera. It has a tragic ending and there are no spoken words at all. All the lines are sung.

A musical, on the other hand, typically has a sentimental plot interspersed with songs and music. A musical typically, but not always, has a happy ending, and includes spoken dialogue in addition to songs. Many times, it also has elaborate dance sequences.

Early musicals included *The Student Prince, Babes in Toyland, The Desert Song,* and the many works of Gilbert and Sullivan such as *The Mikado* and *H.M.S. Pinafore.* More recent musicals that are closely related to opera include *Porgy and Bess, Show Boat,* and *West Side Story.*

Hollywood produced many musicals from 1929 on. Examples of Hollywood musicals include *The Merry Widow, Broadway Rhythm, Anchors Aweigh, Annie Get Your Gun, Seven Brides for Seven Brothers, Kismet, Gigi,* and such all-time classics as *Singin' in the Rain* and *An American in Paris.*

The opera houses may be dwindling in Italy, but musicals are alive and well in the United States.

More questions? Try these websites.

WORD WIZARD

http://wordwizard.com:80/

If you love words, you'll love this site. You have to join (it's free) but it's well worth it. The site describes the origins of hundreds of words and phrases. It also defines slang words and has a dictionary of famous insults, as well as other fascinating sections devoted to words.

PHRASE FINDER

http://www.phrases.org.uk/

Looking for a phrase to describe something? This site will help you out. For instance, enter the word "fish" and you'll see a long list of related phrases such as "kettle of fish," "drink like a fish," and "like shooting fish in a barrel."

DICTIONARY OF PHRASE AND FABLE

http://www.bibliomania.com/2/3/255/frameset.html

Ever wonder where the term "pin money" or "bell, book, and candle" came from? You'll find the explanations for thousands of phrases on this website.

WEBSTER'S DICTIONARY

http://www.m-w.com/

Merriam Webster's Dictionary and Thesaurus are on the Internet. Enter a word in the Dictionary box to find its definition, or enter a word in the Thesaurus box to display synonyms.

ACRONYMS AND ABBREVIATIONS

http://www.ucc.ie/info/net/acronyms/acro.html

You can enter an acronym and see what it stands for, or you can enter a word and see which acronyms contain that word.

Literature

9

**What are the fourteen Oz books written by
L. Frank Baum?
(We're off to see the Wizard.)**

L. Frank Baum wrote fourteen books about Oz. After writing the first two books, he turned out one a year for the next twelve years. The dates and titles of his books are:

1900   *The Wonderful Wizard of Oz*

1904   *The Marvelous Land of Oz*

1907 *Ozma of Oz*

1908 *Dorothy and the Wizard in Oz*

1909 *The Road to Oz*

1910 *The Emerald City of Oz*

1913 *The Patchwork Girl of Oz*

1914 *Tik-Tok of Oz*

1915 *The Scarecrow of Oz*

1916 *Rinkitink in Oz*

1917 *The Lost Princess of Oz*

1918 *The Tin Woodsman of Oz*

1919 *The Magic of Oz*

1920 *Glinda of Oz*

After the death of L. Frank Baum, Ruth Plumly Thompson continued to write the Oz books, producing one a year from 1921 to 1939.

FACTOIDS

According to Baum family legend, L. Frank Baum was telling neighborhood children a fairytale full of wonderful characters he had created. One little girl said, "Oh, please, Mr. Baum, where did they live?" While thinking, Baum glanced around the room and saw a filing cabinet. The top drawer was labeled A-N, the bottom drawer was labeled O-Z. He turned to the little girl and said, "They all lived in the land of Oz."

The Wizard of Oz was a Broadway musical 37 years before the MGM film version was made. It had 293 performances and then went on a tour that lasted 9 years.

L. Frank Baum's most famous book had four different titles (*The Emerald City, From Kansas to Fairyland, The Fairyland of Oz*, and *The Land of Oz*) before it became *The Wonderful Wizard of Oz*.

Australians refer to their country as Oz. They abbreviate Australia as "Aus," which is pronounced "ahs" or "oz." Hence the nickname.

Five pairs of Dorothy's ruby slippers were made for the film. Over 5 million people a year view a pair on display at the Smithsonian Institution in Washington, D.C. Another pair sold for $165,000 at an auction in 1988.

Although written almost a century ago, *The Wonderful Wizard of Oz* is still being published and can be purchased today in most bookstores.

DID YOU KNOW?

Traveling the yellow brick road was hardly smooth going.

Buddy Ebsen of television's *Beverly Hillbillies* fame was the original Tin Man. Unfortunately his lungs became coated with the aluminum powder used in his makeup and he almost died. The studio replaced him with Jack Haley, saying that Buddy Ebsen had pneumonia.

The new Tin Man, Jack Haley, didn't fare much better. He suffered a severe eye infection from the makeup and had to stay at home in a dark room until it cleared up. When he returned to the set, his 40-pound costume prevented him from sitting down and he had to rest on a slant board between takes.

After three days of filming, the director realized that the shiny Tin Man was supposed to be rusting, so they had to scrap the footage and reshoot the scenes with a Tin Man speckled with rust. The mistake cost the studio over $60,000.

The film wasn't even safe for witches. Betty Danko, the stand-in for the Wicked Witch of the East, was hospitalized after the witch's broom exploded during a flying stunt and injured her leg. Margaret Hamilton, the Wicked Witch of the East, suffered third-degree burns when another stunt failed. But Hamilton had her revenge. Her shrill cackle blew out sound tubes when she recorded her dialogue.

A sarus crane, rented from the Los Angeles Zoo, attacked the straw stuffing in Ray Bolger's scarecrow costume and the actor had to hide in his dressing room until the bird was caught. The poor actor also started getting tiny lines in his face because his mask was glued on and peeled off every day for four months.

Weeks after completing her role as the Wicked Witch, Margaret Hamilton complained that her face still had a faint green tint.

The Cowardly Lion costume worn by Bert Lahr was so hot that after each take both Lahr and his costume had to be blow-dried with compressed air.

To add insult to injury, the actors were not allowed to eat in the commissary because it was thought their bizarre costumes might make other studio employees lose their appetites.

There were many potholes along the yellow brick road.

How many pages were in the longest book ever written? (Hope this isn't part of your assigned reading lesson.)

The *Yongle dadian*, an encyclopedia of the Chinese Ming dynasty, had 22,937 chapters in 10,000 volumes. Over 2,000 Chinese scholars worked on the book for 5 years before it was finished.

In modern times, the Spanish encyclopedia *La Enciclopedia Universal Ilustrada Europeo-Americana* has 105,000 pages.

The longest modern work of fiction is the 40-volume novel *Tokugawa Ieyasu* by Sohachi Yamaoka.

Although he did not write lengthy books, Isaac Asimov was one of the most prolific writers of our time, having written over 400 books. His works cover a wide range of both fiction and nonfiction subjects. In fact, he is the only author in this country to have a book listed in every Dewey decimal category.

When speaking of long books, we typically refer to printed works or works created on paper. There are many other types of ancient books such as the 15,000 clay tablets left by the ancient Hittites.

FACTOIDS

Early writing and reading was handled in many different ways. Some writing was written and read left to right, some right to left, some top to bottom, and some back and forth, alternating from line to line. In the sixth century B.C. most Mediterranean cultures agreed to use left-to-right reading and writing. However, the Hebrews kept their right-to-left writing.

The oldest known book to have been printed mechanically is the Gutenberg Bible.

The library of Alexandria was designed to hold all the books that existed in the world at the time (295 B.C.) and contained 700,000 volumes. It was damaged by fire during a siege by Julius Caesar in A.D. 47. Civil wars later inflicted more damage and by A.D. 400 nothing remained of the once great library.

Although libraries in the United States are supported with less than one percent of our tax dollars, they are used by over two thirds of the population.

Some experts believe that the first books were created by the Sumerians over 5,000 years ago. The Sumerians had a cuneiform alphabet with letters made up from a triangular symbol. The symbol could be made with the point facing up, down, left, or right. Combinations of the various symbol positions formed specific letters. A wedge-shaped tool was pressed into clay tablets to form the letters. The tablets were then dried or fired so they would last. Some of these "books" even had clay envelopes.

Before the introduction of the printing press, books were made of vellum (calf or lambskin) because it was extremely durable. In William Randolph Hearst's castle at San Simeon, California, there are lampshades made from fifteenth-century vellum prayer books. Even today the vellum is in excellent condition.

DID YOU KNOW?

It is difficult to speak of books or libraries without mentioning the U.S. Library of Congress, established in 1800. The Library has over 100 million items in its collection and a staff of almost 5,000 people. It is the largest library in the world. It offers unparalleled research services, including materials in more than 450 languages, and is one of the world's leading cultural institutions.

Thomas Jefferson is often called the founder of the Library of Congress. He believed that there was "no subject to which Congress may not have occasion to refer."

In 1815 Thomas Jefferson's library was purchased by Congress and became the core of the Library of Congress. Because of Jefferson's wide range of interests, the Library's collection took on a universal and diverse nature. In fact, even today the Library uses his method of classification rather than the Dewey decimal system.

Today the Library of Congress is experimenting with new electronic technology that will allow its collections to be used by schools and research institutions throughout the United States and, eventually, throughout the world.

Thomas Jefferson believed that the citizens of our country must be informed and involved if democracy is to survive. He laid the foundation for one of the greatest repositories of knowledge in the world so that we can be informed.

Whether we also become involved or not is entirely up to us.

What was the first typewritten manuscript of a novel submitted to a publisher? (Mark this one down.)

In 1874 Mark Twain purchased a Remington typewriter and was the first author to submit a typewritten manuscript to a publisher. The novel was *Tom Sawyer.*

Mark Twain came from a poor family. When he was 11 years old, his father died, and Mark Twain quit school and became a printer, working for his brother Orion for a few years. In 1856 Mark Twain boarded a riverboat headed for New Orleans because he wanted to move to South America to collect cocoa. However, once on the river he changed his mind and persuaded the boat's pilot, Horace Bixby, to train him as a pilot. In 1859 he obtained his pilot's license.

Mark Twain's real name was Samuel Langhorne Clemens. When he started writing, he decided to use a pseudonym. He recalled his happy days on the river and how a crew member would drop a weighted rope into the water to see if it was deep enough for safe travel. Each "mark" was a fathom, or six feet. When the crew member shouted "Mark twain" it meant that there were two marks, or fathoms, and the water was deep enough to prevent the boat from running aground. So Samuel Langhorne Clemens adopted the pseudonym of Mark Twain.

The story that started Mark Twain on the road to fame was "The Celebrated Jumping Frog of Calaveras County," which appeared in a New York periodical, *The Saturday Press*, on November 18, 1865. The story took place in Angels Camp, one of the richest mining areas of the California gold rush. Today, Angels Camp is often called "Frogtown." Each year, during the month of May, the town hosts the Calaveras County Fair and Jumping Frog Jubilee.

In addition to *Tom Sawyer*, Mark Twain wrote many popular books including *The Innocents Abroad, A Connecticut Yankee in King Arthur's Court, The Prince and the Pauper,* and *The Adventures of Huckleberry Finn*.

Mark Twain was born on a day in 1835 when Halley's comet came into view. He died 75 years later when Halley's comet returned.

FACTOIDS

Many typewriter manufacturers started out as companies making arms and munitions, including Remington, Smith-Corona, and Underwood.

Some typewriter patents date back to 1713. The first typewriter that actually worked was built by Pellegrino Turri in 1808 for his friend the Countess Carolina Fantoni da Fivizzono.

In 1867, a Milwaukee, Wisconsin, inventor, Christopher Latham Sholes, built the first practical typewriter. Over the years he continually improved the machine and in 1873 signed a contract with gunsmiths E. Remington and Sons to manufacture his machine. The typewriter was soon renamed the "Remington."

The first typewriters had no shift mechanism and could only produce capital letters. A foot pedal was used for a carriage return.

Typewriters in the twenties and thirties came in many colors, including red, green, gold, and even pink. They also came in marble-textured and wood-grained finishes.

DID YOU KNOW?

The arrangement of keys on a typewriter is called "QWERTY" for the first six letters in the top alphabet row (sometimes people use all 10 letters and call it the "QWERTYUIOP" keyboard). For over 125 years people have been saying that the layout of letters on the typewriter keyboard is awkward, inefficient, confusing to learn, and makes no sense. Yet in spite of the complaints, even sophisticated computers and word processors use the same keyboard layout. Why?

Some writers have accused Sholes (the inventor of the typewriter) of arranging the keyboard so it would slow down fast typists and prevent jamming of his slow machine. The truth is just the opposite. The problem was that if two typebars were close to each other, they would jam if typed in succession. Sholes rearranged the letters so that common combinations, such as "TH," would be far away from each other. This arrangement greatly reduced the jamming problem and eventually led to faster typing speeds.

In the years following the invention of the typewriter, many different keyboards were adopted and quietly died. The most famous was the "Dvořák" keyboard created by Professor August Dvořák of Washington State University. Although developed in 1932, it is still not widely accepted today.

In 1953 a study by the U.S. General Services Administration proved that it doesn't matter what keyboard is used. Good typists type fast while bad typists do not.

Is there a place called Transylvania and was there a real Count Dracula? (There are vamps but are there vampires?)

Transylvania is a region in present-day Northwestern Romania. The boundaries of this region are the Carpathian Mountains to the north and east, the Transylvanian Alps to the south, and the Bihor Mountains to the west. This region was once part of Hungary but became part of Romania in 1918.

Bram Stoker's novel *Dracula* was based on a real person, Vlad III Dracula, who was the Prince of Wallachia (the present-day Romania). His father was Vlad Dracul. *Dracul* is the Romanian word for "devil," and the prince was called Dracula, which means "the son of Dracul," or "the son of the devil."

The "son of the devil" probably suits Dracula because he was ruthless, brutal, and cruel. To punish his enemies or those who opposed him, he would often order them skinned, beheaded, boiled, blinded, burned, or buried alive. However, his favorite method was to impale his victims on stakes, hence he was also known as "Vlad the Impaler." Once he impaled 20,000 Turkish prisoners, and the horrible spectacle became known as "the Forest of the Impaled."

Dracula also believed that the poor were worthless vagrants and thieves. One day he ordered all the poor and sick people in his domain to a great feast. At the end of the feast Dracula had the hall boarded up and set on fire. Not a single person survived.

Dracula was killed in battle and his head was presented as a trophy to the Sultan of Constantinople.

In spite of the horrible acts of torture and murder committed by Vlad the Impaler, there is not a single record or mention of his being a vampire.

No one knows for sure why Bram Stoker patterned the Dracula character after Vlad the Impaler. Some think it was because of the author's friendship with a professor at the University of Budapest who gave him information about Vlad the Impaler. Others believe that

Bram Stoker simply used folktales, historical facts, and his own experiences to create the complex fictional Dracula.

FACTOIDS

Film star Bela Lugosi is well known for his portrayal of Dracula but few people know that he was also an accomplished sculptor.

The word "vampire" was first used in 1734 to describe dead people who left their graves at night and sucked the blood of the living. By 1862 it meant a person who was a bore and by 1911 it meant a woman who intentionally attracts men in order to exploit them. From this came the word "vamp" for a temptress.

The myth that garlic wards off vampires came from the time of the black plague that ravaged Europe in the Middle Ages. Doctors believed the plague was caused by corrupted air and that the pungent garlic would cleanse the air.

There is a scarcity of information about Dracula's creator, Bram Stoker. As his nephew Daniel Farson said, "He is one of the least known authors of one of the best known books ever written."

Today there are many Dracula tours available for people touring Romania. These tours visit such places as Vlad's birthplace, the village of Arefu where Dracula legends still abound, and Curtea Domneasca, Dracula's palace in Bucharest.

When Bram Stoker started working on his novel, he initially called the main character Count Wampyr.

The first World Dracula Congress was organized by the Transylvania Society of Dracula and opened in Bucharest in 1995. The society is a scholarly historical-cultural organization.

Reports of vampires proliferated in Hungary during the first half of the eighteenth century.

DID YOU KNOW?

Although vampires are legendary creatures, there is always a possibility that one could exist. To be on the safe side, it might not hurt to know how to protect yourself in case you run into a vampire. Here are some tips:

Sprinkle mustard or poppy seeds around your house. Vampires have an obsession about counting seeds and will become so involved in the task that they'll lose interest in you or will keep counting until the sun comes up. Sprinkling grain, such as oats or millet, will have the same effect.

Constant bell ringing will drive away vampires. A wind chime is quite effective.

Garlic is a well-known defense. Hang garlic cloves around your neck or mix crushed garlic with water and spray it throughout your house.

Holding a cross or crucifix in front of a vampire will keep it at bay.

Who wrote the first "detective" novel?
(Elementary, my dear Watson.)

Edgar Allan Poe is considered to be the father of the detective novel. In 1841 he introduced the first fictional detective, Auguste C. Dupin, in his novel *The Murders of the Rue Morgue*. This novel started one of the most popular and enduring forms of fiction ever created.

However, the man typically called "the father of English crime fiction" was English writer Wilkie Collins, even though his first crime novel, *The Woman in White*, was published almost twenty years after Poe's *The Murders of the Rue Morgue*. Eight years later, Collins wrote *The Moonstone*, which prompted writer T. S. Eliot to comment, "*The Moonstone* was the first and greatest of all English detective novels." Collins was greatly admired and greatly imitated. The fundamental plot of *The Moonstone* has been copied numerous times and innumerable villains have been patterned after Count Fosco of *The Woman in White*.

In the late 1800s, Sir Arthur Conan Doyle created the brilliant detective Sherlock Holmes. In 1920, one of the greatest mystery writers of all time, Agatha Christie, published her first mystery novel.

Supernatural tales of mystery date back to ancient times and are part of the folklore in every culture. The Gothic novel appeared in the eighteenth century, and by the early nineteenth century horror stories had evolved, such as Mary Wollstonecraft Shelley's novel *Frankenstein*. However, it was Edgar Allan Poe and Wilkie Collins who laid the foundation of today's detective novel.

FACTOIDS

Charles Dickens began writing *The Mystery of Edwin Drood* in 1870 but died before completing it. Ever since that time many people have tried to solve the story's main mystery.

The first woman to write a mystery was Katherine Anne Greene, who wrote *The Leavenworth Case* in 1878.

When asked how it felt to be married to a famous archeologist, Agatha Christie replied, "It's wonderful. The older I get, the better he likes me."

DID YOU KNOW?

Many people want to know what distinguishes a mystery novel from a suspense novel or thriller.

A mystery novel is puzzle-oriented and provides clues so the reader can solve the mystery at the same time as the fictional detective. In a suspense novel the reader usually knows who the guilty person is but is anxious to see if the villain will be caught before committing another crime. Thrillers are typically action novels and often deal with larger issues such as espionage, conspiracy, and terrorism.

Mystery novels themselves fall into different categories. One is the famed "locked-room puzzle," in which the murder occurs in a sealed room with no apparent way for the killer to enter or escape. Another is the "cozy," which occurs in a country house or village and is centered around a group of people who are all suspects.

In the 1920s a magazine called *Black Mask* carried crime and detective stories. Unlike the quaint "cozy" or "puzzle" mysteries, these stories reflected the harsh realities of life. The main characters were often "tough guys" or "hard-boiled" private eyes. This style of raw and violent realism was used by novelists Dashiell Hammett and Raymond Chandler to create a new genre of private-eye novels. Mickey Spillane's fictional hero Mike Hammer is a more recent example of this genre.

Mysteries, both old and new, are becoming increasingly popular in the United States and writers are continually coming up with new ideas. There are mysteries solved by a medieval monk, mysteries that occur in ancient Rome, female detectives, elderly detectives, and one author who has even managed to have a Siamese cat participate in solving the crime.

Whether you prefer to identify with tough loners, be entertained with a group of peculiar suspects in a country manor, solve a seemingly insoluble puzzle, or enjoy mysteries in other lands or other times, you'll probably find just what you want at your local bookstore or public library.

More questions? Try these websites.

BARTLETT'S QUOTATIONS
http://www.cc.columbia.edu/acis/bartleby/bartlett/

You can find famous quotations in one of two ways. You can click on the name of an author to display a number of quotations by that author. Or you can enter a word, such as "heart," and click on Submit. You will then see a number of quotations that contain the word "heart."

PROJECT GUTENBERG
http://promo.net/pg/index.html

The purpose of Project Gutenberg is to provide complete texts of books on the Internet so people can read them. All works provided on-line are in the public domain. Simply click on a letter of the alphabet corresponding to the first letter in the title of the book. For instance, click on "c" to find "A Christmas Carol." When you see the title of the book you want, click on it. Then click on TXT to display a copy of the book on your computer screen.

CLASSIC FICTION, NONFICTION, AND POETRY
http://www.bibliomania.com/

Bibliomania is another site that provides books on the Internet. It features over 50 fictional works by such authors as Jane Austen, Charles Dickens, and Mark Twain, as well as nonfiction books and poetry. Once you click on the title of the book, you will notice that a number of "files" are listed such as: File 1, File 2, File 3, and so on. Click on File 1 to read the first part of the book. Click on File 2 to continue reading the book, and so on until you've finished reading the book.

ANECDOTE: CAN YOU FIX MY KOTO, KATO?

I've answered many questions about music but, to be honest, I had never heard of a koto until Arthur Belefant asked if I could find someone who could repair his koto. Arthur explained that it was a Japanese stringed musical instrument and his had been damaged by water. He had not been able to find anyone who could help him.

Arthur said that he had spoken with a research librarian who was unable to help him but suggested that he get in touch with me. It seems that the librarian once had a question from a patron, couldn't answer it, and asked if I could help. I was able to find the answer for her and she remembered me.

I told Arthur that there was an excellent shop in San Jose, California, that would be able to repair his koto with no problem. He then told me that, unfortunately, he lived in Florida. However, he would be willing to ship the instrument to California if that was the only place where he could have it repaired.

At that point I did some further research and eventually found a store in Florida not far from where Arthur lived. I told Arthur I had called the store in Florida and they had said they could probably repair the damage but they'd need to see the instrument first.

Arthur's last message to me said: "I want to thank you for your fantastic response to my query. I've just come from the store and they said that they can fix my koto. I don't know how you in California managed to find what I was looking for only twenty miles from me, maybe I don't want to know. No one here was able to supply me with the information."

They did fix Arthur's koto. I suspect that even today someone in Florida is listening to soft melodies played by Arthur on a once damaged but now repaired koto.

The Human Body

**Why don't Eskimos die from scurvy?
(Never call them Eskimos!)**

Scurvy is caused by a vitamin C deficiency. If you don't get enough vitamin C, you will get scurvy. This disease is characterized by swollen and bleeding gums with loosened teeth, soreness and stiffness of the joints, bleeding under the skin, and anemia. Eskimos kill caribou and other animals for food. Being less finicky than we are, they eat all of the animal: heart, brains, liver, kidneys, and so on. These organs are rich in vitamins A and C. That's why Eskimos do not get scurvy.

When the correlation between vitamin C and scurvy was discovered hundreds of years ago, British sailors would take lemons or limes on their ships and eat them daily to prevent scurvy. That's where the slang term "limeys" (for Englishmen) comes from.

In the 1800s, different countries sent military expeditions to the arctic. It was quite common for all of the officers to get scurvy, but enlisted men seldom did. Today, we know why. When an animal was killed, the officers ate the best part (steaks, for example) while enlisted men were given the remains (heart, liver, kidneys, and so on). Thus enlisted men were getting vitamins A and C while the officers were not. It appears that rank does not always have its privileges.

One final point of interest: Eskimos call themselves "Inuits." "Eskimo" is a Norwegian word that when freely translated means "stupid people who eat raw meat." If you're ever wandering around the Arctic Circle and run into a native, you'd better not call him an Eskimo.

FACTOIDS

A favorite Inuit dish is made from choice parts of caribou or seal that are cut up into tiny pieces and put in a bowl. A few drops of melted fat and a few drops of blood are added, along with the intestine from a grouse. It is then stirred until it turns fluffy. Yummy!

Only Alaskan natives (Indians, Aleuts, and Inuits) are allowed to hunt for polar bears. It is illegal for anyone else to participate in the hunt.

Rickets, a vitamin deficiency disease, spread throughout Scandinavia during the nineteenth century before the antirachitic effect of cod liver oil was discovered. Inuits have never had a problem with rickets because fish oils are a staple in their diet.

Although Inuits eat the liver of most animals, they will not eat polar bear liver, as it is toxic.

If you're an Inuit, spelling words is never a problem. (Wouldn't it be wonderful if English were the same way?)

In the native Inuktitut language, a word with a single meaning may be pronounced many different ways. A "white person" is a *gallunaaq* or a *kabloona*. Both words mean the same thing. Differences have evolved over time because Inuktitut is an oral rather than a written language.

If you ever run into an Inuit, here are some words that might be handy:

I am hungry. *Kaaktunga* (Kak-toon-ga)

I am cold. *Qiuliqtunga* (K-o-lick-toon-ga)

I am sick. *Aaniajunga* (Ah-nee-a-yung-ga)

I have to use the rest room. *Quisuktunga* (Kwee-soot-toon-ga)

Where am I? *Namiippunga?* (Nah-me-poon-ga?)

Help! *Ikajunga!* (Ick-a-yung-ga!)

Why do I get a headache when I eat ice cream too fast? (Eat it more slowly.)

Not a lot is known about what causes "ice cream headaches" or "brain freeze" as these headaches are commonly called. Scientists know that this type of headache is triggered by cold food or drink hitting the roof of the mouth, but they still have no idea what causes the pain. One theory suggests that pain is caused because the blood vessels constrict from the cold.

Scientists do know that the pain reaches its peak somewhere between 25 and 60 seconds after eating or drinking something too cold and that the temperature of the forehead falls by almost 2 degrees. The pain typically lasts from a few seconds to a minute or two.

Although this type of headache can occur anytime, it is more common during very hot weather or when a person is overheated. Hot weather and ice cream seem to go together, which is probably the reason why most ice cream headaches occur in the summer.

There are two ways to avoid ice cream headaches. One is to eat the ice cream more slowly. The other is to keep the ice cream in the front of your mouth because the back of the mouth is usually associated with these headaches.

FACTOIDS

The United States is the ice cream capital of the world. Each citizen eats an average of 23 quarts a year.

In 1921, the commissioner of Ellis Island decided to treat all arriving immigrants to a taste of something truly American. He served ice cream with their first meal.

New Englanders consume more ice cream per person than anyone else in the United States. They also eat the most vanilla ice cream.

Vanilla and chocolate ice cream are the most popular flavors, accounting for about 50 percent of all ice cream sold. Other popular flavors are butter pecan, strawberry, Neapolitan, chocolate chip, cookies and cream, and vanilla fudge ripple.

During the Victorian period, drinking soda water was considered improper and many towns banned its sale on Sundays. An enterprising druggist concocted a legal confection made of ice cream and syrup. Because it could be eaten on the Sabbath he called it a "Sunday." Later, he changed the spelling to "sundae."

When the first batch of Rocky Road ice cream was made, miniature marshmallows did not exist. The two creators, William Dryer and Joseph Edy, used their wives' sewing scissors to cut the marshmallows into bite-size pieces. Because it was just after the stock market crash of 1929, they decided to name their creation "Rocky Road," not only as a comment on the times but also to make people smile.

No one really knows who invented ice cream. It probably was created in a number of places around the world at various times in history. Many civilizations had wine- or fruit-flavored ices. Some experts believe these were popular thousands of years ago.

It is known that around 200 B.C. in China a soft mixture of milk and rice was solidified by packing it in snow. The Roman Emperor Nero enjoyed mixtures of fruit crushed with snow and honey, and Alexander the Great sent runners to the mountains to bring back snow so he could have a wine-flavored ice.

When Marco Polo returned to Europe from his travels to the Far East, he brought with him a recipe for a tasty ice and milk dessert. These desserts became popular among the rich, and royal chefs kept working to improve the recipe. These recipes were closely guarded secrets for many years.

After ice cream was introduced in the colonies, many of our country's founders became ice cream addicts, including Thomas Jefferson, Alexander Hamilton, Dolley Madison, and George Washington.

The first ice cream plant in the United States was opened a century and a half ago. The owner would never have believed that today annual ice cream sales in this country are over $3 billion.

Do people who are born blind ever dream?
(To sleep, perchance to dream.)

People who are blind from birth do dream, but they do not have visual images as we do. In fact, it's difficult for blind persons to describe their dreams because they have a different frame of reference. You can't ask them, "What did you see in your dream?"

One man who has been blind since birth said, "My dreams are never with shapes or colors. I dream about touching things. Once I dreamed I was being chased by someone with a gun. I heard the horrible blasts from the gun and felt as if the bullets were actually piercing my back."

So blind people do dream, but rather than "see" shapes, textures, and colors, they "hear" and "feel" the dream. Because of this, their dreams probably are much more real than those of sighted people.

It is also interesting that people who can see and become blind later in life will still see images in their dreams. However, the images tend to fade the longer they remain blind.

FACTOIDS

Even when extremely tired, most people have great difficulty sleeping between 9 and 11 A.M. and between 7 and 9 P.M.

When we're sleeping, a biochemical switch in the brain prevents the brain from ordering your muscles to move. If this switch did not work, people would walk, talk, eat, or even commit violent acts while sleeping. This is one of the causes of sleepwalking. In a condition known as "night terrors," victims physically act out their dreams while in a sleepwalking state.

Around the turn of the century, people averaged 9 hours of sleep per night. The chimpanzee gets about 10 hours of sleep a day. Research has shown that if we are removed from the stress of the modern world, we will sleep an average of 10.3 hours a day, about the same as the chimpanzee.

Sleep deprivation has become a national malady. Most of the people in the United States do not get enough sleep. This adversely affects driving and performance at work.

If you are having a nightmare and cannot move, just blink your eyes or wiggle your tongue to break the paralysis.

Astronauts sleeping in a weightless environment tend to draw up their knees and wrap their arms loosely around their torso. This puts the spine in a restful, natural curve, and might be the best position for the rest of us when we sleep.

DID YOU KNOW?

Dreaming is often called a paradox because the body becomes inactive, almost corpselike, but the mind produces the sensation of unlimited freedom of movement. Aside from hallucinations or insanity, dreaming is the only experience we have of living fully in a world without limitations. We may have a dull, boring, routine life but when we dream we can partake of high adventure.

There are many types of dreams. Some are simply "venting" dreams that allow the mind to purge most of the countless images that bombard us daily. Bizarre dreams that make no sense are often venting dreams.

Another type of dream is the "prophetic" dream, which tells us something about the future, often a warning. Although scientists do not understand how a dream can predict the future, there are countless examples that suggest this occurs. One such example comes to us from history.

Augustus Caesar was ill and resting in his tent. A friend had a troubling dream and persuaded Augustus to leave his tent, which he did. Just a few hours later the area was captured by his enemies and the bed on which Augustus had been sleeping was pierced with their swords.

The Bible also has many examples of dream prophecies, such as the impending famine of Egypt revealed to Joseph in a dream about fat and lean cattle.

Whether we believe in dream prophecy or not, it would not be a bad idea to pay a little closer attention to some of our dreams.

What makes us yawn? (Is boredom really a bad thing?)

Some people think that yawning is caused by boredom, while others theorize that we yawn because we need to stretch our neck muscles. However, most authorities agree that yawning is simply a way for the body to compensate for less oxygen in the bloodstream.

Every cell in our body needs a continual supply of oxygen. When we breathe normally, we take air into our lungs, which pass the oxygen to the blood so that oxygen can be carried throughout our body. When we exhale, we get rid of the waste product, carbon dioxide. However, if we're tired, bored, or sitting in a stuffy room, we tend to breathe more slowly than normal and our body doesn't get all the oxygen it needs. Because we also are not getting rid of the carbon dioxide, it builds up in the blood. Our brain senses this and quickly sends a signal to the lungs to take an extradeep breath. This extradeep breath is called a yawn.

When we yawn, we always open our mouths. That's because you can breathe in much more air through your mouth than through your nose. The air isn't as clean because it's not filtered through your nose, but a yawn is designed to take in a lot of air quickly, clean or not.

Although we usually yawn because we are bored or tired, people may also yawn when they're very excited because they need more oxygen to remain attentive.

We aren't the only creatures who yawn. Animals also yawn, for the same reason we do. Watch how a dog or cat takes a big yawn before taking a nap.

If you want to avoid yawning, you should take deep breaths whenever you feel a yawn starting. Sitting comfortably so that oxygen can easily flow through your body or chewing gum to stimulate your mouth muscles can also prevent yawning.

Although we know what causes yawning and how to prevent it, there is one question that no one has yet satisfactorily answered: Why is yawning contagious?

FACTOIDS

The importance of oxygen to our well-being is easily shown by the "rule of four," which states that before permanent damage will occur to our body, we can live four weeks without food, four days without water, and four minutes without air.

Yawning a lot at work is not unusual because so many of today's offices use recirculating heating and cooling systems and oxygen can be easily depleted over time.

Scientists estimate that in the past 300 years, the United States has lost 11 percent of the available oxygen in the air because we have destroyed so much oxygen-producing vegetation.

What blood type is the rarest?
(Blue bloods don't count.)

There are four basic blood types: A, B, O, and AB. The most common is type O. Roughly 40 to 60 percent of the population has this blood type. The rarest is type AB.

Blood type percentages vary among different populations. For instance, although type O is the most common in the United States, type A is the most common in Scandinavians, Australians, and North American Indians.

Here is the breakdown of blood types in the United States:

Type A 40 percent

Type B 10 percent

Type O 46 percent

Type AB 4 percent

If we add the Rh factor, then the rarest blood types of all are type AB Rh-negative (1 percent), type B Rh-negative (2 percent), and type AB Rh-positive (3 percent).

In an emergency, type O blood is a universal donor because it can be given to anyone, while type AB is a universal receiver because a person with this blood type can receive blood from any donor.

The donated blood is separated into a number of components. Red blood cells are used to treat anemia, platelets control bleeding and are used to treat leukemia, white cells are sometimes used to fight infection, and plasma controls bleeding. Other products from donated blood include albumin, immune globulin, and clotting factor concentrates.

FACTOIDS

If all the blood vessels in the average human body were put end to end, they would be 60,000 miles long.

Less than 5 percent of people in the United States donate blood.

Every year over 23 million pints of blood are used in transfusions.

An adult male has about 12 pints of blood in his body, while an adult female has about 9 pints.

If frozen, red blood cells can last up to 10 years.

Two or three drops of blood contain about 1 billion red blood cells. These cells live only for about four months. The body's bone marrow continually produces new red blood cells.

White blood cells fight bacteria and viruses. There are twice as many white cells as red cells in the bone marrow, but there is only one white cell for every 600 red cells in the bloodstream.

DID YOU KNOW?

Although we may marvel at modern technology in collecting, storing, and using blood, it's not all that modern. The first successful blood transfusion occurred in 1665 when Richard Lower, an English physician, kept dogs alive by using blood transfusions.

Subsequently there were many attempts to transfuse animal blood into humans, but these were always fatal and the practice was outlawed, preventing any other significant advances from being made for over 150 years.

Beginning in 1818, doctors once again started advancing the use of blood transfusions. To improve safety, it was suggested that blood be typed and cross-matched between donor and recipient. The first transfusion using blood typing and cross-matching was performed in 1907.

In 1912 physician Roger Lee showed that type O blood could be given to any patient, and that blood from any group could be given to patients with type AB blood.

In 1930 a London hospital established the first blood bank. Seven years later a blood bank was set up at Chicago's Cook County Hospital by the director of therapeutics, Bernard Fantus, who coined the term "blood bank."

In 1939 and 1940 researchers discovered the Rh blood group system. Next to blood typing, it is considered the most important breakthrough in blood transfusion practices.

Beginning with World War II, continued advances made blood transfusions safer, more reliable, and easier to administer. A number of breakthroughs were made, including using Rh-immune globulin to prevent Rh disease in infants of Rh-negative mothers.

It has been well over three centuries since the first successful blood transfusion was used to keep dogs alive. Today approximately 40,000 pints of red blood cells are used to treat accident victims, surgical patients, and people with leukemia, cancer, and other diseases.

Perhaps sharing our blood to heal others or save lives is one of the greatest gifts we can give another human being ... the gift of life itself.

More questions?
Try these websites.

MEDICAL NEWS
http://www.medscape.com/

This site contains the latest medical news, a medical dictionary, and links to such specialties as AIDS, internal medicine, psychiatry, and women's health.

NATIONAL INSTITUTES OF HEALTH
http://www.nih.gov/

This government site contains the latest medical press releases. If you click on Institutes and Offices, you'll find numerous links to other organizations, such as the National Eye Institute, the National Institute on Aging, and the National Library of Medicine.

Music

In the Australian song, what does "waltzing Matilda" mean? (Hint: it's not a woman.)

A "matilda" is a blanket (or swag) usually carried over the shoulder and used to keep its owner warm at night. A "swagman" is an itinerant sheep shearer who wanders about the countryside looking for work. In many ways, he is similar to the American hoboes of the 1930s. Thus, when "waltzing Matilda," the swagman is dancing with his blanket.

This haunting song tells the story of a wandering sheep shearer who is sitting beside a watering hole ("billabong") waiting for his tea ("billy") to boil when he sees a small sheep ("jumpbuck"), kills it, and hides it in his food bag ("tucker bag"). When the authorities arrive and want to see what he is hiding, he jumps into the watering hole, preferring to drown rather than go to prison.

In 1894 there were a series of violent sheep shearer strikes in Australia that eventually led to the breakdown of class distinctions and social privilege. The strikes gained national significance. Shearing sheds and riverboats were burned and men were shot. The song is about this era.

Amid this turmoil, Christina MacPherson wrote a catchy tune called *Craigielee*, and her lover, Banjo Patterson, decided to write some words to keep the tune alive. His words chronicled the fate of one sheep shearer and the song eventually became known as *Waltzing Matilda*.

FACTOIDS

The name "Matilda" was given to women who followed the soldiers in the European Thirty Years' War. Because these women kept the soldiers warm at night, the term was eventually used to describe the blankets that the soldiers carried.

Sheep shearers work an 8-hour day in four 2-hour separate "runs" and are paid according to the number of sheep they shear. An average shearer can shear up to 110 sheep per day.

An excellent film about itinerant sheep shearers is *The Sundowners* (1961) with Robert Mitchum, Deborah Kerr, Peter Ustinov, and Glynnis Johns.

There are over 140 million sheep in Australia (more than in any other country in the world), with individual flocks ranging from a few hundred head to as many as 100,000 sheep or more.

Over 80 percent of all domestic sheep are Australian Merinos, grown for their heavy fleeces of fine-quality wool; the remaining sheep have at least some Merino blood.

Australia produces 32 percent of the world's supply of raw wool, 56 percent of the world's Merino wool, and 73 percent of apparel wool.

Why did Custer choose *Garry Owen* as his regimental song? (They died with their boots on.)

*G*arry *Owen*, or more properly *Garryowen*, was an old Irish quick-step tune popular in the 1860s. The lively beat mimics the rhythm of marching horses.

Predominately Irish regiments used *Garry Owen* as a drinking song. One story is that one of the 7th Cavalry Regiment soldiers was singing the song when Custer heard it and liked it.

The 7th Cavalry Regiment was formed at Fort Riley, Kansas, in 1866 and Custer, then a lieutenant colonel, was put in command. In 1867, Custer adopted the tune as a regimental song and it became the 7th Cavalry's official tune in 1881. Because of this, the 7th Cavalry became known as the Garry Owen Regiment and its troopers were called "Garry Owens." The words were used as a regimental greeting, password, and battle cry.

Although he served in the Civil War and other campaigns, Custer is best remembered for the Battle of the Little Big Horn when he and two battalions under his command were killed by Sioux Indians. None of the 210 soldiers under his command survived. Today, the battle is known as Custer's Last Stand.

FACTOIDS

The only survivor of Custer's Last Stand was a horse, Comanche. Although severely wounded, he eventually recovered and was officially retired with an order that no one would ever ride him again. In later years he developed a liking for beer and the troopers often obliged. He died at age 28, was stuffed and mounted, and is still on display at the University of Kansas.

Custer was 37 years old when he died at Little Big Horn.

Telegraph operator John M. Carnahan stayed on his key for 21 hours to send the news of Custer's defeat to the East.

Park rangers at the Little Big Horn memorial claim they have seen Custer's ghost.

Although Native Americans were at the height of their power at the Battle of the Little Big Horn, the defeat of Custer shocked and enraged America. The government poured so many troops into the area that the Native Americans were eventually forced to surrender.

The 7th Cavalry still exists and is part of the 1st Cavalry Division stationed at Fort Hood, Texas. However the 7th Cavalry now uses armored vehicles instead of horses.

DID YOU KNOW?

Because no one lived to tell what happened, the facts, strategy, and tactics of the Battle of the Little Big Horn have generated countless debates that continue to the present day.

Troops commanded by Brigadier General Alfred Terry had been sent out to locate and rout the Indians. Terry planned a two-pronged attack that would trap the Indians between his force and Custer's 7th Cavalry. However, upon reaching the Little Big Horn River, Custer encountered Indians and abandoned the plan. Although Terry and his troops would not arrive for two days, Custer ordered the 7th Cavalry to attack.

He ordered Captain Benteen and Major Reno to lead the attack on either side of the river while he advanced northwest to surprise the Indian encampment.

Reno attacked first and, being overwhelmed by the Indians, was forced to retreat across the river, losing his tactical advantage. Benteen's forces joined Reno and they dug in and continued to fight.

The Indians were aware of Custer's presence and once Major Reno retreated, the main Indian force attacked Custer's troops, killing them all in less than an hour.

Today the debate still rages. Was Custer an arrogant, ambitious soldier who sacrificed his men while trying to make a name for himself? Or was he a courageous soldier, fighting to save his men against insurmountable odds?

Unfortunately, the only person who knows for sure is General George Armstrong Custer.

What was the last song the musicians on the *Titanic* played? (The fall of a Titan.)

The eyewitness accounts of *Titanic* survivors disagree as to what the band was playing as the ship went under. Many said it was *Nearer My God to Thee*, while others said it was *Autumn*, a tune popular during that time but virtually unknown today. The producers of the most recent film probably chose *Nearer My God to Thee* because it is still a familiar melody.

As the ill-fated ship began to sink, the band moved to the deck and began playing in an effort to calm the passengers who were waiting to be rescued.

Although behavioral psychologists talk about how people panic during a disaster, they find it difficult to explain the reaction of the *Titanic's* passengers in comparison to those of other maritime disasters. In typical panic situations, the individual completely disregards the lives of fellow passengers.

Yet the *Titanic* passengers reacted in the opposite way. Although everyone knew that the ship was sinking and that there were not enough lifeboats for everyone, there was little panic. In fact, many men refused to board the lifeboats until all of the women and children had been rescued first. The crew performed heroically before and after the ship sank. One man exchanged his life jacket for a sweater; he said that if he were about to die, he wanted to die like a gentleman.

But perhaps the most heroic action was that of a small band of musicians still playing melodious music as the ship sank beneath the waves.

If the *Titanic* were built today, it would cost at least $400 million.

The ship was known as the R.M.S. *Titanic*; "R.M.S." stands for Royal Mail Steamer.

At 882 feet, the ship was longer than the tallest skyscraper in New York at that time.

It took over 22 tons of soap, grease, and train oil to launch the giant ship.

Christopher Columbus's ship the *Santa Maria* weighed less than the *Titanic's* rudder.

Although there were four funnels on the *Titanic*, only the first three were used. The fourth was an air ventilator.

The *Titanic* was the first ocean liner to have a swimming pool and gym. It also had an infirmary and associated operating room.

DID YOU KNOW?

The *Titanic's* double-bottomed hull was divided into 16 watertight compartments, four of which could be flooded without affecting buoyancy. The *Titanic* was thought to be unsinkable.

That fateful night, seven iceberg warnings were sent to the *Titanic*. The last and most important was ignored because the radio room was so busy sending passengers' messages to friends, relatives, and business associates.

Shortly before midnight on April 14, a lookout in the crow's nest spotted an iceberg, but the warning came too late for the *Titanic* to avoid a collision. The iceberg sliced a 200-foot gash in the ship's side and six of the watertight compartments began flooding.

Knowing the ship was doomed, the captain ordered an evacuation. The problem was that there were only enough lifeboats for about half of the 2,200 passengers. The radio operators sent out frantic international distress signals.

Many lifeboats were lowered when only partially full because officers thought the davits would not hold the weight of a fully loaded lifeboat. Of those lowered, only one returned to pick up passengers even though most could easily have carried more people.

More lives would have been lost except for the construction of the double hull and watertight compartments that prevented the ship from sinking immediately. The *Titanic* sank two hours and twenty minutes after the collision.

Many survivors saw a nearby ship that must have seen the Titanic's signal flares but never responded to help. It was thought to have been the steamer *Californian* but a later investigation proved nothing.

In answer to the radio distress call, the steamer *Carpathia* arrived nearly two hours after the sinking and picked up the survivors.

Of the over 2,200 people on board, only slightly more than 700 survived. The brave musicians were not among them.

What makes the sound when you rub your finger along the edge of a glass? (The armonica came before the harmonica.)

A vibrating object produces waves that propagate in all directions. If the waves are at a certain frequency they are called "sound" waves. When our ears sense the waves, we hear the sound. If you rub your finger along the edge of a glass you make the glass vibrate. Although the vibration is very small it is enough to make a sound.

The unusual sound made by rubbing a wineglass is due to a sound spectrum rather than a single tone. When you rub a moist finger along the rim of a wineglass the rim vibrates where the finger touches it and then vibrates at a different cycle when the finger is moved from that point. This causes a fundamental tone as well as a number of harmonic overtones. However, most of the sound "theory" related to wineglasses is still a mystery to scientists.

The faster an object vibrates, the higher the pitch of the sound. For example, a cello has very long strings that vibrate slowly, causing a low range of tones. On the other hand, a violin has shorter strings that vibrate much faster and cause a higher range of tones.

As an experiment take an empty water glass, hit it lightly with a spoon, and listen to the sound. Now fill the glass almost full of water, hit it lightly again, and listen to the sound. You'll note that the tone is much lower when the glass is nearly full of water.

When you hit the empty glass, you cause the entire wall of the glass to vibrate rapidly, which produces a high tone. When the glass is almost full of water, it takes the vibrations longer to get through the water so they are slower and the tone is much lower.

If you take eight glasses and fill each one with more water than the previous one, you can actually produce the eight notes of the scale (you have to experiment in order to fill each glass with the proper amount of water to get the tone you want). You can then play songs by tapping the appropriate glass to produce the notes you want to play.

FACTOIDS

Instruments made of glass existed in fourteenth-century China and in fifteenth-century Europe. In the 1700s performers created music by rubbing the rims of finely tuned wineglasses.

Benjamin Franklin invented an instrument he called the "glass armonica." It had 35 custom-blown glass bowls fitted on a horizontal rod. Each bowl was "tuned" and so did not need to be filled with water. Because a treadle rotated the bowls, he could "play" up to ten at a time. The armonica was the first musical instrument invented by an American.

Mozart and Beethoven, among others, composed music for the glass armonica.

Around 1800, doctors claimed that listening to musical glasses was bad for the health and could cause premature births, convulsions in animals, and depression that could result in suicide. In some German states the glass armonica was banned by order of the police.

The "harmonica" was invented by Friedrich Buschmann of Berlin in 1821, 60 years after Benjamin Franklin's invention of the armonica.

DID YOU KNOW?

Although few people have heard of it, the armonica is still alive and well.

In 1956 the American Academy of Arts and Sciences, the Franklin Savings Bank, the Corning Glass Company, and a team of engineering students from the Massachusetts Institute of Technology tried to reproduce Franklin's armonica. They failed.

However, Gerhard Finkenbeiner, a brilliant German inventor, made the first successful modern armonica in 1982. Since then he has made more than 100 glass armonicas, including one with three octaves.

In addition to the armonica, other glass instruments exist today. For over 20 years, the Glass Orchestra of Canada has been performing music on custom glass instruments that they designed and made themselves. The orchestra uses 1,000 pounds of glass instruments during its performances.

The Glass Orchestra has received rave reviews and still performs twice a year in Toronto, Canada.

It seems that glass music is not broken after all.

What gave Roger Miller the inspiration to write *King of the Road*? (Our country should be grateful to these "kings of the road.")

In 1964, Roger Miller saw a road sign west of Chicago, Illinois, that read "Trailers for Sale or Rent." After writing that as the first line, he gave up. Some time later he was in a Boise, Idaho, airport gift shop and saw a statuette of a hobo that inspired him to finish the song. People who know Roger Miller usually refer to it as "that hobo song."

Although Roger Miller had two hits in 1964, *Dang Me* and *Chug-a-Lug*, his 1965 hit *King of the Road* won six Grammy Awards. The following year he had a variety show on NBC. He also became part owner of a Nashville, Tennessee, hotel aptly named King of the Road.

In his early career, Roger Miller wrote songs performed by stars such as Ray Price, Faron Young, Porter Wagoner, and Johnny Paycheck. These songs included *Invitation to the Blues, Half a Mind, Billy Bayou,* and *Home*.

Although his recording career slowed down after 1967, in 1973 he was inducted into the Nashville Songwriters' Hall of Fame. During the 1980s he won a Tony Award for writing the score to the Broadway musical *Big River* (based on Mark Twain's *Huckleberry Finn*), was the voice of the rooster in Walt Disney's animated film *Robin Hood*, recorded *Old Friends* with Ray Price and Willie Nelson, and in 1987 won the Pioneer Award from the Academy of Country Music.

Roger Miller died in 1992 from a tumor under his vocal cords. He was just 56 years old. Three years later he was posthumously inducted into the Country Music Hall of Fame.

Roger Miller always had a great sense of humor. When asked how he would like to be remembered, he said, "I just don't want to be forgotten."

He probably never will be forgotten.

Roger Miller once remarked that his hometown of Erick, Oklahoma, was so small that the city limit signs were back-to-back. When asked the location of the home he grew up in, Roger Miller replied, "It's close to extinction."

While in grade school, Roger Miller picked cotton on the weekends so he could earn enough money to buy a guitar. After quitting school in the eighth grade, he herded cattle and rode bulls in rodeos.

After reading a letter from former Yale professor Rocco Landesman asking him to write the musical score for *Big River*, Roger Miller told his wife, "He made me an offer I couldn't understand."

DID YOU KNOW?

A hobo is not a tramp or a bum. The saying goes that "a hobo is a man who travels to find work, a tramp is a man who travels but refuses to work, and a bum is a man who won't travel and won't work." Just look at this list of people who at one time were hoboes: Supreme Court Justice William O. Douglas, Pulitzer Prize-winning author James Michener, attorney Melvin Belli, and, of course, Roger Miller.

In 1935 an estimated 1.5 million people rode freight trains as hoboes across the country.

After the Civil War many soldiers had no home to return to so they wandered through the countryside in search of work, often as migrant farmhands. Because they often carried their own tools, including hoes, they were given the name "hoe boys," which was later shortened to "hobo."

As the country expanded westward, so did the hoboes. They were a big part of the workforce the railroads needed to lay track.

During the Great Depression in the 1930s, men once again took to the road to find work. Willing to work in remote areas accessible only by freight train, they were the core workforce that built the great dams and other structures in this country.

Hoboes still exist today, although most people wouldn't recognize them as such. These are men who treasure personal freedom, love the land, and seek new adventures. You might find them building a pipeline through virgin land or working in an oil field or a lumber camp.

Our country owes a lot not to tramps or bums but to the hoboes of the past.

More questions?
Try these websites.

BROADCAST MUSIC INC.
http://www.bmi.com/

You can search for any song by title, writer, or publisher and find relevant information. Broadcast Music Inc. (BMI) is a nonprofit organization. There are over 3 million songs in this database.

LYRICS
http://www.garlic.com/kpranger/lyrics.htm

If you're looking for the lyrics to a particular song, you might find them here. This site contains links to other sites that contain song lyrics.

Odds

and Ends

What is the world's fastest roller coaster?
(Ready for takeoff?)

If you like drag racing or taking off in a jet fighter, you'll love the "Superman, the Escape" roller coaster at Magic Mountain in Valencia, California. The first roller coaster to break the 100 mph barrier, it is currently the world's fastest roller coaster.

This high-speed ride launches 15-passenger cars from a standstill to 100 mph in 7 seconds with a force of 4.5 Gs as it heads skyward.

At the top, which is 42 stories high, riders experience 6.5 seconds of weightlessness and free-fall backward for the return trip.

The fastest inverted roller coaster is the "Raptor" at the Cedar Point amusement park in Sandusky, Ohio. This gut-wrenching ride features a "cobra roll" that flips passengers over, spirals them upside down into a 180-degree roll, and then repeats these twisting movements in the reverse order, all at speeds of almost 60 mph.

Cedar Point also has one of the fastest and steepest stand-up roller coasters. Riders speed over part of a lagoon and, among other thrills, experience four upside-down inversions at 60 mph while standing up.

FACTOIDS

The Cedar Point amusement park has more roller coasters than any other amusement park. The park's 12 roller coasters are in *The Guinness Book of Records* and the park is known as the roller coaster capital of the world.

Before the advent of the roller coaster, people paid to drive their cars over an undulating track.

Many weddings are performed on roller coasters, and one minister specializes in such weddings.

Modern roller coasters take two to three years to design and cost $8 million on up.

There is a market for used roller coasters. It is cheaper to take one apart, move it, and reassemble it than to build a new one.

The longest roller coaster in the United States is the 1.4-mile "Beast" at Kings Island, Ohio.

The oldest operating roller coaster in the United States is the "Zippin Pippin" at Libertyland amusement park in Memphis, Tennessee. It was built in 1915.

DID YOU KNOW?

The origin of the roller coaster dates back to the 1700s when Russians created "ice slides" at country fairs. The slide was a steep drop made entirely of ice with a series of small bumps at the end. Riders sat on a straw patch on top of a block of ice and hung on to a rope tied to the ice block.

A French businessman who liked the idea decided to build an ice slide in France. Unfortunately, the ice melted and he ended up with a "slush slide." He then tried an all-weather version by using a waxed wooden slope and a wooden sled with rollers on the bottom.

Because it took skill to use these sleds, there were many accidents. As a result, a crude track was built to ensure that the rider would descend in a straight line.

The beginnings of the American roller coaster come from the Mauch Chunk Railway, originally devised as a transportation system for coal mines. The mine was at the top of a mountain and the Mauch Chunk port was 18 miles away, all downhill. The miners simply loaded the coal cars and then pushed them off the top of the mountain. Gravity did the rest and the cars eventually ended up at the port.

Used for coal mining during the day, the Mauch Chunk Railway became a pleasure ride at night. People paid one dollar to ride a car down the main track. This "ride" exceeded today's roller coasters, being an 18-mile ride at a speed of 100 mph. The rail- way operated from 1870 until the 1930s with an exemplary safety record.

Roller-coaster designs continued to evolve. Today's innovations include corkscrews, loop-the-loops, suspended cars, inverted cars, and stand-up coasters.

What is the difference between green and blue mailboxes? (Really a relay.)

Blue mailboxes are for customers to deposit mail. Green mailboxes are used only by U.S. Postal Service employees and are called "relay boxes." (If you ever try to put a letter in a "green" box, you'll quickly discover there's no opening.)

The post office leaves mail in a green box for the postal

employee responsible for that route. In this way, postal employees who deliver mail on foot aren't burdened with a heavy mailbag; they take mail from the relay boxes as needed.

It's efficiencies like this that help make the Postal Service profitable. In fact, it has been self-supporting since 1982 and receives no government subsidies of any kind. Since 1982, the Postal Service has depended exclusively on postage and fees rather than taxpayer revenue for its operations.

Green mailboxes are only one of the many tools used by the Postal Service to maintain an efficient operation that processes 177 billion pieces of mail annually or about 580 million pieces of mail a day. The national delivery network now reaches 125 million addresses.

With successful and efficient automation programs, Postal Service employees are 500 percent more productive than those in Germany, 250 percent more productive than those in France and the United Kingdom, and 33 percent more productive than those in Japan.

FACTOIDS

The U.S. Postal Service handles 40 percent of the world's mail volume while Japan, the second largest carrier of cards and letters, handles only 8 percent.

The Japanese pay 80 cents and the Germans pay 64 cents for first-class mail. America's 33 cents for first-class mail is the lowest in the industrialized world.

As the nation's largest civilian employer, with 729,000 career employees, the Postal Service employs more workers on American soil than General Motors, Ford, and the Chrysler Corporation combined.

The Postal Service maintains a fleet of over 200,000 vehicles and contracts for space on almost half of all commercial flights.

In 1639 the first public mailbox was installed in Burbank's Tavern in Boston, Massachusetts.

The zip code (which is an acronym for Zone Improvement

Plan) was created in 1963 by then postmaster general James Edward Day.

The Postal Service delivers more mail in 1 day than Federal Express does in a year, and more mail in 3 days than the United Parcel Service (UPS) does in a year.

A postal museum, established at the Smithsonian in 1886, houses a collection of more than 16 million mail-related items.

Why don't beeswax candles drip? (Candle, candle, burning bright.)

Although beeswax resembles other waxes, its molecular structure is unique.

Typical paraffin candles consist of hydrocarbon molecules that react with oxygen in the candle flame and are transformed into water and carbon dioxide, which are then vaporized. Because paraffin molecules are large, not all of them are vaporized and many simply melt in the flame and drip down the side of the candle.

Beeswax molecules are small by comparison. The wax is completely vaporized by the flame, leaving no ash or wax residue. In addition to the smokeless and dripless characteristics, beeswax candles have a higher melting point, burn longer and more cleanly, and give off more light than other wax candles.

Honey bees consume 7 pounds of honey for each pound of wax they produce. The resultant wax is white, odorless, and tasteless. The so-called natural yellow color and pleasant aroma come not from the wax itself but from the pollen and honey stored in the wax honeycomb.

Beeswax was not used to make candles until around A.D. 300, when the Catholic Church mandated that for certain rituals candles had to contain at least 51 percent pure beeswax, the rest of the candle being either mineral wax or tallow. Some ritual candles today consist of 56 percent to 100 percent pure beeswax.

Beeswax candles found in Egyptian tombs are still pliable, even though they are thousands of years old. Beeswax candles salvaged from sunken ships are still in good condition even though they have been underwater for hundreds of years.

Beeswax is used in the manufacture of lipsticks, floor wax, and other products. So far, no one has been able to produce a good imitation of beeswax candles using other types of waxes. Beeswax candles remain unique to this day.

In the Middle Ages, it was customary to give a child a candle during baptism. This is the origin of putting candles on a birthday cake.

DID YOU KNOW?

The history of candles is not a well-lit path. Although many believe that candles originated over 3,000 years ago, no one knows for sure.

The Romans are given credit for developing the type of candle used today. At night these candles lit homes and places of worship as well as the way for travelers. The Romans made their candles from tallow, which was made from cattle or sheep suet.

Ancient peoples made candles from a variety of ingredients. Many used tallow, or animal fat. The Japanese used wax from an insect, the Chinese extracted oil from the tallow tree seed, and early American settlers made wax by boiling berries from the wax myrtle tree. In India wax was obtained from cinnamon, and in South America wax was obtained by scraping the leaves of the wax palm. American Indians simply stuck a spear through a candlefish and lit it.

All candles were made by dipping up until the fifteenth century when wooden molds were created by a French inventor.

However, almost all modern candle-making techniques date from the 1800s when stearic acid was first created. The braided wick was also developed at this time.

Before the braided wick, the tops of candlewicks had to be trimmed periodically. Villages with street lanterns would hire men to trim the wicks. Because of the height of the lanterns, the wick trimmers wore stilts while doing their job. The new braided wick put them out of business. The wick curled at the top, providing a better flow of oxygen to the rest of the wick. The top of the wick vaporized and the ashes fell off. There was no need to trim it.

In spite of all our modern electrical lighting, people still love the pleasant aroma and soft light given off by candles. Americans spend over $2 billion a year on candles, and sales have increased from 10 percent to 15 percent a year during the 1990s.

Today's customers aren't concerned about the light given off by the candle. Research indicates that the most important factors to consider when selecting a candle are shape, color, and scent. With a typical candle maker offering one or two thousand varieties of candles, there is no shortage of variety from which to choose.

Did Thomas Crapper really invent the toilet? (Flushed with pride.)

Although Thomas Crapper, born in 1836, was a real person and did have a successful plumbing career, most authorities agree that this common myth is simply not true. He held nine patents, four for improving drains, three for water closets, one for pipe joints, and one for manhole covers.

However, the "Silent Valveless Water Waste Preventer" system that allowed a toilet to flush effectively was invented by Albert Giblin, who worked for Crapper. Some authorities believe that Giblin let Crapper use his invention, while others believe that Crapper purchased the patent rights and then marketed the new device.

Crapper had three plumbing shops, one of which operated under the Crapper name until it closed in 1966.

During World War I, U.S. solders spent some time in England before going to the battle lines. They saw the words "T. Crapper-Chelsea" painted on the toilet tanks and coined the slang word "crapper" for a toilet.

FACTOIDS

The first flushing toilet was in use almost 4,000 years ago at the Minoan Palace of Knossos on the island of Crete. Unfortunately, this useful invention was lost and, although an Englishman invented a toilet (called a water closet) in 1775, so many people made fun of it that he never made another. It was another 200 years before another toilet appeared.

During the industrial revolution people moved in great numbers to the cities. A toilet was simply a glass or metal jar that people emptied by simply tossing the contents into the street below. However, common courtesy dictated that passersby be warned with the shout "gardyloos," "gardez l'eau," or "watch out for the water." When an Englishman pronounced "l'eau" it sounded more like "loo," which even today is the English slang word for toilet.

As more and more people began living close to one another, the problem of human waste disposal became acute. The famous Roman aqueducts that carried drinking water were not built until 500 years after the first sewers of Rome were built.

DID YOU KNOW?

When we think of a toilet, we usually also think of toilet paper.

Many methods were used before toilet paper was invented. Many regions used leaves, ancient Romans used a stick with a sponge attached, and American colonists used corncobs. In the 1700s people realized that the daily newspaper was good for more than just reading, and in the late 1800s the Sears catalog ended up in many outhouses.

In 1879 the Scott brothers invented toilet paper that consisted of single squares of a very coarse paper similar to crepe paper. It was not until almost thirty years later that toilet paper appeared in rolls of soft, fluffy paper. Although Americans like such toilet paper, the English still prefer it to be very coarse.

During the 1970s the United States experienced shortages of many items, such as gasoline and raisins. Famous talk show host

Johnny Carson quipped, "You know what's disappearing from the supermarket shelves? Toilet paper. There's an acute shortage of toilet paper in the United States." That did it. The next day many of the 20 million viewers ran to the stores and bought all the toilet paper they could find. By noon, most stores were completely out.

Although Carson explained on his next show that it had all been a joke and apologized, people still saw empty shelves in the stores and panicked. Scott Paper Company ran a video showing all of their plants in full production. It didn't help.

It took three weeks before the shelves were restocked. The shortage was finally over, the only shortage in American history caused by the consumer.

What is the name and breed of the RCA dog? (His master's voice.)

His name was Nipper. He was a mongrel, part bull terrier with some fox terrier.

Nipper was born in Bristol, England, in 1884. When his owner died, he was cared for by two brothers. One brother, Francis Barrud, had a photographic studio and often took Nipper with him to work. While in the studio, Nipper listened attentively to the old phonograph. Barrud thought the dog, who was then 11 years old, might be hoping to hear his dead master's voice. The thought inspired him to paint a picture of Nipper and the phonograph. He titled the finished painting *His Master's Voice*.

Thinking his painting was too dark, Francis went to the Gramophone Company in London hoping to borrow a brass horn as an object to brighten up the painting. While there, he asked the owner if he might like to buy his painting. The owner agreed, with the stipulation that Barrud would replace the Edison cylinder phonograph with his company's gramophone.

The deal was made and the painting became a trademark. It was called *Dog and Trumpet*.

Emile Berliner, inventor of the disc gramophone, visited the

Gramophone Company and liked the painting so much that he began using the trademark in the United States. He later founded the company that became the Victor Talking Machine Company and eventually Radio Corporation of America (RCA).

Nipper's current successor is a dog rescued from death row at an animal research laboratory by an agency that was searching for a dog to play the RCA mascot. This modern Nipper travels first class and wants his filet mignon cut into small pieces. When he travels, his own limousine always meets him at his destination. Nipper's salary is used to save other animals from experiments.

FACTOIDS

Nipper is not the only famous dog star.

Tiger was the dog on *The Brady Bunch*.

Old Yeller was so named because of his yellow color and his "yelling" bark.

Comic strip dog Marmaduke and cartoon character Scooby Doo are both Great Danes.

The first muppet that Jim Henson created was Rowlf the dog.

The only dog to ever appear in a Shakespearean play was Crab in *The Two Gentlemen of Verona*.

The very first seeing-eye dog was Buddy, a German shepherd.

Every box of Cracker Jack popcorn has a picture of Sailor Jack and his dog Bingo.

In 1957, the first dog traveled in space aboard the Russian satellite *Sputnik 2*. The dog's name was Laika, which means "the barker."

DID YOU KNOW?

In 1901 the first model of the Victor Talking Machine Company was a machine with a single-spring motor, a wooden tone arm, and an outside mounted horn. From these humble beginnings came the now famous Radio Corporation of America, or RCA.

In addition to being a leading supplier of radios, RCA transmitted the first radio photograph, the predecessor of today's facsimile machines, across the Atlantic Ocean in 1924. Just two years later RCA, General Electric, and Westinghouse formed the National Broadcasting Company (NBC).

RCA's president David Sarnoff did not stop with radio. He envisioned every home equipped with not only a sound-receiving device but a screen mirroring the sights of life. Some mechanical televisions had already shown crude pictures. An engineer, Vladimir Zworykin, had produced an "iconoscope" camera and a "kinescope" receiver.

Sarnoff met with Zworykin and asked how much money and time it would cost to develop a system that could be sold. Zworykin replied that it would take $100,000 and a year and a half.

Ten years and $50 million later, Sarnoff introduced television at the 1939 world's fair and a new industry was born.

What is the average number of flowers used on a Rose Parade float? (A rose by any other name is still a rose.)

The number of flowers on a float in the annual Pasadena, California, Rose Parade varies depending on both the size and complexity of the float. A float will have anywhere from 30,000 to over 150,000 flowers. It takes 700 to 900 hours of labor to apply the flowers to each float.

Float builders start with a custom-built chassis and engine. They construct a framework of steel and chicken wire that is sprayed with plastic. The process is called "cocooning" because the sprayed frame resembles a cocoon. The plastic is painted in the colors of the flowers that will be applied at the last minute.

Every square inch of the entire float must be covered with flowers, leaves, seeds, or bark. Between Christmas and New Year's Day, an army of volunteers glues the flowers to the floats, sometimes one petal at a time.

FACTOIDS

A single Rose Parade float is decorated with more flowers than an average florist will use in five years.

Most floats are now built by professional companies and take almost a year to build.

In 1902 the first football game associated with the Rose Parade saw Stanford University so mauled by the University of Michigan that Stanford quit after the third quarter when the score was 49-0. The following year, the Tournament of Roses committee decided to hold Roman-style chariot races instead of a football game. Football did not return until 13 years later.

Each Rose Parade features over 300 horses and riders. A variety of horse breeds are represented, including Andalusians, Peruvian pasos, Bashkir curlies, golden palominos, and miniature horses.

The first marching band was the 20-member Monrovia Town Band in the 1891 Rose Parade. Today 400-member marching bands are quite common. Over 200 bands compete to be one of the 22 bands participating in the parade.

DID YOU KNOW?

In 1890, former residents of the East and Midwest wanted to show off the mild winter weather in their new home of Pasadena, California. At a meeting of the Pasadena Valley Hunt Club, Professor Charles F. Holder said, "Here our flowers are blooming and our oranges are about to bear. Let's hold a festival to tell the world about our paradise." Because of all the flowers, he suggested the festival be called the "Tournament of Roses."

As the festival became more popular, it included marching bands and motorized floats and, in 1900, ostrich races, bronco busting, and a race between a camel and an elephant. (Believe it or not, the elephant won the race.)

From a simple beginning, the Tournament of Roses Parade, known as the Rose Parade, has grown to over a million spectators lining the streets to watch. In addition, an estimated 425 million television viewers in over 100 countries watch the parade, making it one of the largest such events in the world.

Before refrigeration was invented, where did the iceman get the ice he delivered to homes during the summer? (The iceman cometh.)

If large blocks of ice are stored in well-insulated buildings and covered with sawdust, the ice can last for most of the year without melting. Years ago it was common practice during the winter to cut large blocks of ice out of a frozen pond and store them in an "icehouse." The ice was cut into smaller blocks for delivery and transported to families in the neighborhood.

Few people realize that transporting ice around the world was once an extremely lucrative business. Schooners transported ice from Alaska to other parts of the country as well as to Mexico, Central America, and South America. Ice from New England was shipped to the West Indies and other parts of the world.

In the mid-1800s, ice distributors in Seattle and San Francisco wanted harder and thicker ice and an Alaskan company invested heavily in the ice trade by ordering seven new steamers to haul the ice. Each winter the company cut about 10,000 tons of ice from a local lake. A crew of 150 to 200 people cut the ice, moved it into an icehouse, and covered it with sawdust to keep it from melting. The following summer the ice was transported by steamer to the distributors.

A typical New England icehouse was built next to a pond or lake and was framed using 2-by-10 pine or spruce studs. An inner wall was built 10 inches from the outer wall and the space between was filled with sawdust for insulation. A layer of sawdust was also spread on the floor. The ice was normally cut into 250-pound blocks. When the icehouse was full, all the ice was covered with either sawdust or hay. Because of the insulation the ice melted very slowly and lasted almost all year.

In the 1870s new refrigeration techniques made manual cutting of ice from lakes obsolete. As a result, the once flourishing world ice trade melted away.

FACTOIDS

One ice business that has not melted is that of creating ice sculptures. Many ice sculptures are created by chefs to adorn banquet tables, but there are also worldwide competitions. Although not well publicized, ice sculpture competition is part of the Olympics Culture and Art Festival. To qualify for the Nagano Winter Olympics, Steve Brice and Kevin Roscoe created a 2.5-ton ice sculpture called *Moment of Truth*. It depicted a man fighting a lion and included an intricate net made of ice.

For those who do not want to spend years learning the art, numerous companies sell fiberglass molds. You simply fill them with water, freeze them, and peel off the mold to reveal your "sculpture." Prices range from $40 for a onetime-only mold of a heart or horn of plenty to over $1,500 for a reusable mold of a sailfish that is 3.5 feet long.

DID YOU KNOW?

Another form of ice, called dry ice, is really not ice at all but is compressed carbon dioxide. Carbon dioxide has the unique property of changing directly from a solid to a gas. Dry ice can be purchased as either rectangular or square blocks, or as disks, pellets, or snow.

Although the primary use of dry ice is to keep perishable products such as ice cream and meat refrigerated during shipping, it also has some rather unusual uses.

For example, dry ice pellets are often used instead of sand blasting to clean structural walls.

Dry ice is also one of the two most common substances used to seed clouds to produce rain (the other is silver or lead iodide).

Although some people like to play with dry ice, such as by adding water to a container full of dry ice to create an artificial fog, the ice can be dangerous. It should never be handled without using gloves, as it can cause severe burns.

Also, never store dry ice in an airtight container. If you do, it will explode!

More questions?
Try these websites.

EARTH AND MOON VIEWER
http://www.fourmilab.ch/earthview/vplanet.html

You can view the earth from the moon, or the moon from the earth. You can see a view of most major cities as seen from a satellite, as well as many other fascinating views such as the world's current cloud cover.

LIBRARY REFERENCE
http://www.lkwdpl.org/

A storehouse of information divided into ten major categories. You can find everything from a list of Supreme Court decisions to the closest ATM.

CELEBRITY ADDRESSES
http://www.geocities.com/SiliconValley/1954/address

If you want to write to famous actors, actresses, or singers, this site gives you their mailing addresses.

INTERNET PUBLIC LIBRARY
http://www.ipl.org/

This site has a wealth of information on subjects ranging from antique bottle collectors to phrenology.

ANECDOTE: WHICH CAME FIRST, THE CHICKEN
OR THE EXERCISE MACHINE?

I've often been asked, "Which came first, the chicken or the egg?" When J. Mark Davis asked me that question once again, I sent him my answer and thought no more about it.

The next day I received a thank-you and a fascinating e-mail. It seems that Mark is the inventor of the "Eggsercizer." He is a consultant for nuclear power industries, and as he traveled from plant to plant, he often squeezed a tennis ball to work out his hand and arm muscles. One night he couldn't sleep and decided to get a snack from the refrigerator. When he opened the refrigerator door the first thing he saw was an egg, and a new idea was born.

Mark realized that the egg shape matched the natural contour of the hand. So he decided to make rubber objects in the shape of eggs. Mark called them Eggsercizers and manufactured them to look like egg-shaped footballs, basketballs, soccer balls, baseballs, golf balls, and so on.

Mark was delighted with my answer to his question and told me, "I usually tell people I know which came first, the chicken or the egg. Your explanation makes more sense and I will now have to change my marketing strategy for the trade shows."

A few weeks later, Mark kindly sent me and my staff a number of Eggsercizers. He told me that he had "eggspress"-mailed them. When they arrived I sent him a note of thanks and could not resist telling him that they were "eggsactly" as "eggsciting" as "eggspected."

Mark and I have been exchanging e-mail for some time now and he has sent me a copy of his book on marketing as well as some of the new products he has invented. He is a true inventor, entrepreneur, and author.

A short time ago, I noticed that J. Mark Davis had been profiled in *People* magazine because of his invention. In the meantime, my daily workout with my baseball Eggsercizer is guaranteeing that I have a very strong handshake, which I'll definitely need if I ever have a chance to personally meet Mark Davis, the inventor of the egg-shaped exercise tool.

Off

the Wall

How many licks does it take to reach the center of a Tootsie Pop? (Sucking doesn't count.)

In the commercial, wise Mr. Owl decides to find out and counts, "Ah-one [lick], ah-two [lick], ah-three [CRUNCH]." He just didn't have the willpower to keep licking. If he had, he would have found out that it takes approximately 142 licks to reach the center.

A group of curious college students were not satisfied with Mr. Owl's answer and decided to conduct a study to find how many licks it takes. To do this, they set up some simple ground rules:

1. No one could put the entire Tootsie Pop in their mouth. That would be "sucking" and only "licking" was allowed.
2. Everyone had the same flavor as a "control."
3. Each person could choose whether to lick on only one side or all around the pop.
4. The goal was reached when the licker "tasted Tootsie."

The lickers ended up in one of three groups:

• 75 to 100 licks group. These people tend to be too excited about the experiment or not excited enough. The excited ones were candy fanatics who couldn't resist biting. The apathetic ones just wanted to get the experiment over and didn't want to taste the center anyway.

• 125 to 150 licks group. These were the most serious experimenters, keeping meticulous notes and striving to use true scientific principles for the experiment. To them, even a Tootsie Pop was fair game for scientific investigation.

• 175 to 200 licks group. These people tend to savor candy, let a Life Saver completely melt in their mouth without ever biting it, etc. You know the type. The ones who always have candy long after yours is gone.

Although it took the experimenters from 75 to 200 licks to reach the center, standard statistical methods were used to determine the 142-lick average.

FACTOIDS

If you find a Tootsie Pop wrapper with an Indian shooting at a star, you can turn it in for a free Tootsie Pop.

About 100 years ago, candy maker Leo Hirshfield came up with the treat and named it for his 5-year-old daughter, Clara, his "Little Tootsie." At the same time electric lights were just starting to flicker on across America and Utah became the forty-fifth state.

Each year Tootsie Roll Industries produces enough candy to stretch from the earth to the moon and back.

The company experimented with brightly packaged "Mutant Fruitants" suckers that changed colors and flavors on the way to a Tootsie Roll center.

Oddly enough, Tootsie Rolls and Tootsie Pops aren't classified as chocolate under the definitions federal officials use when collecting data on the candy industry.

DID YOU KNOW?

In today's often male-dominated corporate world, Tootsie Roll Industries is owned and operated by a woman, Ellen Gordon.

The company strives to maintain a familylike atmosphere. At the Chicago plant, all employees are greeted by name and the 1,700 workers at the various plants are allowed to eat sweets while on the job.

In addition to its main product, Tootsie Roll Industries produces other candy, including: Mason Dots, Cella's, Charleston Chews, Sugar Daddys, Sugar Babies, Blue Razzberry, Junior Mints, Zip-A-Dee-Doo-Da Pops, Tootsie Pops, Blow Pops, and Caramel Apple Pops.

The company has done well even when the candy industry has been in a slump. It has paid dividends for 53 years, increased sales each year for the past 19 years, and boosted annual earnings for the past 14 years.

Glamour and other magazines have recommended Tootsie Rolls because they are small and low in fat.

But perhaps the candy's enduring success is due to durability. As Ellen Gordon once said, "We have some that were made in 1938 that we still eat. And if you can't bite it when it's that old, you certainly can lick it."

How long would it take to vacuum the state of Ohio? (You'd better get some help!)

You must be ambitious if you want to vacuum the entire state of Ohio. It would take you 33,683 years! You should probably recruit some help before undertaking this project.

To calculate the answer, certain assumptions were made:

1. Lake Erie forms part of the state of Ohio and you do not want to vacuum the lake.

2. Ohio is flat. Although it is a flat state, it's assumed to be extremely flat: no boulders, ravines, hills, or hummocks. The calculations did not consider the extra time needed to push the vacuum up a hill or move a boulder so you can vacuum under it.

3. It takes approximately one second to vacuum one square foot.

Here, then, is the computation:

Area of Ohio: 41,330 square miles

Lake Erie portion: 3,277 square miles

Part of Ohio to be cleaned: 38,103 square miles (41,330 minus 3,227)

Convert square miles to square feet: 1,062,250,675,200 square feet

If you can vacuum one square foot in one second, then it will take you:

1,062,250,675,200 seconds or

17,704,177,920 minutes or

295,069,632 hours or

12,294,568 days or

33,683 years!

FACTOIDS

Because of the popularity of vacuum cleaners made by the Hoover Company, the English use the word "hoover" instead of "vacuum." A typical expression is "I hoovered the carpet today."

The first vacuum cleaner, invented by Cecil Booth, was so large it had to be drawn up to a house by horses; a team of men was required to use it.

Early vacuum cleaners were operated manually. Two people were needed: one to operate the bellows and the other to move the mouthpiece over the floor. The dust was blown into the air.

Most vacuum cleaners were sold by door-to-door salesmen until the late 1940s because the vacuums were expensive and a relatively new concept.

The 1944 Sears catalog mentioned the vacuum cleaner in the index but didn't include a picture because so few were sold.

DID YOU KNOW?

It all started because M. R. Bissell, a china shop proprietor in Grand Rapids, suffered from allergy headaches caused by the dusty straw used to pack the china.

Bissell designed a "carpet sweeper" with a knob that adjusted the brushes to compensate for variations in floor surface and a box to capture the dust.

The carpet sweeper didn't catch on until the mid-1800s when many companies started producing them and giving them distinctive names such as "Weed," "Boston," "Welcome," "Whirlwind," and "Lady's Friend." They wanted to make the consumer feel that the lady of the house would be a superior mother and housewife.

Unfortunately, the carpet sweepers didn't perform well enough. It was up to a British bridge builder, Booth, to make the first practical vacuum cleaner. Booth sent vans to houses and used his machine to suck the dust out via long tubes. While earlier vacuums simply blew the dust around, Booth's machine sucked the dust through a filter – the same method used in today's vacuum cleaners.

In 1905 a small, portable, electric vacuum cleaner was developed by Murry Spangler, who improved on Booth's machine. U.S. industrialist W. H. Hoover manufactured it. He called his company the Hoover Suction Sweeper Company, which became the Hoover Company in 1922.

Sold door-to-door in the 1940s, vacuum cleaners finally became widely accepted in the 1950s and many well-known companies such as Regina and Eureka were formed.

Even today, you can buy a Hoover or Eureka vacuum cleaner.

Which came first, the chicken or the egg? (Please don't ask why the chicken crossed the road.)

There are two answers, depending on whether you are a creationist or an evolutionist.

If you are a creationist, you believe that God created man and all of the animals on the earth. It wouldn't make a lot of sense for God to create an egg, so the chicken must have come first. After all, if God created the egg first, there would be no hen to hatch it or to take care of the baby chick once it was hatched.

If you are an evolutionist, you believe that animals evolve into different species over time. Therefore, the chicken must have evolved from a former chickenlike creature. At some point in time this creature laid an egg that hatched into a modern chicken. It couldn't have been a chicken egg, because there was no such thing as a chicken yet. The first chicken egg could only have been laid by the first chicken.

Therefore, it doesn't matter if you are a creationist or an evolutionist, the answer is the same. The chicken came before the egg.

In fact there is an old proverb that says "He who wants eggs must endure the clucking of the hen."

FACTOIDS

The color of the egg yolk depends on what the hen has been eating. In this country, adding artificial colors is not allowed so some producers add marigold petals to the hen's food to create a more orange yolk.

Hindus do not eat eggs because they believe them to be a valuable source of life.

Some religions believe that in the beginning there was a master egg. The creator of the universe hatched from this egg and then produced other eggs from which all living things came, each from its own egg.

The color of an eggshell has nothing to do with nutritional value but is dependent on the breed of the chicken. Brown-feathered chickens, such as Rhode Island Reds, lay brown eggs; white-feathered chickens, such as White Leghorns, lay white eggs. Brown eggs are often more expensive simply because brown hens tend to be larger and require more food.

The number on an egg carton is the date when the eggs were packed. For example, a 3 indicates January 3 while a 365 indicates December 31.

In China and Russia eggs were valued so much that replicas were carved from precious stones and set with valuable gems.

To prevent a hen from laying her eggs in a hiding place, a natural or artificial egg can be placed in the nest to entice the hen to lay her eggs there. From this practice comes the expression "nest egg," which means putting aside money for future use.

DID YOU KNOW?

Columbus's ships transported the first chickens to this country. They were a strain that had originated in Asia and were considered more valuable for their eggs than for their meat because they laid eggs year-round.

From this small beginning a mammoth industry has evolved. There are now approximately 240 million laying hens in the United States producing approximately 66 billion eggs a year (meaning that the average hen lays an egg 275 days out of the year).

What is the correct way to eat an Oreo cookie? (To dunk or not to dunk, that is the question.)

There are many correct ways to eat an Oreo cookie. It really seems to be a matter of taste (pardon the pun). Some people plop the whole cookie into their mouths at once. Some nibble on the cookie slowly so it doesn't break and drop crumbs. Others dunk their cookies in milk, then take a bite. Many separate the cookie, lick off the cream, and then eat the cookie (these people are called "twisters"). We've heard of one woman who eats only the cream and then gives the rest of the cookie to either her dog or her husband.

In 1912 consumers wanted an English-style biscuit (cookies are called "biscuits" in England) and the Oreo cookie was produced to meet this demand. For the first three years, consumers had their choice of either vanilla or lemon cream. Now only vanilla cream is available. An Oreo cookie is 29 percent cream and 71 percent cookie.

Who coined the word "Oreo" is unknown; in fact the name itself is shrouded in mystery. One theory is that someone took the letters "RE" out of "cream" and placed it between two letter "O's" which represent the two parts of the cookie. Some think the name came from the French word or, meaning "gold," while others think it came from the Greek word *oreo*, which means "hill" or "mountain."

Not knowing what the name Oreo means has not bothered the cookie-hungry public. The Oreo is the most popular cookie in the United States and over 9 billion are eaten every year (the chocolate chip cookie is a close second at 7 billion a year).

FACTOIDS

Of the people who dunk their Oreo cookies, 82 percent dunk them in milk and 2 percent dunk them in peanut butter. Others dunk in hot chocolate or some other drink.

It takes 90 minutes to make a single Oreo cookie and each cookie has 90 ridges.

Each year there is an "Oreo stacking contest" held at 15,000 supermarkets throughout the country. Contestants compete in two age groups (7 and under and 8 to 12) to see how many cookies they can stack in 30 seconds. The national stacking finals are held in Universal Studios, Florida.

If all of the cream filling used to produce a one-year supply of Oreos were used to decorate wedding cakes, there would be enough to decorate all of the wedding cakes made in the United States for the next two years.

Over 40 percent of consumers dunk Oreo cookies all of the time. If everyone dunked every cookie they ate, cows would have to produce over 42 million extra gallons of milk just to satisfy the additional dunkers.

DID YOU KNOW?

Authorities believe that the earliest cookies were made in seventeenth-century Persia (now Iran), which was one of the first countries to produce sugar. The word "cookie," however, comes from the Dutch word *koekje*. It is pronounced "kook-yah" and means "little cake." The Germans call cookies *keks*, and the Italians call them *biscotti*.

One of the most popular cookies in the United States is the chocolate chip cookie. Most people don't realize that it is a relatively modern cookie and wasn't created until 1930. That was the year that Ruth and Kenneth Wakefield bought the Toll House Inn in Whitman, Massachusetts.

One day Ruth Wakefield was making cookies when she discovered she had run out of baker's chocolate. A friend, Andrew Nestle, had give her some semisweet chocolate bars so she broke them up and mixed them with the dough. She assumed the chocolate and dough would mix together, resulting in all-chocolate cookies. But the chocolate didn't mix and the baked cookies were full of the broken chocolate pieces. She named her new creation "Toll House cookies."

Although the original Toll House Inn burned down on New Year's Eve in 1984, most of us will still be eating many Toll House cookies in the years to come.

What can I do with the small slivers of soap left over in the shower? (Use them up, wear them out, make them do, or do without.)

There are at least four methods for saving those slivers of leftover soap.

The first is to simply moisten the sliver, then moisten a new bar of soap. Place the sliver on the new bar and press firmly around its edges to attach it. After a few uses it will become part of the new bar.

A second method is to drop the slivers into a jar with some water and let them sit for a period of time. Eventually the water will melt the soap and you can use the mixture as a liquid soap or shampoo. (For faster results, mix the water and soap slivers in a blender.)

Another method is to put all of the leftover soap slivers into a mesh bag. When you think you've collected enough, tie the ends of the bag and slip the top of the bag over an outdoor water faucet handle. It can help at cleanup time after you've been gardening or doing some other outdoor chore. It's also handy for taking on camping trips.

Soap has a long and interesting history. Although soap making was recorded as long ago as 2800 B.C., soap was not commonly used for cleaning until thousands of years later. Ancient Greeks and Romans rubbed their bodies with olive oil and sand and scraped off the mixture with a wooden scraper called a "strigil." Although Romans bathed, they added oils and other ingredients to the water, not soap.

FACTOIDS

Around 2000 B.C. soap was used as a medication for wounds, but not for cleansing.

Prior to the eighteenth century soap was used primarily to do laundry because personal cleanliness was not a social custom up until then. In the eighteenth century water was thought to be a "magical" fluid and bathing became popular as a medical treatment. As bathing became more acceptable, so did soap.

The B. J. Johnson Company made a soap consisting of only palm oil and olive oil. The soap, called "Palmolive," was so popular that the company was renamed after it.

William Procter and James Gamble made candles and soap and sold their products house to house out of a wheelbarrow. Their company, Procter & Gamble, introduced Ivory soap to the public in 1879.

DID YOU KNOW?

Children are often much more interested in soap bubbles than in soap itself. Although bubbles are a part of nature, soap bubble blowing didn't become popular until the nineteenth century and was limited to bubble pipes until the early 1940s. It was then that a chemical company, Chemtoy, started bottling bubble solution. Today, bubble solution is one of the best-selling toys in the world.

In recent years bubble blowing has become quite exotic. David Stein of New York created the biggest bubble ever blown, 50 feet long and 2 feet in diameter. An entertainer, Professor Bubbles, has actually encased five people at one time in a gigantic bubble. People have blown bubbles of various shapes, including square bubbles, and bubble-making displays are now in many science museums.

More questions?
Try these websites.

USELESS INFORMATION

http://home.nycap.rr.com/useless/contents.html

Visit this site for over 60 true stories, such as the woman who survived the sinking of the *Titanic* and then survived two other shipwrecks.

THIS ONE CAN DRIVE YOU CRAZY

http://complete-access.com/puzzle.html

Have you ever seen the quiz that asks "What does 16 = O in a P mean?" The answer is "16 ounces in a pound." This site has 30 of these curious questions. If you don't know the answer, just click on the question to find out.

Religion

Who are the Shi'i Muslims and what do they believe? (The Five Pillars of Islam.)

A Muslim is a follower of the Islamic religion. There are two major branches of Islam. Most Muslims are Sunnites who follow the orthodox faith, while a small minority are Shi'ites, followers of the only major sect outside the orthodox Muslim religion. Shi'ites were a political faction in the early days of Islam. They supported 'Ali, a son-in-law of Muhammad and the spiritual and temporal leader of the Muslims. 'Ali was killed striving to maintain his authority. Over time, the Shi'ites created a religious movement that sought to maintain the authority of 'Ali's descendants. The majority of Muslims, the Sunnites, preferred to accept the authority of any ruler who maintained the religion and kept order in the Islamic world.

The Shi'i Muslims believe that an exemplary leader, or "imam," was transformed into a mystical being who was a manifestation of God as well as the primordial light that gave true knowledge to man. Of the twelve imams, the last was Muhammad, who disappeared in the ninth century. Today the Shi'i holy men interpret law and doctrine while waiting for the end of time when the imam will return to dispense truth and justice throughout the world.

Although the Shi'ites believe that man is fallible and truth can come only from the imam, the more practical Sunnites believe that the consensus of the Islamic community is a valid source of both knowledge and decision making.

In contrast to the Sunnites, the Shi'ites believe in free will and the ability of humans to know the difference between good and evil.

FACTOIDS

Muslims believe in one God, Allah, and that Muhammad was Allah's prophet. The name of the religion, Islam, means "submission to God's will."

Islam is the second largest religion in the world and is the major religion in over 48 countries. In the United States, it is the third largest after Christianity and Judaism. Islam is also one of the fastest-growing religions in the world.

Muslims believe that there were many prophets in the past including Adam, Noah, Moses, and Jesus. They believe that Muhammad was the last prophet to receive a revelation from God in the form of the Koran, or Book of God.

Although it is historically younger than Judaism and Christianity, Muslims consider Islam to be the oldest religion and one that corrects the corrupted versions of the Jewish and Christian scriptures.

Islam divides all people into two main groups.

The first group consists of those who possess divine books, or books inspired by God. This group includes Christians (the Bible), Jews (the Torah), and Zoroastrians (the Avesta). People in this group are called "People of the Book."

The second group includes any religion not based on divine revelation. People in this group are called "heathens."

Although it is surprising to many, Muslims are quite tolerant toward "People of the Book." Even when conquered by the Muslims, Jews and Christians were given freedom of worship and were also well protected from harm.

The "Five Pillars" of Islam are strict rules that every Muslim must follow. They are:

1. *Profession of faith.* There is no God but God and Muhammad is the messenger of God.

2. *Daily worship.* Muslims must pray five times a day.

3. *Giving of alms.* Unlike other religions that require tithing on a person's income, Islam requires Muslims to tithe on their accumulated wealth.

4. *Annual fasting.* Once a year, during the entire month of Ramadan, Muslims must fast from dawn to dusk while abstaining from food, drink, and sex.

5. *Pilgrimage.* All adults who are physically and financially able must make a pilgrimage to Mecca at least once during their lifetime.

Although Islam is one of the three major religions in the United States, it is probably the one most misunderstood by most Americans.

When did the Roman Catholic Church begin using the calendar we use today? (A red-letter day!)

The calendar we use today (known as the Gregorian calendar because it was instituted by Pope Gregory XIII) replaced the former Julian calendar in 1582. Within a year it was adopted by most Catholic countries but was not adopted in England until 1752, in China until 1912, in Russia until 1918, and in Greece until 1923. Most Muslim countries do not use this calendar.

The problem with the former Julian calendar was its inaccuracy. It calculated the year as being 365¼ days long while it is actually 365 days, 5 hours, 48 minutes, and 46 seconds long. Because of this, the calendar lost a day each century. When Pope Gregory instituted the new calendar, the Julian calendar was already 14 days off.

Although the Gregorian calendar kept leap years for the most part, it eliminated leap years occurring at the century mark unless the century is exactly divisible by four. Thus, 1700, 1800, and 1900 were not leap years, but 2000 will be a leap year.

FACTOIDS

The names of our months are derived from Roman names. The first six months are named after gods (Janus, Mars, Aprilis, Maia, and Juno) or festivals (Februa), the next two months are named after emperors (Julius and Augustus), and the last four are simply the Latin names for seven, eight, nine, and ten (septem, octo, novem, and decem).

Only three Roman names remain for our days of the week: Saturday (Saturn's day), Sunday (Sun's day), and Monday (Moon's day). The rest are named after gods of Norse mythology: Tiu, the god of war (Tiu's day), Wodin, the supreme deity (Wodin's day), Thor the god of thunder (Thor's day), and Frigg, the wife of Woden (Frigg's day).

When dividing time we use both natural and artificial systems. Natural divisions are the day (time it takes the earth to rotate once on its axis), the month (time it takes the moon to complete its phase cycle), and year (the time it takes the earth to orbit the sun). Hours and weeks are purely artificial. In fact, some ancient societies had weeks of eight, ten, or thirteen days.

After the introduction of the Gregorian calendar, it was common to mark holy days in red letters on church calendars to note that they were special days. Because any day that had a red letter was significant, the phrase "red-letter day" came to mean any day of special meaning.

DID YOU KNOW?

One of the most impressive calendars is the Aztec calendar discovered in 1790. It is a circular stone 12 feet in diameter and weighing almost 25 tons.

The center of the calendar stone is the face of the Aztec sun god. Four squares around his face represent the four previous suns, or worlds, and how they came to end: by wild animals, by wind, by fire, and by flood. Aztecs believed that they lived in the fifth and final world.

The Aztec calendar depicts both a civil and a religious year. The Aztec civil year, which is an agricultural or solar year, was divided into 18 months of 20 days, ending with 5 extra days considered to be extremely unlucky.

In addition to the 365-day civil calendar, the Aztecs had a 260-day religious calendar that consisted of twenty 13-day weeks. Both calendars are shown on this single stone.

The name for a year on the civil calendar was different from the name for the same year on the religious calendar. However, every 52 years, the name of the year was identical on both calendars. This was a sacred time because the Aztecs believed the world could come to an end during this period if they did not perform the proper sacred rites.

All of the people let their home fires die out. The priests then held a somber religious ritual that lasted for days. When the ritual was over, the priests lit a new sacred fire on the breast of a sacrificial victim, the people took some of the sacred fire to rekindle their hearth fires, and a time of feasting began.

The Aztecs knew then that the world could not end for another 52 years.

Why are the signs on Pennsylvania Dutch barns called "hex" signs? (Have the signs kept away phones, electricity, and automobiles?)

The colorful hex signs painted on Pennsylvania Dutch barns were used to protect crops and animals from disease and injury caused by witches' spells and to ward off the evil eye. The word "hex" has two meanings. One meaning comes from the Old High German word *hexe* meaning "witch." The other meaning comes from the Greek word for six. The hex symbol combines both meanings because it is a hexagram, or six-sided figure, designed to ward off witches.

The hexagram is considered a powerful symbol for many reasons. It symbolizes the combination of the male (an upward-pointing triangle) and the female (a downward-pointing triangle). The two triangles can also symbolize "above" and "below," referring to man's relationship with God.

The Star of David is a hexagram but its origin is not known. In ancient times it was most often found in non-Jewish contexts. In the 1600s Emperor Ferdinand approved a seal for the Jewish community of Prague in the form of a six-pointed star with each point having the letter M, G, N, D, V, and D, or Mogen David (King David). In 1897 the six-pointed star was adopted at the First Zionist Congress and is now on the flag of Israel.

Today most Pennsylvania Dutch hex signs are circles rather than six-pointed stars. They are decorated with geometrical patterns or intricate bird and flower designs. Each symbol represents certain ideas, and the entire hex sign represents a legend that has particular meaning for the family to which it belongs.

Typical symbols include a sun wheel (warmth and fertility), stars (protection against fires), tulips (faith, hope, and charity), oak leaf (long life), and wheat (abundance). Commonly used colors are blue (protection and peace), yellow (health), and green (fertility and growth).

FACTOIDS

Designs similar to those used on hex signs also adorned the Pennsylvania Dutch birth and marriage certificates, Bibles, and some furniture.

Early hex signs were carefully hand-painted directly on walls, doors, books, and barns. Today most hex signs are silk-screened on round disks that can be mounted anywhere.

Some of the first settlers in Pennsylvania practiced "pow-wowing," or the art of healing by using incantations and magic amulets.

The early Pennsylvania Dutch settlers were superstitious people but were also quite sensible and practical. Their practical side is evidenced in the legends of Tyl, a mythical immigrant about whom many stories were told. All the stories had the same basic plot – a practical man who always succeeds in outwitting his wily opponent or the devil.

A number of Pennsylvania Dutch families still maintain parts of their culture, especially in their cooking. A traditional dessert is shoofly pie, made of molasses and dough crumbs.

DID YOU KNOW?

It is difficult to think of the Pennsylvania Dutch settlers without thinking about the Amish. The Amish are a group of conservative Christians who settled in eastern Pennsylvania and still have large settlements there. They stress peace, humility, family, community, and separation from the world.

Pennsylvania is known for having at least three pacifist religions: the Amish, the Brethren, and the Quakers.

Most Amish speak three languages: Pennsylvania Dutch (a German dialect) at home, High German during worship services, and English.

The Amish are best known for their severity of dress and lack of modern conveniences. Men wear broad-brimmed black hats and plain clothes fastened with hooks rather than buttons. They have full beards but no mustaches. Women wear long full dresses, bonnets, and black shoes and stockings. No one wears jewelry of any kind.

The Old Order Amish do not use telephones or electric lights. Instead of driving automobiles, they drive horses and buggies. Children go to private one-room schoolhouses and attend only through the eighth grade. After that, they work on the family's farm or in its business until they marry.

The Amish do change, however. They carefully examine new ideas and gadgets and will accept them only if they help keep their life simple and their families together.

Although theirs is not a large religion, the Amish are to be admired for being pacifists in a warlike world, for maintaining a simple lifestyle that tends to keep them from becoming materialistic, and for placing great importance on family and community.

What is the religious makeup of the United States? (Why do other countries think we are materialistic?)

Christianity is the dominant religion in the United States and is embraced by 87 percent of the people, who belong to one of four major Christian Churches: Protestant (58 percent), Roman Catholic (27 percent), Mormon (1 percent), and Eastern Orthodox (1 percent).

Of the remaining population, 3 percent embrace Judaism,

3 percent belong to lesser-known religions, and the rest have no religious preference.

Christianity has the most followers worldwide, with its members accounting for 32 percent of the world's population. Islam is second, accounting for 17 percent of the world's population. However, the growth of Christianity is stable while Islam is expanding rapidly.

There are many hundreds of religious groups in the United States that are typically labeled as denominations, sects, or cults. Unfortunately, there are no hard-and-fast rules and the category a religion is placed in is often left to the whim of the writer or "expert" who is discussing it. For instance, the Church of Jesus Christ of Latter-day Saints (the Mormon Church) at one time or another has been called a denomination, a sect, and a cult.

A denomination usually refers to an established religious group that has existed for some time and has members throughout the country. Examples are the Methodist Church and the Episcopal Church.

A sect refers to a small group that has sprung from an established religion. Although it adheres to many beliefs of the parent religion, it often introduces new and original concepts. A modern example of a sect is one of the groups that have broken away from the Mormon Church so male members can still have multiple wives, a practice outlawed by the Mormon Church.

A cult brings up images of an evil religious group using brainwashing to control its followers. However, that is the media definition. A cult can also be any emerging religion that has few followers and differs in beliefs from most established religions. As with any organized group of people, a cult can be bad or it can be good.

FACTOIDS

Over half of the people in the United States claim that religion is very important in their lives and about 40 percent attend church once a week, making church attendance in the United States higher than in any other country. On the other hand, less than 3 percent of the people in Japan and Russia attend church once a week.

Although religion tends to decline in developed nations, it remains healthy in countries where people fear the government or where economic downturns are common.

Latin America was colonized by northern Europeans who also converted the majority of inhabitants to Christianity. In a bizarre role reversal, Latin American countries are now sending missionaries to northern European countries where the collapse of religion is particularly dramatic.

DID YOU KNOW?

One of the founding principles of the United States was "freedom of religion." Because of that, our country is rich with many diverse religious beliefs, traditions, and rituals.

Some of these little-known religions, such as Zoroastrianism and Shamanism, date back hundreds of years. Others are relatively modern but are not often understood by the general public. These include Christian Science, Spiritists, Unitarians, Unity Church, Neo-Pagans, Science of Mind, and so on.

Not all beliefs follow conventional religious thought. Wicca came from ancient pagan beliefs and Santeria is a combination of Roman Catholicism and ancient African traditions.

Although we preach "freedom of religion," we too often condemn those who do not believe as we do. Animal sacrifices in Santeria are condemned by Christians even though the Bible praises the same sacrifices when performed by ancient Israelites.

We do not have to embrace the religion of others, but understanding what others believe and why can help us become more understanding and tolerant of others.

Isn't that really what freedom of religion is all about?

What is the history and significance of the Infant of Prague? (An infant protected a city from the ravages of war.)

The Infant of Prague is a statue of Jesus as a child. It stands in the Lady of Victory Church in the Czech Republic city of Prague. In the seventeenth century a statue of the child Jesus was transported to the Czech Republic (called Bohemia at the time) and given to an order of Carmelite nuns in the city of Prague.

The statue is 18.5 inches high, made of wax, and covered with a long elaborate gown. The outstretched arms welcome those looking at it.

Roman Catholics have long venerated the child Jesus, so it was not unusual for such a statue to be given to Catholic nuns. When Polyxena, the granddaughter of Doña Isabella Manrique, donated the statue to the nuns she told them, "I am giving you what I most esteem of my possessions." At this point the statue became known as the Infant Jesus of Prague.

In 1628 Prague was invaded by the Saxons and Swedes and the Carmelite nuns were forced to flee, leaving the statue behind. Almost 10 years later a young priest found the statue, minus its arms, buried in the ruins of the Lady of Victory Church. Its hands were gone. The priest prayed for financial aid to repair the statue and claimed that the Divine Infant spoke to him, saying, "Place me near the entrance of the sacristy and you will receive aid." A few days later a man came by the sacristy and repaired the statue.

This and other reported miracles caused an increase in devotion to the Infant of Prague statue among both the masses and the nobles. One of these nobles, Bernard Ignatius, presented a gift of a little gold crown set with precious stones and jewels, which is still on the statue.

Although Prague later endured many wars and years of unrest, the Lady of Victory Church and the statue remained unscathed. In fact, Prague escaped the ravages of both World War I and World War II.

FACTOIDS

The Christmas carol "Good King Wenceslas" (who "looked out on the feast of Stephen") was based on an actual king of Prague.

In the fourteenth century a Bohemian king was named Charles IV, emperor of the Holy Roman Empire, and chose Prague as the capital. During his reign, Charles IV had a totally useless wall constructed in the city. By being paid to build the wall, the workers retained their pride and didn't have to rely on charity. The wall was called the "Hunger Wall."

The fight to overthrow communism in Czechoslovakia was led by Vaclav Havel, a playwright who later became president of the new Czech Republic.

Because of its castles and gothic buildings, Prague is called the "City of a Hundred Spires."

DID YOU KNOW?

The famous composer Antonín Dvořák, whose music still has wide popularity, was a citizen of Prague. He used Bohemian folklore as his inspiration and often embellished traditional melodies, as in his famous *Slavonic Dances*.

When Dvořák was 51, the founder of the U.S. National Conservatory of Music, Mrs. Jeanette Thurber, asked him to come to the United States. After numerous refusals Mrs. Thurber's persistence paid off and he finally accepted her offer. He wanted to study the social and political culture of the United States. Dvořák arrived in New York and almost instantly fell in love with the United States.

Dvořák did return to his beloved Prague. But he left behind a wonderful gift: a musical work based on the rich culture of our country, his ninth symphony, *From the New World*.

More questions?
Try these websites.

FINDING PASSAGES IN SCRIPTURES
http://bible.gospelcom.net/cgi-bin/bible

The Bible Gateway lets you enter a passage or key words to find the associated reference in the Bible.

BRIEF DESCRIPTION OF MAJOR WORLD'S RELIGIONS
http://www.omsakthi.org/religions.html

Provides a short history and synopsis of Buddhism, Christianity, Confucianism, Hinduism, Islam, Janism, Judaism, Shintoism, Sikhism, Taoism, and Zoroastrianism.

Science

Is it true that toilets in Australia flush in the opposite direction from those in the United States? (Down the drain.)

Theoretically, draining water swirls clockwise north of the equator and counterclockwise south of the equator, but the effect is so minimal you would probably not be able to see it.

A phenomenon called the Coriolis effect causes the different rotation directions in different parts of the world. It's also the reason that tropical storms rotate counterclockwise in the northern hemisphere (where they are called hurricanes) or clockwise in the southern hemisphere (where they are called typhoons).

Scientists conducted an experiment in which all of the variables were carefully controlled such as water temperature and effects of friction. They even started by deliberately swirling the water in the wrong direction. They concluded that although water does spiral down the drain in opposite directions in the two hemispheres, the effect is so slight that you would not be able to see it in a sink or toilet.

The Coriolis force is so subtle on a small scale that other rotational forces can easily overcome it, causing the water to swirl in either direction.

In the early nineteenth century Gustave Gaspard de Coriolis introduced the theory of the Coriolis effect, which states that an object moving in a straight line above the surface of the earth (and not parallel to the equator) will appear to curve because the earth is turning under it.

FACTOIDS

In an African country near the equator, some enterprising people have set up two toilets, one on either side of the equator. For a fee, they claim they can demonstrate that the toilets flush in the opposite directions. However, it isn't true.

If you fill your sink and then pull out the plug, water always goes down the drain in the same direction. However, this is not due to the Coriolis effect; rather, it is because the faucet is usually slightly off-center or there is some irregularity in the sink itself.

The idea of the Coriolis effect did not come about because of an interest in weather or ocean currents but was based on improved ways of killing. As the range of cannons increased, soldiers noticed that if they aimed at a target to the north, the cannonball usually landed east of their target. The cannonball was fired in a straight line but the rotation of the earth caused the trajectory to curve.

To see the Coriolis effect, get on a merry-go-round and throw a ball to a child across from you on the ground. The ball will appear to go to one side instead of going straight.

Although pilots may not know the name of the Coriolis effect, they certainly know its dangers. They use terms such as "graveyard spin" and "graveyard spiral."

If a pilot performs a rapid roll and then levels off, the inertia of the roll causes him to lean opposite to the direction of the roll even after it has stopped. If the pilot should quickly look down while turning, the Coriolis effect takes hold and he feels as if the plane is descending. Because he thinks he is descending, the pilot might pull back on the stick to gain more altitude, causing the plane to stall and go into a spin.

In a long continued spin the pilot may feel he is spinning in the opposite direction after he makes a correction. Because he thinks he has overcorrected, he counters the spin and goes back to the original spinning pattern. This is the "graveyard spin" because that's probably where the pilot is heading.

My grandmother told me that when she visited Ireland she saw the sun turn green. Is that possible? (Green sun, blue moon, what next!)

It's not only possible, it does happen. What your grandmother saw is known as a "green flash."

If it's very clear when the sun is setting or rising on the horizon, you can see a green flash of light on the horizon that lasts for a few seconds. In order to see it, you need a distant horizon with a distinct edge. That's why a green flash is typically seen over the ocean. If conditions are just right, you will see a brief flash of green or a green flame that shoots up from the horizon.

When the sun rises or sets, the spectrum of light waves must pass through the greatest atmospheric thickness of the day. Because water vapor in the atmosphere absorbs the yellow and orange rays and scatters the violet rays, only the red and blue-green light travels toward you. The longer red waves are cut off by the horizon but the shorter blue-green rays are refracted, or bent, and linger for a second before disappearing.

Another way to understand the green flash is to imagine four suns, a yellow-orange sun, a violet sun, a red sun, and a blue-green sun. Imagine each one on top of the other like four stacked poker chips standing on edge.

The yellow-orange sun is absorbed by the atmosphere and disappears. The violet sun is scattered and disappears, leaving only the red and blue-green suns. The red sun is closer to the horizon than the blue-green sun and it sets first, followed almost immediately by the blue-green sun. In that instant, you can see the upper part of the blue-green sun which appears as a green flash.

One scientist always looks for a green flash whenever there is a clear horizon. After ten years of looking, he is still waiting to see it. It is indeed rare to observe a green flash.

FACTOIDS

The temperature of the sun can go as high as 15 million degrees Fahrenheit. The coolest parts of the sun are about 10,000 degrees Fahrenheit.

Like people, stars are born, mature, grow old, and die. Our sun (which is a star) is middle-aged.

The sun contains over 99.8 percent of the total mass in our solar system, while Jupiter contains most of the rest. The fractional percentage that is left is made up of our earth and moon and the remaining planets and asteroids.

When light rays are scattered because of atmospheric haze, results can be more than just beautiful sunsets. For instance, after the volcanic island of Krakatoa exploded, the moon actually looked blue. (There is no proof that this is the origin of the expression "a blue moon," however. This phrase was used long before the explosion of Krakatoa.)

Many ancient cultures have worshipped the sun, including the ancient Egyptians, Mayans, Incas, and Hindus. In our country, Native Americans such as the Hopi and Zuni revered the sun. In Japan, the royal family was believed to have descended from the sun goddess, Amaterasu.

Scientists believe that the mysterious stones at Stonehenge in England are actually a solar observatory built almost 5,000 years ago. Another ancient method of identifying important times in the sun's orbit around the earth is a simple spiral rock carving in New Mexico's Chaco Canyon. At noon on the day of the summer solstice, the center of the spiral is penetrated by a dagger of sunlight. At the winter solstice, a dagger of sunlight strikes each side of the spiral.

A controversial archeological site is the Bighorn medicine wheel in northern Wyoming (so named because Native Americans often use the name "medicine" for an object believed to give control over natural or magical forces). The wheel, made up of rocks carefully positioned on the ground, has 27 spokes and a circumference of 245 feet. Scientists believe it was constructed about 2,500 years ago.

It's not just the wheel that is intriguing. All across Wyoming giant stone arrows point the way to the medicine wheel. Some of these arrows are 200 miles away. It appears that some ancient peoples wanted to make sure that anyone could find the wheel, but the wheel's importance is unknown today.

Perhaps scientists will one day unlock the secrets of the Bighorn medicine wheel.

How are magnets made? (Are people attracted to you because of your magnetic personality?)

First you need an object that can be magnetized. Wood or glass, for example, cannot be magnetized. Any material that can be magnetized is called ferromagnetic. "Soft" ferromagnetic materials will lose their magnetism once they are removed from a magnetic field, while "hard" ferromagnetic materials such as iron retain their magnetism. The only three elements that can be permanently magnetized are iron, nickel, and cobalt. Some elements, such as chromium, exhibit paramagnetism, which means they can only be made into a very weak magnet.

To make a magnet out of a piece of ferromagnetic material, you must place the object in a magnetic field. As the field cuts through the object, most of the electrons within the material are aligned in the same direction, and the object becomes magnetized. An object can be placed in a magnetic field in one of two ways.

The first method is simply to stroke the object with another magnet. The second method is to pass an electric current through the object; an electric current creates a magnetic field. This method is used to create industrial electromagnets.

An electromagnet is a large coil of wire wound against a soft ferromagnetic core. It is usually hung from some type of crane. The core remains magnetized only while an electric current flows through the wire. One use of industrial electromagnets is in automobile wrecking yards. The crane is positioned so that the electromagnet touches the top of the automobile. When the electricity is turned on, the magnet lifts the automobile. The crane is then swung around to where the automobile is to be placed, the electricity is turned off, and the automobile drops into the desired spot.

In recent years scientists have come up with a number of alloys to produce small but extremely powerful magnets. An alnico magnet, for example, is an alloy of aluminum, nickel, and iron. Some powdered materials are also made into magnets. Barium ferrite magnets, for example, are used as the focusing magnets for television tubes.

FACTOIDS

The earth can be thought of as a giant magnet. A compass helps us find directions because it can point to the earth's magnetic pole. Earth's magnetic field is also the cause of the spectacular aurora borealis, or northern lights.

Natural magnets have been used for over 3,000 years.

Today's computers would not be possible if not for magnets. The computer's memory and all storage devices such as disks and tapes are made of tiny magnets.

More than half of the permanent magnets in the world are produced by Japan.

A typical home contains at least 150 magnets, found in electric motors, loudspeakers, microwave ovens, CD players, VCRs, and computers.

Experimental high-speed trains in Japan use magnetic levitation to allow the trains to float above the track, thereby eliminating the friction that would slow them down.

DID YOU KNOW?

The ancient Chinese and Greeks knew about rare and mystical stones with the power to attract iron. These were natural magnets of iron-rich ore called "lodestones." This was the only form of magnetism known until 1821.

The first Greeks to discover the lodestone lived near the city of Magnesia. This is where the word "magnet" comes from, meaning "the stone of Magnesia." Milk of magnesia was also named after this city but it doesn't contain any magnets.

Around a thousand years ago, the Chinese found that stroking a steel needle with a lodestone caused it to become magnetic. They also found that if the needle was freely suspended, it would always point north-south. Thus the compass was invented.

The magnetic compass was soon introduced to Europe and Columbus used it when he crossed the Atlantic.

It's difficult to tell where Columbus might have landed without a compass. He could have landed anywhere. And if that had happened, the Spanish and later the British might have colonized some other land and where would the United States be today? Magnets can be extremely important.

What makes the sound when you snap your fingers? (Shame, shame on you.)

When you rub two fingers together, the loudest sound occurs when the air is forced out between the middle finger and the palm and the air strikes the palm. You can test this theory by first snapping your fingers and listening to the sound. Next, place a soft tissue or piece of cloth on your palm and try snapping your fingers. The sound will be very muffled.

Our fingers have many uses outside of the obvious ones. We rub two fingers together when we say "shame on you." Some authorities believe that this gesture evolved from the practice of crossing two fingers to make the sign of the cross in order to ward off evil. The finger strokes in the "shame on you" gesture symbolize pushing away or repelling the evil one.

Our decimal numbering system, which has 10 numbers, is based on our fingers. Ancient people kept track of things by counting on their fingers. Because we have 10 fingers, we devised a numerical system based on 10 digits. In fact, the word "digit" can mean either a finger or a number. Some cultures, however, used a different numerical system. The ancient Mayans, for example, used a system with 20 digits rather than 10.

Some cultures use their fingers to do complex arithmetic. Koreans have a "finger math" that is also taught in some places in the United States. Teachers who work with visually impaired students teach this Korean "finger-calculator method," called "chisanbop," that lets students do multiplication problems such as 18 times 26 using nothing but their fingers.

One of the most fascinating features of our fingers is our fingerprints. Every person in the world has a unique set of fingerprints, unlike any other. However, most experts believe that identical twins have identical fingerprints 95 percent of the time. The use of fingerprint identification has become a major tool in apprehending criminals.

FACTOIDS

Latent fingerprints (the prints left at a crime scene as opposed to those on a fingerprint card) can be left on any surface, including paper and human skin. Some techniques used to make latent fingerprints visible include lasers, powders, alternate light sources, and subjecting them to glue fumes.

In ancient Babylon, fingerprints on clay tablets were used for business transactions; in fourteenth-century Persia, many government papers had fingerprints on them; and in Nova Scotia, a prehistoric picture shows a hand with ridge patterns.

Wearing latex gloves does not necessarily keep a criminal from being apprehended if the criminal leaves the gloves at the crime scene. When tight-fitting, nonporous gloves are removed, fingerprints remain on the insides of the gloves and can be detected by a number of different methods.

The first mention of fingerprints occurred in 1686 when a professor of anatomy, Marcello Malpighi, described the ridges, loops, and spirals of fingerprints. In 1823, another professor of anatomy, John Evangelist Purkinji, described 9 basic fingerprint patterns. However, neither man considered using fingerprints to identify individuals.

DID YOU KNOW?

Prior to using fingerprints to identify individuals, a system of measuring bony parts of the body was used. This system was devised in the late 1800s by Alphonse Bertillon, a French anthropologist. Bertillon measured certain bony body parts and then used a formula to come up with a value that would apply to only one person in the world and would not change during that person's lifetime. This technique, named the Bertillon system after its inventor, was accepted as valid for 30 years.

In 1903, a bizarre event triggered the end of the Bertillon system. A man by the name of Will West was sent to the federal penitentiary in Leavenworth, Kansas. The problem was that the penitentiary already had an inmate named William West. When photographs of the two men were compared, they were identical. When the authorities used Bertillon measurements, they indicated that both men were the same person. Finally, their fingerprints were compared, proving they were indeed two different individuals. When authorities reviewed prison records and correspondence from the men's families, they discovered that Will West and William West were identical twins.

In that same year, the New York state prison system began using fingerprints to identify criminals, and a year later fingerprint identification was started at the Leavenworth penitentiary.

Thanks to the West brothers, today we only have to put an inked thumbprint on a piece of paper rather than have all of our bony body parts measured.

Does hot water freeze faster than cold water? (Should you heat the water to cool it faster?)

This is a frequently asked question. If both the cold and hot water are identical in composition, then the cold water will freeze faster. However, 50 percent of people asked this question believe just the opposite. Why?

People tend to think that hot water will freeze faster because they are basing their opinion on real-life experience. When water is boiled until all the trapped air bubbles are released, it will freeze faster than cold water. But hot water doesn't freeze faster because it's hot but because it has a different composition from the cold water that still has the trapped air bubbles.

When you heat water you promote evaporation that causes two cooling effects. First, some of the mass is carried off so there is actually less water to be cooled. Second, during evaporation the hottest molecules are released into the air first, thus lowering the temperature of the remaining water. This is why you can cool your soup by blowing on it. When you blow on the soup, it removes the water vapor hovering above it and helps evaporation.

The folklore about hot water freezing faster probably started more than a century ago when water was carried in wooden buckets, which help retain the heat and increase evaporation. Nowadays, when water is kept in a metal bucket, a large amount of heat is transferred through the metal sides and cooling is not dependent on evaporation. In a modern experiment using wooden buckets a bucket of hot water froze 10 percent faster than a bucket of water at room temperature.

FACTOIDS

It takes about 1,500 gallons of water to produce a typical fast-food lunch of a hamburger, french fries, and a soft drink. This includes the water required to raise the potatoes and the grain used to make the bun and feed the cattle.

Your body requires about 9 glasses of water a day. You can be dehydrated by 5 percent before you even feel thirsty.

The volume of water on earth today is the same as it was 3 billion years ago.

Two thirds of your body and three fourths of your brain are water.

Of all the water on the earth, only 1 percent is available for human consumption.

On average, you use about 2 gallons of water just to brush your teeth and from 4 to 6 gallons every time you flush the toilet.

About 39,000 gallons of water are needed to manufacture a domestic automobile.

DID YOU KNOW?

When we think of water, we usually think of a liquid. However, when water is solid, it's ice. The largest and most impressive ice is in the form of gigantic icebergs that float in the North Atlantic Ocean.

The tallest known iceberg was sighted in 1967 near Greenland. It was 550 feet tall, or taller than a 50-story skyscraper. Another iceberg was approximately the size of the entire state of Rhode Island.

Most icebergs come from glaciers on the western side of Greenland. Between 10,000 and 15,000 icebergs shear off from these glaciers every year.

Icebergs have always been dangerous to ships because about 90 percent of the iceberg is hidden below the waterline, making it difficult to see how large it is. However, modern devices such as radar and satellites minimize the danger.

Nevertheless, to be safe, if you decide to take an ocean cruise in the near future, you should do so in the summer, and go south rather than north. A cruise in the South Pacific Ocean would be even better.

Why do some paints, stickers, and toys glow in the dark? (Have you ever seen a real frog glow?)

A material that glows in the dark after being exposed to light contains molecules that absorb energy for long periods of time, then later release that energy as light. The phenomenon is called "phosphorescence" and the materials are said to be "phosphorescent."

Electrons in a molecule are normally arranged in a state of the least possible energy. However, when a molecule is exposed to light it may absorb a particle of light, called a "photon." The photon rearranges the electrons to a highly energetic state. If the material is phosphorescent, the extra energy from the photon becomes trapped in the molecule. Eventually, the electrons shift to a lower energy state and the extra energy that had been trapped is released as a photon of light.

Electrons escape randomly rather than all at the same time. As these higher-energy electrons release light to return to their original states, fewer and fewer are left to escape. That is why the glow continually diminishes until it fades into nothing.

Three types of substances can glow in the dark. The first is the phosphorescent material that absorbs light and then gradually releases it, like the phosphorescent material we just described.

The second type can emit light without any outside help. For example, the firefly has the rare chemical luciferin and the enzyme luciferase in its abdomen. These interact with oxygen to produce the glow.

Radioactive materials are the third type. These emit high-energy rays that react with surrounding materials to produce light. Radium is a good example of a radioactive material that gives off light.

Around 1852 the term "fluorescence" was coined. Phosphorescence refers to a material that absorbs light and releases it over a period of time. Fluorescence refers to a material that absorbs light in one spectral color and immediately emits light in a different spectral color. If you've ever seen a mineral glow under an ultraviolet light (black light) then you've seen fluorescence.

FACTOIDS

Some female fireflies do not have wings and look very much like flat larvae. These are called "glowworms." Most glowworms give off a greenish light, but the "railroad worm" also has a red headlight.

Some frogs eat so many fireflies that they also glow.

The rhythmic flashes of the firefly are used to attract fireflies of the opposite sex.

Some fish give off definitive patterns of light to help them either form or maintain schools.

White phosphorus glows in the dark when exposed to air rather than light. However, the chemical reaction between it and the air can also cause it to explode into flames. It is extremely dangerous and has been used in warfare for years.

DID YOU KNOW?

If you live near an ocean or have ever taken a cruise at night, you may have seen the waves glowing with a blue-green tint or noticed that the wake of the ship was luminous.

This light is produced by large numbers of phosphorescent marine life such as plankton, jellyfish, and small crustaceans. They generate a heatless light by chemical means. The light produced is almost always blue-green. Some squids also surround themselves with a luminous light when in danger.

The deep-sea angler fish uses its light to great advantage. The lights in its mouth attract and illuminate prey which quickly fall victim to this predator.

Most of us have seen phosphorescent stickers, toys, and light sticks. But if you've ever seen the beauty of luminous ocean waves at night, you are indeed fortunate.

Why aren't there 100 seconds in a minute and 100 minutes in an hour instead of 60? (Some people never did learn to use fractions.)

About 5,000 years ago there was a great city, Uruk, in Sumeria, an area we now call the Middle East. It was here that the earliest known writing was found, as well as a system of mathematics. This early numbering system was based on the number 60 rather than the number 10 as in our system. The ancient Sumerians divided each hour into 60 minutes and each minute into 60 seconds. Although their numbering system has not been used for centuries, their system of dividing hours into minutes and minutes into seconds survived and is still used today.

In our modern numbering system we use fractions to denote a part of something. For example, if we divide 10 by 3, our answer is $3\frac{1}{3}$. However, if we want an answer without fractions, then we have only two choices because the number 10 can only be divided evenly by the numbers 2 and 5. (If we divide 10 by 1, we still get 10 so we don't consider that combination here.) If we divide 10 by 2, the answer is 5 or "half," and if we divide 10 by 5, the answer is 2 or "one fifth."

The ancient Sumerians didn't know how to write fractions, yet they often needed to know what a "half" or a "third" of something was. To solve this problem, an Uruk mathematician decided to base the Sumerian numbering system on the number 60, which can easily be divided by both halves and thirds. Although 10 can only be divided by 2 or 5 if a whole number answer is desired, 60 can be divided by 10 different numbers that provide answers without fractions (2, 3, 4, 5, 6, 10, 12, 15, 20, and 30).

FACTOIDS

Scientists have found chemical traces of wine proving that ancient Sumerians were drinking wine more than 7,000 years ago.

Sumerians were probably the earliest fish farmers. They kept fish in artificial ponds over 4,000 years ago.

A form of duplicating designs was invented by the Sumerians. They would inscribe a cylindrical stone with a design. This stone was then rolled over a soft clay tablet, leaving a reverse impression of the design. This principle of using a roller to duplicate a design is similar to the basic principle of a modern printing press.

The concept of multiplication was devised by the Sumerians.

Wagons were in use over 5,000 years ago. In Sumeria, the wagons had solid wheels. Copper nails were used to nail a leather tire to the wooden wheel. The wagons were pulled by oxen or by the Assyrian onager (wild ass), which is now nearly extinct.

The cuneiform writing of the Sumerians was not deciphered until the early nineteenth century.

What is the star closest to our sun? (Close but oh, so far.)

Generally speaking, the star closest to our sun is Alpha Centauri, which is 4.35 light-years away. However, it is actually a triple star system. Alpha Centauri A and Alpha Centauri B form a binary star, or two stars that orbit each other. Alpha Centauri A is larger than our sun while Alpha Centauri B is slightly smaller. The third star, Alpha Centauri C, is actually the nearest individual star to our sun and is 4.22 light-years away. It is significantly smaller than our sun, and because it is so faint, it was not discovered until 1915. Because of its closeness, it is often called Proxima Centauri.

Alpha Centauri intrigues scientists because it is one of the few stars in the galaxy that might offer life conditions similar to those in our solar system. To determine if a star possibly harbors planets that could support life, scientists have come up with five tests. Proxima Centauri fails all five, Alpha Centauri B passes most, but Alpha Centauri A passes all five.

The first test is that a star must fuse hydrogen into helium at the core, thereby generating heat and light.

The second test is that a star must be the right temperature. If it's too hot, it may burn out too quickly and if it's too cold it may not produce the energy needed to sustain life.

The third test is that the star must be stable. Instability would cause a star's brightness to vary considerably, so that it would alternately freeze or burn any life on a nearby planet.

The fourth test is that a star must be old enough to give any surrounding planets time to evolve life.

The fifth and final test is that the star must have the chemical elements such as carbon, nitrogen, oxygen, and iron needed to produce planets and life.

FACTOIDS

Although 4.35 light-years seems like a small number, if you started a journey to Alpha Centauri as a baby and traveled at 10,000 mph, you would die of old age before you had completed less than 10 percent of the journey. Take heart, however, because after only 45,000 years of travel you would be halfway there.

The Hubble Space Telescope is currently checking for the existence of planets around Alpha Centauri.

The fastest-known star doesn't have a name, just a number (PSR 2224+65), but it's traveling through space at 1,000 miles per second (that's well over 3.5 million miles per hour).

The asteroid that came closest to hitting the Earth was the size of a house and passed by on December 9, 1994, narrowly missing us by only 60,000 miles.

DID YOU KNOW?

Scientists and amateurs alike believe that there could be a planet orbiting Alpha Centauri. If Alpha Centauri is so much like our sun, wouldn't its planet be similar to our earth? Not likely.

Although the planet's terrain would probably be similar to earth's continents, islands, and oceans, the planet would be different in most other ways.

Temperatures would be much higher than those on earth and could be lethal to humans trying to live in the tropical regions. Life would prefer the cooler highlands. The Arctic and Antarctic regions would probably be quite balmy, never reaching cold temperatures like earth.

The planet would be covered with clouds and the sky would be seen only rarely. The atmospheric pressure would be one and a half times that of earth's. Although humans could tolerate it, they would probably move to higher elevations not only to live in atmospheric pressures similar to ours but also to escape the intense heat.

Because of the cloud cover and high temperatures, the weather would often be violent, spawning cloudbursts and hurricanes. The frequent rainfall would cause rapid erosion so there would be fewer high mountains. There would also be more rivers, lakes, and wetlands.

Although the planet would not be a Garden of Eden, humans could survive there. In fact, knowing how well people have adapted to extreme climatic conditions here on earth, humans would probably prosper.

A NASA expert stated that "we will discover extraterrestrial life in the next 25 years." Perhaps it won't be on Mars after all. It just could be a planet orbiting Alpha Centauri.

Why are the oceans salty but not lakes?

Most of the salt in the oceans comes from rocks containing various salts. Wind, rain, and erosion gradually wear down mountains and rocks. Rain then dissolves the salts into streams that eventually reach the sea. This has been going on for millions of years and that's why the oceans are salty.

Although water vapor evaporates, rises from the ocean, and is carried to the land, the heavier salt is left behind. As the river waters from new rainstorms feed the oceans, they carry more salt. Thus, after every rainstorm the oceans become just a little bit saltier.

Most lakes are relatively new compared to the age of the earth, and the salt from rainwater has not had time to build up. In addition, many lakes have outlet streams or rivers to let the water out when it reaches a certain height. The lakes may also be in a cooler climate, which prevents a high degree of evaporation.

The famous salty lakes, such as the Great Salt Lake in Utah, the Salton Sea in Southern California, and the Dead Sea in the Middle East have no outlets. All are in desert climates and a lot of water is lost through evaporation. The new water coming in carries salt and these lakes build up salt deposits just as the oceans do.

FACTOIDS

Flecks of gold are suspended in seawater. If all of it were mined and distributed, every person on earth would get about 9 pounds of gold.

Although ocean water is warmer near the shore where it's shallow, the average temperature of the deep ocean is just a little above freezing, around 39 degrees Fahrenheit.

The deepest-known spot in all of the oceans is the Mariana Trench in the Pacific Ocean, which is almost 7 miles deep.

Of all the water on earth, 97 percent is salt water, 2 percent is frozen water trapped in glaciers and ice caps, and the remaining 1 percent is fresh water.

Although we speak of different oceans, such as the Atlantic and Pacific, or of the Seven Seas, all oceans are connected and flow into one another.

The difference between low and high tides at the Bay of Fundy in Nova Scotia, Canada, can be as much as 50 feet, or the height of a 3-story building. They are the highest tides in the world.

The largest tidal wave ever measured was 210 feet, about 18 stories above sea level. It hit the coast of Siberia in 1737.

DID YOU KNOW?

Even fresh water contains salt but not enough to be noticeable. If you were to take a glass of fresh water and add a pinch of salt, it might still taste fresh or it might seem slightly salty, depending on your personal taste.

However, if you add a teaspoon of salt to a glass of water virtually everyone will complain it's too salty to drink. That is almost the same proportion of water and salt as in the oceans. In fact, ocean water is about 220 times more salty than fresh water in a lake.

To give you an idea of how much salt this is, if all of the salt in the world's oceans were removed and spread over all of the earth's land, it would form a layer about as high as a 40-story office building.

However, this salt is not distributed evenly throughout the oceans. The Red Sea and Persian Gulf are very salty because evaporation is high. The Sargasso Sea in the North Atlantic is also very salty because the water temperature is high and it is too far from land to receive an influx of fresh water. On the other hand, some parts of the ocean are hardly salty at all. For example, water from the Columbia River in Oregon is so powerful that it travels over 200 miles from shore before mixing with seawater.

Is it true that opals contain a lot of water? (More valuable than diamonds?)

Opals usually contain 4 to 9 percent water, but some may contain up to 30 percent water. These precious stones are formed from lumps of silica and are actually silicon dioxide and water. The water in the stone cannot escape unless the opal is heated to extreme temperatures.

Most opal is more than 60 million years old and is typically found where hot springs once flowed. The silica in the springs lined the walls of cracks, vents, and cavities in the bedrock. When the hot springs dried up, the silica hardened into opal. It is one of the few gemstones that is sedimentary in origin.

An opal has an extraordinary ability to refract light and reflect specific wavelengths of light. This capability is so unique that the term "opalescence" was coined to describe it. Each tiny sphere of silica within an opal refracts a single pure spectral color depending on the size and spacing of the sphere. Looking at an opal can be like looking at water droplets in a rainbow.

When buying an opal you should consider the color of its "fire," the intensity of its "sparkle," and the rarity of the color. An opal is not subtle. Even in indirect light it shows flashes and flares of a mystical inner fire.

But most of all, you should choose one that simply appeals to you.

FACTOIDS

High-quality opals can bring as much as $80,000 per carat, making them more valuable than diamonds.

Arabs believed that opals have a fiery color because they fell from heaven in flashes of lightning.

Archeologists have found 6,000-year-old opal ornaments in African caves.

Opals were set in the crown of the Holy Roman Emperor and in the crown jewels of France.

The ancient Aztecs mined opals in Central and South America.

Opals are considered to be very magical. They are reputed to have healing powers and are used for various rituals. Black opals are the choice of witches. However, wearing a black opal near the heart is said to ward off evil and protect travelers.

Although opals are found in various parts of the world, 90 percent of the world's gem-quality opals come from southern Australia. All black opals come from Australia.

It is said that Cleopatra wore an opal to attract the gaze of Mark Antony.

DID YOU KNOW?

Opals have a special meaning for the Aboriginal people living in Australia. They believe that they have lived in Australia since Dreamtime, the beginning of all creation. Archeologists have proven that the Aborigines have lived in Australia for tens of thousands of years. To them an opal is something that a Dreaming ancestor left behind as a sign of the ancestor's presence. One legend tells the story of how the people received the gift of fire from opals.

The people sent a pelican to explore the country so he could come back and tell them what was there. The pelican carried provisions of water and fish in his beak to sustain him on the long journey. But before he had flown very far, he became ill and landed on top of a hill. As the pelican rested, he saw that the ground before him was a kaleidoscope of color. He did not realize that he was looking at a field of opals.

Being curious, the pelican pecked at the flashing stones with his beak until he accidentally created a spark that lit the nearby dry grass. The flames grew larger and spread a great distance until they reached a group of people camping near a creek. The people took the fire and for the first time were able to cook their fish and meat. Their creator had given them the gift of fire.

More questions? Try these websites.

ASK DOCTOR MATH

http://forum.swarthmore.edu/dr.math/drmath.college.html

Dr. Math answers questions about all branches of mathematics. When you go to this site, don't be frightened when you see Answers: College Level and Beyond. Just click on All Levels to find answers at the elementary, middle, and high school levels. If you have a specific question, you can e-mail Dr. Math. Whenever I've written him, he's always answered.

ANECDOTE: A VISIT FROM THE DUTCH ROYAL NAVY

I've always enjoyed helping people. If I can find an answer to someone's question, then that's a reward in itself. However, there are times when the reward is much more tangible ... and totally unexpected.

Rob Dijxhoorn, who lives in the Netherlands, sent me an e-mail asking for some specific information relating to computers. I responded that same day and thought no more about it. Just another question, another answer, all in a day's work.

I didn't know until later that Rob was very excited when he received my response. He was thrilled not only because he had an answer that no one else had been able to give him, but also because the answer came all the way from California and had arrived the very next day.

Some months later Rob came to San Francisco on vacation and wanted to thank me personally. All he had was my e-mail address, which contained an acronym for the facility I worked in. He asked the hotel clerk what the acronym meant and the clerk told him. He then called directory assistance, asked for the phone number of the facility, called the receptionist, and asked for the street address. Rob then asked someone at the hotel for directions, rented a car, and drove the 50 miles from his hotel to the building where I worked.

That morning the receptionist called to tell me that I had a visitor in the lobby. When I met my visitor and he introduced himself, I was shocked that someone had come so far just to shake my hand and thank me personally. It turns out that Rob is a former officer in the Dutch Royal Navy and a mathematics professor. I was thoroughly impressed with the effort he had made to find me and I introduced him to my staff. We all had a memorable visit with Rob. In fact, we had another wonderful visit the following year and hope to have many more in the years to come.

That one visitor from the Netherlands made up for the tens of thousands of people we've helped who never bother to say "thanks."

My Dutch friend, Rob Dijxhoorn, and I still keep in touch.

Sports

**What does "packers" refer to in the name
of the Green Bay Packers football team?
(A team that produced a true star –
Bart, that is.)**

The official Green Bay Packers media guide states that in 1919,
Curly Lambeau and George Calhoun were talking on a street
corner in the city of Green Bay, Wisconsin, and decided to start up a
football team. They later convinced Curly's employer to put up
money for the equipment and let them use the company athletic
field for practice. Curly worked for the Indian Packing Company, and
because early publicity identified the new team as a company

project, the team was named the "Packers." It's been called that ever since.

However, Curly Lambeau's first wife tells the story differently. When she was still Curly's sweetheart, his father wanted him to return to Notre Dame University in the fall. Curly hated school and had a good job with the Indian Packing Company. However, he thought the only way to keep playing football was to return to Notre Dame University until Calhoun suggested that he could play for the town team. The Indian Packing Company gave them $500 for uniforms and equipment and Curly was elected team captain.

The first season was highly successful. The Green Bay Packers beat 10 opponents in a row before being beaten by another company-sponsored team from Beloit, Michigan.

Some consider 1921 to be the birth year of the Packers. This was the year that the fledgling National Football League (NFL) granted a franchise to the owners of the Acme Packing Corporation (successor to the Indian Packing Company) to host a team in the city of Green Bay.

The owners of the Acme Packing Corporation lost the franchise in 1922 for using college players under assumed names. The franchise was later awarded to Curly that same year. Low attendance and other financial problems forced the Packers to seek help from local merchants. In 1923 Curly, Calhoun, and others formed a corporation that was awarded a franchise in June of the same year. The corporation, with some revisions, still exists today.

FACTOIDS

In 1931 the Packers became the first team to win the NFL title three years in a row. In later years the team won nine NFL titles and two Super Bowls.

Vince Lombardi was the only Packer coach who never posed with the team for the official team photo.

Although quarterback Lynn Dickey recovered more fumbles than any other Packer, most of the fumbles were his own.

Unlike other professional football teams, Green Bay is a

nonprofit organization. All of the team's profits are either reinvested in the franchise or donated to charities or other worthwhile programs. In 1950 stock in the Green Bay Packers was $25 per share. Today it is still $25 per share.

Ray Nitschke played in more postseason games than any other Packer.

DID YOU KNOW?

Perhaps one of the greatest Packers is also an unsung hero, Bart Starr. Quiet and soft-spoken, Starr never displayed the ego common among superstars. Under his direction, the Packers defeated the Giants in the first title game ever played at Green Bay and the first million-dollar gate in professional football history.

But in spite of the fact that Starr had thrown three touchdown passes, the press raved about Paul Hornung's great catches. After the game a national sports columnist was asked about Starr and replied, "Who's that?"

The following year Starr led his team to victory while a 50 mph wind whistled through Yankee Stadium. While his opponents complained about the horrible weather, Starr completed 9 out of 21 passes and didn't fumble once.

In 1967 the Packers played in weather that was 13 degrees below zero. During the final minute of the game, Starr executed a one-yard quarterback sneak that gave the Packers their third consecutive NFL title.

Although players and coaches on other teams recognized Starr as one of the best quarterbacks in the league, the modest Starr replied, "There are two big reasons for any success I've had. One is Coach Lombardi and the second is the best offensive team in the pro ranks."

With all of the superegos in today's professional sports, it's refreshing to think about the "forgotten hero" of the Green Bay Packers: quarterback Bart Starr, who said, "I do the best I can."

Who was the model for the Heisman trophy? (With a snarl, not a smile.)

The model was Warren Mulrey of the Fordham University football team, chosen by John Heisman, director of the Downtown Athletic Club of New York. The Heisman trophy was designed by sculptor Frank Eliscu.

The Heisman trophy is a statue of a football carrier with his right arm extended as if to straight-arm a would-be tackler. It is 21 inches high, stands on a black onyx base, and weighs about 70 pounds.

Originally there was a smile on the face of the statue but Heisman made Eliscu replace the smile with a snarl, arguing that football players were fighters. Other consultants wanted the fingers on the runner's hand extended. Eliscu replied, "That may be good football but it is not good sculpture because they can be broken off too easily."

Eliscu used a newspaper picture for some of the details of the uniform. The picture was of Jay Berwanger of the University of Chicago. It showed him with his stockings folded over the tops of his shoes and his legs bare, which was the style at that time.

Perhaps the picture was prophetic. Jay Berwanger was the first player to win the Heisman trophy.

FACTOIDS

John Heisman helped legalize the forward pass and originated the "center snap" and "hike" signals. He also was the first coach to use the quarterback as a defensive safety and use him to run interference on end runs.

Archie Griffin is the only player to win the Heisman trophy twice.

The trophy was originally called the DAC (Downtown Athletic Club) trophy but was renamed the Heisman trophy after John

Heisman died in 1936. In the same year the rules were changed so that all college players in the United States could compete, rather than just those east of the Mississippi River.

John Heisman was a Shakespearean actor during the off season. When coaching, he often reverted to more eloquent language such as saying "prolate spheroid" for "football."

Most Heisman trophy winners have also made a name for themselves in professional football, including Paul Hornung, Roger Staubach, O. J. Simpson, Jim Plunkett, Tony Dorsett, Billy Sims, Marcus Allen, and Barry Sanders, to name just a few.

During his career, John Heisman coached at six colleges with a total record of 185 wins, 68 losses, and 18 ties.

DID YOU KNOW?

Although American football started in the eighteenth century, it was really just a combination of rugby and soccer. It wasn't until 1880 that the game was changed to resemble modern-day football.

In 1905 there were so many football deaths and injuries that President Theodore Roosevelt called for more rule changes to make the game safer. Blocking with extended arms was outlawed and new formations were introduced. The forward pass was legalized at this time, with the help of John Heisman, but did not gain the popularity or finesse we recognize today until Knute Rockne at Notre Dame perfected it.

Perhaps one incident that prompted President Roosevelt to make football safer was the fact that his second cousin, William Roosevelt, broke his leg when playing for Stanford in the first Rose Bowl in 1902. In spite of his injury, he continued playing for another 15 minutes until he was forced to leave the game because of broken ribs. To add insult, Stanford was destroyed by Michigan, 49-0.

In 1934, three men decided to create a trophy for the best collegiate football player of the year. The three were John Heisman, director of athletics at the Downtown Athletic Club of New York; Lou Little, coach of Columbia University; and Jim Crowley, coach of

Fordham University. The trophy was first presented in 1935.

Although Heisman's name will always be remembered because of the trophy named after him, it's rather sad that he isn't remembered for his other contributions to the great sport of football.

How did the "seventh-inning stretch" originate? (Respect for a president?)

Most authorities believe the seventh-inning stretch began in 1910 when President William Howard Taft left a game early and everyone stood up out of respect for the president.

A variation is that President Taft, who weighed more than 300 pounds, found that sitting for an entire game made him uncomfortable. Thus he would often stand up and stretch at about the seventh inning. Fans thought he was getting up to leave so they also stood up to show respect. Soon, everyone began stretching in the seventh inning.

There is, however, another reference dating back to 1869. It states, "The spectators all arise between halves of the seventh inning, extend their legs and arms and sometimes walk about. In so doing they enjoy the relief afforded by relaxation from a long posture upon hard benches."

The term itself, however, cannot be traced back further than 1920.

FACTOIDS

Interesting quotes from baseball players:

Pitcher Dan Quisenberry said, "Once I tried to drown myself with a shower nozzle after I gave up a homer in the ninth. I found out you can't."

When the owner of the Dodgers offered to send Babe Herman on a trip around the world, Herman replied, "Frankly, I'd prefer someplace else."

After officiating for the longest game on record (over eight hours), umpire Jack Lietz remarked, "We went the whole game without going to the bathroom."

When speaking about hitter Willie Stargell, Sparky Anderson commented, "He's got enough power to hit home runs in any park ... including Yellowstone!"

The worst epithet hurled by clean-living Padres pitcher Bruce Hurst was "Oh, go wash your car!"

DID YOU KNOW?

Did Doubleday really start it all?

Ingrained in American sports folklore is the story of how baseball was invented by Abner Doubleday, a young West Point cadet. Supposedly, Doubleday invented the game in the summer of 1839 in the village of Cooperstown, New York. So much credence is given to this story that today's Baseball Hall of Fame is located in Cooperstown.

The story originated in 1907, in the final report of a committee commissioned by major-league executives to inquire into the origins of "America's National Game."

The story of Doubleday, who was also famous as a Union general during the Civil War, was based on the somewhat dubious testimony of Abner Graves, a retired mining engineer. Graves claimed to have witnessed the event. This account appealed to committeeman Albert G. Spalding, a former star baseball player and club owner who was also a famous sporting goods tycoon and a fanatically patriotic American.

The term "baseball" (originally "base-ball") dates from 1744, when *The Little Pretty Pocket Book* described a game involving a pitcher who throws a ball to a batter who tries to hit it, runs to a base, and returns to score a run. The book contained an illustration showing a batter holding a bat with a curious flat, fanlike end, a catcher behind him, and a pitcher preparing to throw a small ball underhand. The two bases are marked by posts instead of the modern bags and flat home plate.

Many other early references to bat-and-ball games involving bases are known: "playing at base" at the American Army camp at Valley Forge in 1778; the forbidding of students to "play with balls and sticks" on the common of Princeton College in 1787; a note in the memoirs of Thurlow Weed, an upstate New York newspaper editor and politician, of an organized baseball club in 1825; a newspaper report in the 1820s that the Rochester, New York, baseball club had about 50 members at practice; and at Harvard an 1829 reminiscence by the elder Oliver Wendell Holmes that he played a good deal of ball at college.

What is the difference between billiards, snooker, and pool? (Are you waiting for a cue?)

It is common to use the term "billiards" for all games played on a billiard table that may or may not have pockets. However, there is a more precise definition.

Carom, or French billiards, is played on a table without pockets and only three balls are used, two white and one red. One white ball is the "cue" ball, and the remaining balls are "object" balls. To score a point, called a "carom" or "billiard," a player must hit the cue ball so that it then hits the other two balls in succession. In some games, the cue ball must also hit a cushion one or more times to complete a carom. Carom is now a generic term for any game played on a table without pockets.

Snooker is played on a table that has six pockets. The game is played with a cue ball and 21 other balls; 15 are red and 6 are numbered, colored balls. A player must first shoot a red ball into a pocket. The player then tries shooting any other colored ball into a pocket. If successful, the player continues to alternately hit red and colored balls into a pocket. Every red ball remains in the pocket but each colored ball is removed and set on the table again. Once all of the red balls are in the pockets, the six colored balls must be shot into pockets in their numerical order.

Pool, which is also called "pocket billiards," is also played on a six-pocket table. However, the pockets are usually wider than those on a snooker table. The game is played with a cue ball and numbered balls. Solid colors are used for balls 1 through 8, and stripes for balls 9 through 15. There are many varieties of pool games. When "Chicago" is played, for example, all balls must be sunk in rotation. In "straight pool" balls can be sunk in any order. However, the player must indicate the ball and the pocket, and gets one point only if successful.

FACTOIDS

Rudolph "Minnesota Fats" Wanderone was one of the best-known figures in the history of pool. Originally nicknamed "Brooklyn Fats" or "New York Fats," he renamed himself "Minnesota Fats" when the movie *The Hustler* appeared in the early 1960s.

When only 18, Willie Hoppe won his first world's billiards title by defeating Maurice Vignaus, the renowned French champion. Hoppe went on to win more than a dozen titles. Most consider him to be the greatest all-around billiard player of all time.

The record for an exhibition game unbroken run of 526 balls was set by Willie Mosconi. He also won the World Pocket Billiards title 15 times from 1940 to 1957. In world championship competition, the highest unbroken run of 182 balls was set by Joe Procita. He was competing against Willie Mosconi at the time.

In the nineteenth century billiards were often played at racetracks while people waited for race results to be posted. Sometimes a number of wagerers would pool their bets on a long shot in the race. If they won, the money was counted out on a billiard table. Hence the name, "pool" table.

Billiard balls used to be made of ivory or Belgian clay. Today they are usually made of cast phenolic resin, a strong plastic with small particles imbedded in it to add strength.

Billiards started out as a lawn game sometime in the fifteenth century. Wooden sticks were used to shove, rather than hit, the balls. The term "billiard" comes from the French words *billart* (one of the sticks) and *bille* (a ball).

When the game was moved indoors it was played on a table with six pockets. The table also had a hoop used as a target. Eventually these disappeared, leaving only the pockets. The game was played by people in all walks of life and was so popular that even Shakespeare mentions it in *Antony and Cleopatra*.

The wooden stick, called a "mace," had a large head that made it difficult to use. Players often turned the mace around and used its handle to hit the ball. This eventually led to the development of the cue stick in the 1600s.

In *The Music Man* Professor Howard Hill said that pool was "the first step toward moral degradation." But, let's face it, he was trying to sell musical instruments for a band. In spite of his concern, pool has lost the stigma of smoky dens of iniquity and has become socially acceptable.

Why is a dartboard laid out the way it is? (Go for the bull's-eye on this one.)

To be perfectly honest, no one knows for sure why a dartboard is designed the way it is and not that many people even have opinions about it.

It is known that a form of darts was a training game for English archers in the Middle Ages and that the indoor dart game became popular in English inns and taverns in the nineteenth century. It is also known how the "bull's-eye" originated. When darts were first played they were thrown at the end of a keg. There was a cork in the keg's center where it was tapped. This cork center eventually became the "bull's-eye."

Around 30 years ago there were many regional dartboards, each with a different design. One example is the "Log-End" board, which is nothing more than the sawed-off log from the bottom end of an elm tree.

Although some regional boards are still used today, one board has become the standard and is used in all major competitions. This board is called by such names as Clock, Treble, Standard, London, or Number One. The main feature is the treble ring that permits many different types of games to be played.

There are 20 numbers around the outer edge of the board and each number is at the large side of a "wedge." The wedge is divided into four parts: two large scoring areas, a doubles area (the outer ring), and the triples area (the inner ring).

Although no one knows how the numbering sequence originated, it is the same on virtually every board. The 20 is flanked by the two low numbers 5 and 1, 19 is flanked by 3 and 7, 18 by 1 and 4, and 17 by 2 and 3. The four odd numbers (17, 3, 19, and 7) are clustered near the bottom and three pairs of even numbers fall together (18 and 4, 6 and 10, and 16 and 8).

FACTOIDS

"Diddle for the middle" is a slang expression used for the start of a game when opposing players each throw a single dart at the bull's-eye. The person who is the closest starts the game.

When throwing darts, each player stands 7 feet 9.25 inches from the board which is hung 5 feet 8 inches above the floor.

If someone calls you a "chucker" it's an insult. The name refers to someone who doesn't care and just "chucks" the darts at the board without aiming.

Although darts have been around for centuries and became popular in English taverns and inns during the nineteenth century, it was not until about 1970 that the sport became so popular that major competitions were televised.

People traditionally equate the game of darts with England. However, the game has become so popular in the United States that there are over three times as many dart players here as there are in England. Annual prizes for major tournaments held in the United States can exceed a million dollars a year. The major world championships are the Winmau World Masters, the World Darts Federation (WDF) World Cup, the Embassy World Professional Darts Championship, and the News of the World Championships.

Perhaps it's due to our love affair with high technology that in the 1980s coin-operated electronic dart machines appeared. These are extremely popular in the United States. With the electronic dart games, new dart rules had to be created. Some of these are rather interesting:

If a dart sticks in the board but the machine fails to score it, you lose those points.

If the dart bounces off the board, it does not score and cannot be thrown again.

However, the basic rule of electronic darts is rather frightening for those who do not like high technology:

The machine is always right, no exceptions.

In football, why is it called a "down" instead of a chance, or try, or attempt? (Another way of saying, "I give up"?)

In football the term "down" has been used since the late nineteenth century when the game was more rowdy than it is today. If the runner fell to one knee he could get up and run again. When a ball carrier was tackled, he would yell "Down" to let his opponents know that he couldn't go any farther. This kept players on the other team from piling on the downed ball carrier.

Today's game hardly resembles early football. From colonial

times until the late 1800s, football did not involve the foot at all. The ball was dribbled or was carried by a runner. By 1820, players were allowed to bat the ball with their fists and the game became known as ballown.

A typical team consisted of 2 backs, 16 runners, and 2 rovers, but playing the game was hardly orderly. There were no set rules and the few rules that did exist were often arbitrarily changed from game to game. Many colleges made up their own rules, some of which promoted violence. No college had any firmly established rules and the number of players allowed on each side was usually agreed upon just before the game.

In the 1850s a round rubber ball was introduced. Players began developing the skills necessary to kick the ball long distances as well as the soccer style of dribbling the ball with the foot or using the foot to pass the ball to a teammate.

In 1875, when Harvard University had a match with Yale University, the rules were a combination of rugby rules and rules from the existing American game of ballown. Within five years an association was formed to standardize football rules among the colleges.

Football became a popular but often deadly sport. In 1909, for example, 33 college athletes died while playing football and almost 250 suffered major injuries. More rule changes were introduced to promote skill rather than roughness as the way to win a game.

The game of football has continued to evolve and has become highly refined. It is now the most popular of all college sports.

FACTOIDS

It is always difficult to pick the greatest college football games of all time. However, here are two of the ten games that many writers, coaches, and players have voted to be among the greatest.

Stanford versus California, 1982. John Elway had moved Stanford into field goal range and when Mark Harmon booted the ball through the uprights, Stanford took a 20–19 lead with only four seconds left to play. When Stanford kicked off for the final play of the game, California's Kevin Moen ran down the field and then lateraled the ball to his linebacker Richard Rogers. As Rogers was being tackled, he flipped the ball to Dwight Garner, who threw it backward to Mariet Ford. Ford raced down the sideline. The Stanford band, not realizing the game was not over, streamed onto the field in a victory celebration and hemmed Ford in. Ford flipped the ball over his head and it was caught by Kevin Moen who charged into the end zone, making one of the most bizarre touchdowns in college play. California won the game 25–21.

Miami versus Boston College, 1984. Although played in a driving rain and on a muddy field, this game saw the Miami quarterback, Bernie Kosar, pass for almost 450 yards and the Boston College quarterback, Doug Flutie, pass for over 470 yards. In the fourth quarter, the lead changed three times. Miami was leading 45–41 when Boston College made the last play of the game. On their own 48-yard line, Boston College's Flutie threw a desperation pass as time ran out. Gerard Phelan had beaten the Miami defenders, caught the pass, and fell backward into the end zone. Boston College had won. The pass that won the game went down in history as one of the most famous "Hail Mary" passes.

DID YOU KNOW?

Football enthusiasts each have their own idea as to who contributed the most to modern college football. Knute Rockne, who made the forward pass popular, trained the "Gipper" and the "Four Horsemen," and invented the "platoon system" of substituting complete teams, is always high on the list.

There are too many others to mention them all here, but there is one who is rarely mentioned, Walter Chauncey Camp, who died in 1925.

It was Camp who helped change the game from a combination of rugby and ballown to what it is today. Some of his innovations included the 11-man team, the quarterback position, the scrimmage line, and signal calling. One of his greatest innovations was the rule that requires a team to surrender the ball if it does not advance a specified number of yards from the scrimmage line.

We remember some names, we've never heard of others. Yet we should thank all of the innovators who have made college football the popular and exciting sport that it is today.

How did the sport of hockey get started? (Zamboni is not a hockey player.)

Historians believe that ice hockey is derived from a game played by the Micmac Native Americans and was later adopted by settlers in Canada. However, the settlers introduced some facets of field hockey into the Micmac game, which eventually evolved into a game called "shinty." This game was played on ice, but players used their sticks to hit a ball instead of a puck. The puck was first used in 1860. The exciting sport of ice hockey has been described as being a game of "blood, sweat, and beauty."

The National Hockey League (NHL) was created in 1917 and consisted of both Canadian and American professional teams.

Over the years, hockey has produced legendary superstars. One of the most famous was Bobby Hull, who was an all-star 12 times. He was a fast skater, clocked at skating almost 30 mph, and had a devastating slapshot clocked at 118 mph. During one season he played with his mouth wired shut because of a broken jaw but still scored 58 goals.

You can argue about who is the best hockey player of all time, but almost everyone agrees that the greatest defenseman of all time was Bobby Orr. A goalie on an opposing team once said, "The first thing I did when I saw Bobby Orr bearing down on me was to pray, if I had time!"

In the 1970–1971 season Orr scored an amazing 139 points, including 102 assists. It was the first time any player had scored 100 assists in a single season and only two players have done it since, Gretzky and Lemieux. Orr's record is even more astonishing because he was a defenseman. In 1998 the *Hockey News* named Wayne Gretzky the greatest player of all time. Bobby Orr was second.

The great Gordie Howe had his record of all-time leading scorer broken by the great Wayne Gretzky. Howe's record had been 1,851 points during his playing lifetime. Wayne Gretzky recently took retirement.

FACTOIDS

When Bobby Hull left the Blackhawks in 1972 to join the World Hockey Association (WHA), the drop in attendance over the next ten years is estimated to have cost the Blackhawks over $1 billion in lost revenues.

The Scandinavian game of "bandy" (or "banty") is similar to hockey but uses a ball rather than a puck, making it a much faster game.

When tenor Luciano Pavarotti performed in the San Jose, California, arena (home of the Sharks hockey team), he sang on a stage that sat on 10,000 gallons of frozen water.

DID YOU KNOW?

A key element in the sport of ice hockey is the ice itself. It's only been in recent years that scientists have made major discoveries to help us understand the properties of ice.

Hockey players talk about "fast ice" and "slow ice." When the ice is "fast" it means that it is harder, colder, and smoother. "Soft" ice is warm, soft, and rough. Scientists have recently found that ice has a semifluid layer that coats the surface and makes it slippery. When the ice is minus 250 degrees Fahrenheit, this layer is only the thickness of a molecule. As ice temperature rises, the number of these slippery layers increases.

The ice in a hockey arena is made by pumping freezing salt water through a system of pipes embedded in a large piece of concrete. When the concrete is cold enough, water is poured onto its surface. After a few layers of ice have been laid down, the hockey markings and advertisements are painted on and another eight to ten layers of ice added on top. When finished, the ice is only an inch thick.

A hockey fan doesn't care that much about how ice is made or its consistency. Whether the ice is "slow" or "fast," hockey is a fast, rough, exciting sport to watch.

More questions?
Try these websites.

PROFESSIONAL FOOTBALL
http://www.nfl.com/

This is the official site of the National Football League and includes news, standings, statistics, links to all of the teams' websites, and more.

PROFESSIONAL BASEBALL
http://www.majorleaguebaseball.com/

This official site of major-league baseball includes sections on players, current scores, scheduled games, best records in baseball history, and much more.

Transportation and Travel

How does a traffic signal know that a car is waiting for a green light? (No, driving back and forth won't fool the detector.)

Traffic lights are controlled in many different ways. The simplest method uses an internal timer that specifies how long a light should stay a particular color.

Other lights are controlled by a "low-tech" controller that can be programmed for a specific sequence to handle normal traffic patterns. During peak traffic times, the light stays green longer on the main streets. However, during times of light traffic, the lights are controlled by detectors – a few loops of wire embedded in the center of each lane near the intersection. An electric current is sent through the wire loop creating a magnetic field.

When an automobile passes over the wire, the metal absorbs some of the energy causing a signal to be transmitted to the controller. This lets the controller know that there is an automobile in the lane and that it should change the light to green. This method of traffic control has been used for decades.

FACTOIDS

The traffic signal was invented by Garrett A. Morgan in the 1920s. The early signals did not have lights and displayed either a red STOP sign or a green go sign. A simple electric clock controlled the movement of the signs.

Traffic speed limits vary greatly from country to country. In a Dutch "shared street" the speed limit is a walking pace, while there is no speed limit at all on the German autobahn, although it is recommended not to drive faster than 80 mph.

Strict Orthodox Jews are not allowed to do any work on the Sabbath, including using mechanical devices such as a "Walk" button. To prevent the devout from being stuck at a traffic signal forever after leaving the synagogue, Los Angeles traffic engineers have programmed nearby traffic signals to provide automatic walk times during the Sabbath.

The city of Los Angeles has three times more automobiles than people.

In 1928, Charlie Adler invented a device that could respond to the sound of an automobile horn. It was placed on a utility pole along with a sign saying SOUND HORN TO CLEAR SIGNAL. When a driver honked, the light turned green. Not popular with local residents, the invention was short-lived.

DID YOU KNOW?

Today traffic engineers must consider more than automobiles. They also need to consider bicycles, fire engines, horses, buses, commuter trains, blind people, and people in wheelchairs.

One new innovation is a microwave radar unit that detects pedestrians in a crosswalk and makes sure they have time to cross the street before the light changes. Another is a high-tech video imaging system with four cameras per intersection. Whenever a vehicle enters the camera's field of vision, it trips a sensing device.

Another fascinating device being tested in Los Angeles is designed to prevent collisions between horses and bicycles, which have occurred in the past. A microwave "horse detector" has been installed at the intersection of an equestrian path and a bicycle path to warn bicyclists when a horse approaches.

The City of Los Angeles has always been in the forefront of traffic control technology. The city is now experimenting with a "thinking computer" that analyzes traffic patterns when a baseball game is over. Baseball games end at different times, so a timing device will not work. Engineers use the computer to define typical traffic patterns that occur after a game. Then, for subsequent games, the computer sets traffic lights to this "after-game" pattern to give preference to traffic moving away from the stadium.

The next time you get stuck at a red light for what seems to be an eternity, remember that many hard-working engineers are constantly seeking ways to give you a green light as quickly as possible.

Why do they drive on the left side of the road in England? (It depends on which hand you use to hold your sword.)

During the Middle Ages people traveled on the left side of the road for protection. If a stranger was coming from the opposite direction or was passing you, it was important to keep your sword handy in your right hand in case the stranger turned out to be an enemy. In A.D. 1300 Pope Boniface VIII mandated that all pilgrims going to Rome had to travel on the left side of the road.

Over 400 years later farmers hauling their products to town in large wagons usually rode on the horses rather than in the wagon. The farmer sat on the horse that was on the left and at the back of the team, thereby keeping his right arm free to whip the team if needed. Sitting on the left also made it easier to look down and make sure the wagon wheels didn't hit those of other passing wagons. In this way people started driving on the right side of the road. During the French Revolution Napoleon enforced a keep-right rule in France and in all countries he occupied.

The English, however, didn't drive huge wagons and the driver sat on the right side of the wagon seat, so that when he whipped the horses the whip wouldn't get hung up on the load behind him. Because of this, the English continued to drive on the left side of the road and this practice has continued to this day.

There is an old saying that if everything is coming your way, you're either in the wrong lane or you're in England.

FACTOIDS

President Theodore Roosevelt once said that he had ridden in an automobile only twice in his life and that was enough. Yet he became the first president to own an automobile and the first to drive one.

A month before Clyde Barrow of Bonnie and Clyde fame was killed in a shootout with police, he wrote a letter to Henry Ford telling him what a "dandy" automobile he had made.

Starting with Calvin Coolidge in 1924, the Lincoln became the official automobile for the president of the U.S. The tradition was broken by Ronald Reagan, who preferred a Cadillac.

In 1906 a Stanley Steamer reached the unbelievable speed of 127 mph at Ormond Beach, Florida.

Instead of a steering wheel, early U.S. automobiles had a stick similar to a joystick in an airplane. It was mounted in the middle of the automobile in front of the front seat, forcing the driver to also sit in the middle. When steering wheels came into use, some were on the left and some were on the right. It was not until after 1913 that the left-hand steering wheel became standard.

Driving on the left side of the road is only a minor problem compared to some others when driving an automobile in England.

Because most English roads evolved from footpaths and cart trails, they are seldom very straight. The name of the road also changes at each village or town, and it is rare for the same name to last for more than a few miles. English roads only rarely have a shoulder and are usually flanked by trees, hedges, or rock walls. If there's a problem and you can't simply pull off the road, you'll hit something.

Most terrifying of all is the "roundabout" (in Boston they're called "rotaries" and are just as maddening). A roundabout is a circle with a number of roads leading into it at odd angles. When you enter a roundabout, you are supposed to go around the circle until you see the road you want, then exit. In practice, however, this is a test of courage. There are no stop signs or rules for yielding. Sometimes you can go round and round while trying unsuccessfully to maneuver your automobile through the swirling traffic to reach the edge of the roundabout and your exit.

If you've ever driven in England, you'll long for the streets and highways of the United States. If you've ever driven in Boston, there's a good chance you might have considered moving further west.

Why are the roofs of some school buses painted white? (It's not to hide pigeon droppings.)

School buses with white roofs are usually used in areas of the country where it gets very hot. Because the white roof tends to reflect the heat better than a yellow roof, the inside of the bus stays cooler.

In 1939 delegates from all of the states attended the first National Minimum Standards Conference to decide on a uniform color for school buses. By being of a uniform color, school buses nationwide would be instantly recognizable. When picking a color, one consideration was cost because bus manufacturers charged extra for any special color. The second consideration was safety. The delegates decided that yellow was easier to see in fog, rain, and bad weather than any other color. The selected color was called National School Bus Chrome Yellow.

Although there is no federal law that requires school buses to be painted yellow, most states follow the recommendation. In some states, however, some of the school buses are painted white.

The federal government regulates the manufacture of school buses but once the bus is on the road, the individual state assumes all responsibility.

FACTOIDS

Transporting students to school is the largest system of public transportation in the United States. Roughly 10 billion student trips a year are taken to school in school buses. Another 900 million students use public transit to get to school.

Approximately 40,000 yellow school buses are manufactured every year.

Although school bus accidents and fatalities do occur, the National Safety Council claims that school buses are the safest form of ground transportation in the United States. Riding a school bus is about 40 times safer than riding in the family car.

School buses travel an average of 100 billion pupil-passenger-miles per year.

Large school buses do not have seat belts. Each student is surrounded by energy-absorbing materials such as thick foam seats and seat frames that bend to absorb crash impacts. In addition, the entire bus is designed to absorb energy in a crash. Only New York and New Jersey have laws making school bus seat belts mandatory.

Why don't they make dirigibles anymore? (A little hot air goes a long way.)

Dirigibles were popular from their inception in 1900 until their demise in the late 1930s. These large airships carried 50 passengers in style and luxury equal to that found in any lavish hotel. Dirigibles ushered in a new era of travel and promised to be the safest air travel at the time, logging over a million passenger miles without a single loss of life. Then one disaster after another occurred, which along with the outbreak of World War II marked the death of the dirigibles. However, dirigibles have recently started to make a comeback. In September 1997, the Zeppelin NT made its maiden flight. It is the first in a line of dirigibles manufactured by a German firm, Zeppelin Luftschifftechnik GmbH.

A dirigible is different from a blimp. A blimp is a large balloon that is stretched at both ends to make it egg-shaped. The blimp, like a balloon, keeps its shape because of the gas inside. However, a blimp can buckle when strained by heavy loads or violent weather.

The U.S. Navy constructed four nonrigid (blimp) airships in 1958 that were each 403 feet long. Two years later one of them exploded and crashed, and the other three were retired in 1962.

Today's blimps are used primarily for advertising and often tour sports events, fairs, and other attractions.

A dirigible has a rigid metal framework attached to a sturdy metal keel. The entire structure is covered with fabric and is then inflated with gas, typically hydrogen (modern dirigibles use helium). The first dirigible of this type was designed by a retired German army officer, Ferdinand Graf von Zeppelin. His airships were so successful that even today many people call all dirigibles "zeppelins."

FACTOIDS

The first German dirigible was built in 1900. One of the most famous of the subsequent zeppelins was the *Graf Zeppelin*, which was built in

1928 and made transatlantic flights for the next nine years. During that time, it made 590 flights (including 144 trips across the ocean) and flew more than a million miles.

Blimps were used during World War I as antisubmarine patrol craft. British-built blimps were called "Class B airships" or, more simply, "B airships." The origin of the blimp's name is unclear but the consensus is that the name is a combination of "B airships" and "limp," which describes the blimp's construction.

The German dirigible company founded by Ferdinand Graf von Zeppelin in 1908 still exists today.

The U.S. dirigible *Shenandoah*, which means "Daughter of the Skies" in a Native American language, was the first dirigible to use nonflammable helium instead of the dangerous flammable hydrogen.

In 1929, just a year after it was built, the *Graf Zeppelin* made a flight lasting 21 days and covering 21,500 miles.

The largest dirigible ever made was the German *Hindenburg*, which was 804 feet long and could carry 235 tons. It was bigger than a Boeing 747 and almost as big as the *Titanic*. In 1937, while landing at Lakehurst, New Jersey, the *Hindenburg* burst into flames and crashed. The airship was completely destroyed and 36 people lost their lives. Experts still argue as to the cause of the crash. Some think it was a static electric spark, others believe it was sabotage.

Many historical dirigible events took place at the Lakehurst Naval Air Station in New Jersey. The *Shenandoah* made its maiden flight there, the *Graf Zeppelin's* historic endurance flight began and ended there, and the *Hindenburg's* fiery crash there led to the death of rigid airships around the world.

DID YOU KNOW?

The *Hindenburg* disaster is well documented and many people have heard about it or seen films of its fiery crash. Three other dirigible disasters also occurred in the United States. However, these dirigibles were built for the U.S. Navy.

In 1925, the Navy dirigible *Shenandoah* was ripped apart during a thunderstorm. Winds of 70 mph ripped the control cabin from the airship and eight crew members riding in it were killed, as were others in the tail section.

The bow section remained aloft and carried seven men over Ohio farmland. A farmer managed to grab one of the mooring ropes and tie it around two tree stumps. The crew members all jumped to safety.

When it was all over, 14 men had died, 29 had survived, and the dirigible's wreckage was strewn across 12 miles of farmland.

The Navy dirigible *Akron* was destroyed in 1933. Two years later, the Navy dirigible *Macon* was returning from a successful scouting mission when it ran into severe winds off of Point Sur, south of Monterey, California. A crosswind hit the ship, tore off its upper fins, and the ship started to fall. To lighten the dirigible, the crew threw overboard everything they could find. The *Macon* started rising until it reached an altitude of 5,000 feet. Then it started falling again and minutes later gracefully settled into the ocean. Two crew members died: one jumped out of the falling ship, the other tried to retrieve his belongings and drowned. Of the 83-man crew, 81 survived.

The Navy never built another dirigible.

How many people in the world visit zoos in a single year? (Lions and tigers and bears, oh, my!)

About half of the people in the United States, or around 100 million people, visit zoos in a single year. Roughly 10 percent of the world's population, or 600 million people, visit zoos worldwide.

The world zoo attendance figures may be misleading because it is difficult to determine the number of zoos in the world. There are approximately 1,000 zoos worldwide that belong to national, regional, or international zoo federations. However, if the word "zoo" is defined as any institution exhibiting wild or nondomestic animals to the public then there are probably over 10,000 zoos in the world.

FACTOIDS

Hippopotamus is a Greek word meaning "river horse."

Vampire bats need two tablespoonfuls of blood each day. They land near a sleeping victim and approach on foot to avoid waking the intended prey. The bat uses a heat sensor to determine where the blood is close to the skin and then makes a small incision (one fifth of an inch long) to extract the blood.

The oldest-known animal was an Aldabra tortoise who lived to be more than 152 years old.

Bamboo makes up 99 percent of a panda's diet. The panda spends about 12 hours a day eating from 23 to 36 pounds of bamboo.

The finicky koala eats only the leaves from the eucalyptus tree. On top of that, although there are more than 500 species of eucalyptus trees in Australia, the discriminating koala will eat the leaves of only about 20 species.

Bats can fly up to 60 miles per hour and as high as 10,000 feet.

The South American capybara is the world's largest rodent and can weigh up to 145 pounds.

A giraffe's tongue can be up to a foot and a half long.

For most of the year cactus is the only food available for peccaries. They break off portions of the cactus and use their feet to expose the inner part. They eat small pieces and can consume the spines without suffering any ill effects.

A baby gorilla learns to crawl and walk twice as fast as a human baby.

DID YOU KNOW?

One of the most famous zoos in the United States is the San Diego Zoo. It was founded in 1916 by a local physician who had a collection of 50 animals in his 100-acre zoo. One person, named Army, took care of all the animals. Army had only one arm but as the good doctor said, "It was all that he needed." With far too many animals for a one-armed zookeeper, the zoo now has over 1,000 people on its staff.

Renowned for being one of the first zoos in the country to keep animals in a naturalistic setting, the San Diego Zoo has maintained this tradition by opening new natural habitats in recent years. These include an aviary, Gorilla Tropics, Pygmy Chimpanzees, Hippo Beach, and the Polar Bear Plunge.

The Pygmy Chimpanzees is a 6,000-square-foot exhibit of the typical habitat that is home to the bonobo, or "pygmy," chimpanzee. These primates have slender shoulders and a distinctive "center part" in the hair on their heads. But the bonobos are not the only interesting part of the exhibit.

During a violent Southern California windstorm, all of the young palm trees in a nursery were blown over and tossed into a jumbled heap. They were left there for a few years before being set upright and planted in the Pygmy Chimpanzees exhibit. These "twisted" palms are now one of the fascinating features of the exhibit, growing in a variety of erratic shapes that create an appealing climbing framework for the playful bonobos.

More questions? Try these websites.

MAPQUEST
http://www.mapquest.com/

This is a fascinating and useful site for the traveler. I suggest you start by clicking on TripQuest. You can enter your home address and the address of where you want to go. When you select Calculate Directions, you'll see a map marked with a driving route along with written driving directions. You can also select Door-to-Door Options to see the shortest or the fastest route, or things you'd like to avoid, such as frontage roads. If you're making a longer trip, select City to City.

This site also has trip and moving guides.

FIND LATITUDE AND LONGITUDE

http://www.census.gov/cgi-bin/gazetteer

Simply enter the name of a city or a zip code to find its latitude and longitude, population, and zip codes. This site also provides links to census tables for that city.

FOREIGN LANGUAGES FOR TRAVELERS

http://www.travlang.com/languages/index.html

This is a wonderful site if you're planning a trip to a foreign country. Select the language you speak and then choose the language of the country you're going to visit. At this point you have many options.

For instance, you can click on Basic Words to see both the English and foreign language equivalents. You can also listen to them if you have a Real Audio player (if not, you can download the player free of charge).

You can also enter a word or phrase in English and see the translation.

There are also links to dictionaries, such as an English-to-Spanish dictionary, as well as other information pages.

United
States

**What is the average height of a person in the
United States? (Are people in other
countries looking down on us?)**

The average height for a U.S. male is 5 feet 9 inches, while the average height for a female is 5 feet 4 inches.

Although U.S. residents are taller than they were 100 years ago, we are no longer the tallest people in the world. On the average, people in Sweden are about half an inch taller, while the Dutch and Norwegians are a full inch taller.

Authorities do not know for sure why we have been surpassed

in height. Although we are the most advanced nation in the world when it comes to medical technology and knowledge of nutrition, some scientists think that much of our population either does not fully understand good nutrition or does not have adequate health care, or both.

Even with a knowledge of good nutrition, many people simply do not eat properly. Perhaps that is why over one third of the population over 20 years of age is overweight.

In spite of the fact that we are no longer the tallest people and tend to be overweight, the average life expectancy in this country has increased to 79 years, from 75. This is encouraging compared to the poor citizens of Botswana who have a life expectancy of only 40 years, but it's not nearly as good as the lucky citizens of Andorra who can plan to live until they are almost 87. In fact, you can expect to live until 80 or older in Australia, New Zealand, Belgium, Canada, England, France, Germany, Greece, Iceland, Israel, Italy, Holland, Norway, Sweden, and many of the island nations such as Palau, the Republic of Fiji, and the Federated States of Micronesia.

FACTOIDS

The tallest man in the world was Robert Pershing Wadlow of Alton, Illinois. He was just slightly over 8 feet 11 inches tall.

The average height of a Pygmy is 4 feet 6 inches.

In the ancient world, people from civilized countries such as Egypt and Greece were shorter than the invading barbarians. The population centers of modern civilization are home to the descendants of the barbarians.

The average female from the Scandinavian countries is taller than the average Asian male.

Chang, an 8-foot giant who lived in England, had a 5-foot-high table in his home. The doors of his house were enlarged until they nearly reached the ceiling and special high windows were installed. It is rumored that when he strolled through the village at night, he would light his cigar from the gas streetlights.

Many people believe that in past centuries people were smaller. This belief is usually based on a number of premises such as shorter armor, lower doorways, and low ceilings belowdecks on a ship.

However, if we look at historical figures we find that Charles II was over 6 feet tall as was Mary, Queen of Scots.

We are accustomed to seeing 8-foot ceilings in our homes. When we see an older house with 6-or 7-foot ceilings we assume that it's because people were shorter then. However, ceilings were not lower because people were smaller. Ceilings were lower in order to save heat and reduce drafts.

Because Charles II's suit of armor could only fit a man 5 feet tall, people assume that he was short. This isn't true. He was over 6 feet tall. The suit of armor was made for him when he was still an adolescent.

Perhaps maintaining that people centuries ago were shorter in stature gives us a sense of superiority. But like it or not, they were not much shorter than us.

Who was the youngest American to go up in space? (This lady went into orbit.)

The youngest astronaut from the United States was Sally Ride. She was 32 years and 23 days old when she took off on Space Shuttle *Challenger* (flight STS-7) in June 1983.

The oldest astronaut to fly in space was John Glenn, who was 77 when he flew on Space Shuttle *Discovery* (flight STS-95) on October 29, 1998. He was also the first U.S. astronaut to orbit the earth, which he did on February 20, 1962.

The first woman to become a shuttle commander is Eileen Collins, who commanded Space Shuttle *Columbia* (flight STS-93) in 1995. She was also the first woman pilot on a space shuttle mission.

The first black American astronaut was Guion S. Bluford, who flew on Space Shuttle *Challenger* (flight STS-8) as a mission specialist in 1983.

The first woman in space was the Russian astronaut Valentina Tereshkova, who piloted the spaceship *Vostok 6* in 1963 (*vostok* means "east" in Russian). The first woman to perform a space walk was also a Russian, Svetlana Savitskaya, who performed the maneuver in 1984 while on *Soyuz T12* (*soyuz* means "union" in Russian).

One of NASA's goals is to help industry create new rocket systems that would eventually make space flight so simple and routine that many ordinary citizens could go into orbit in the future.

FACTOIDS

To remain in orbit, a space shuttle must maintain a speed of approximately 17,500 miles an hour.

Twenty-seven humans have flown to the moon and twelve have actually walked on its surface.

Rockets were used as long as 1,000 years ago by the Chinese as military weapons. In the fourteenth century, rockets were used as fireworks in Italy. In fact the word "rocket" comes from the Italian word rocchetta.

The first man-made object to leave our solar system was *Pioneer 10*, launched in 1972. *Pioneer 10* has passed the orbits of all nine known planets and left our solar system with all of its systems still functioning properly. No one knows where it is today.

A centrifuge is used to help astronauts become accustomed to the G-forces they will encounter during liftoff of a space vehicle. Russian astronauts refer to their centrifuge as "the devil's merry-go-round."

Although it cannot be seen by the naked eye, the American flag is still on the moon. In fact it's the only official American flag that is not taken down at night.

Each space shuttle mission costs around $450 million.

While watching space shuttle flights on television, many viewers have seen astronauts work, eat, and exercise. But there is one aspect of space living that few people know about but often wonder about. How do astronauts keep clean and how do they go to the bathroom?

Astronauts brush their teeth in the same way they do on earth. Because there are no showers on a space shuttle, they must get by with sponge baths until they return home.

There is a toilet on the space shuttle. It's designed to look as much as possible as those on earth. However, it uses flowing air instead of flowing water to move waste. Once through the system, solid waste is compressed and stored for disposal after landing. Waste water is vented into space. The space station *Mir* (*mir* means "peace" in Russian) recycles waste water.

All of the air is filtered to remove bacteria and odors and is then recycled into the space shuttle cabin.

If you truly want to be an astronaut, you may have to forget many of the comforts you now routinely enjoy at home.

What is the book that the Statue of Liberty is holding? (A symbol of two countries that each shed blood for freedom.)

The Statue of Liberty holds a torch in her right hand and in her left hand she carries a tablet with JULY 4, 1776 inscribed on it in Roman numerals. The statue is a symbol of American freedom and a beacon lighting the way for immigrants.

The Statue of Liberty was a gift from the people of France to commemorate the U.S. centennial. The torch represents "Liberty Enlightening the World," which was the original name of the statue. The crown of 7 spokes represents the 7 seas and the 7 continents. The 25 windows in the crown represent the 25 gemstones found on earth.

Broken chains symbolizing the overthrow of tyranny lie at the statue's feet.

The statue consists of an iron framework covered with thin sheets of hammered copper. It is 151 feet high and weighs 225 tons. After it was completed, it was dismantled and sent to the United States in 214 packing cases.

When the sculptor, Frederick Auguste Bartholdi, came to this country to find a suitable site for the statue, he spotted Bedloe's Island as he sailed into New York harbor and knew that was the spot for his statue. The 12-acre island was renamed Liberty Island and the statue replaced Fort Wood, an old fortification.

The cornerstone was laid on August 4, 1884. Two years later the Statue of Liberty was unveiled by President Grover Cleveland, who said, "We will not forget that liberty here made her home; nor shall her chosen altar be neglected."

Nearby Ellis Island was an immigration station through which passed more than 12 million immigrants from 1892 to 1954. In 1903, the now famous words from a poem by Emma Lazarus were inscribed on the base of the statue:

Give me your tired, your poor,
Your huddled masses yearning to breathe free,
The wretched refuse of your teeming shore,
Send these, the homeless, tempest-tossed, to me:
I lift my lamp beside the golden door.

FACTOIDS

The statue's metal framework was built by Gustave Eiffel, who later built the Eiffel Tower in Paris.

The statue was formally presented to the United States by Ferdinand de Lesseps, who built the Suez Canal.

All of the statue's features are large: each fingernail is the size of a sheet of typing paper, the nose is $4\frac{1}{2}$ feet long, index fingers are 2 feet taller than a man, and each arm is 42 feet long.

The sculptor's mother was the model for Liberty's face.

Eighty metric tons of copper cover the statue, an amount exceeded by only a few projects before or after. No historical records exist to indicate where the copper was mined but Bell Laboratories finally solved the mystery. The copper came from Norway.

Oxidation of the copper sheeting has turned the copper green. When first erected, the Statue of Liberty showed a rich copper color. It has never been painted green.

Although scheduled to be dedicated at the U.S. centennial in 1876, the dedication did not take place until 10 years later because it took longer to erect the statue than planned.

DID YOU KNOW?

Between 1892 and 1954, immigrants to the United States were usually fleeing religious persecution, political oppression, or economic hardship. The first symbol they saw upon entering the United States through the New York harbor was the Statue of Liberty. But the first place they landed was Ellis Island, the site of an immigration station. There were other immigration ports in the United States but Ellis Island is the most famous.

Native Americans called it Kioshk, or Gull Island. Dutch settlers later named it Little Oyster Island because of the oysters found in its sand. Eventually it was owned by Samuel Ellis and has been called Ellis Island ever since.

During the peak immigration years, Ellis Island became a small city with an average staff of 500 to 850 people, including immigration officers, engineers, doctors, nurses, cooks, and guards. It had dormitories, kitchens, a bathhouse, and even a small hospital.

Although many immigrants were allowed to stay in the United States, many others failed some of the numerous medical, legal, and mental tests. They were rejected and sent home in tears. For them, the dream of freedom was shattered.

Today Ellis Island is a museum. Its two theaters often show a documentary film about the immigrants. The film's simple title sums up both the hopes and broken dreams of the immigrants: *Island of Hope, Island of Tears.*

What caused the fire that destroyed San Francisco? (It wasn't Mrs. O'Leary's cow from Chicago.)

A major earthquake was the direct cause of the 1906 San Francisco fire. The magnitude is estimated to have been 7.7 to 7.9 on the Richter scale. During and after the earthquake many fires started all over the city, ignited by flames and pilot lights in furnaces and stoves, broken gas lines, shorting electrical lines, and ruptured storage tanks holding flammable materials.

Many buildings collapsed because of the earthquake and became much more vulnerable to fire. They were nothing more than a pile of kindling, the gaps in the roofs and walls acting as chimneys to help fuel the fire.

Although the San Francisco firemen were thought to be the best in the nation, they were virtually helpless because the earthquake had also broken most of the water mains. Leaking gas lines ignited fires all over the city until the gas works blew up, finally stopping the flow of gas.

The fire destroyed almost 500 city blocks over 5 square miles. Over 28,000 buildings were destroyed or damaged so badly that they had to be demolished.

The fire burned for four days and nights. When it was over, 250,000 people were homeless, 500 were dead (some authorities claim the death toll was in the thousands), and hundreds were injured.

FACTOIDS

The San Francisco earthquake broke more than 270 miles of ground, with up to 21 feet of displacement in some areas.

The shaking lasted only 45 to 60 seconds but was enough to do catastrophic damage. To those in the earthquake, it seemed to last for an eternity.

Residents as far north as southern Oregon, as far south as Los Angeles, and as far inland as central Nevada felt the earthquake.

When the ground was displaced, it moved at a speed of about 3 mph, but the rupture itself propagated at a speed of 5,800 mph.

A telegraph station in San Diego, California, sent newspaper reports of the disaster to the U.S.S. *Chicago* anchored in San Diego harbor. The ship steamed at full speed to San Francisco to aid the stricken city. This was the first time that telegraphy was used in a major natural disaster.

One fire chief was killed when a chimney from a hotel crashed through the fire station where he was living.

The earthquake shock covered an area of about 375,000 square miles. About half of this area was in the Pacific Ocean. Damage occurred along a 400-mile north/south corridor, out to 30 miles on either side of the fault zone.

There were 135 aftershocks on the same day as the great quake. Many damaged buildings that had survived the main earthquake collapsed when hit by an aftershock.

DID YOU KNOW?

In the late 1800s and early 1900s, cities were overpopulated and buildings were constructed quickly and cheaply out of wood, which was a definite fire hazard. As a result, city after city had its downtown area destroyed by fire.

The three major cities destroyed by fire were Chicago in 1871, San Francisco in 1906, and more recently, Texas City, Texas, in 1947.

A fable states that Mrs. O'Leary's cow knocked over a lantern in a barn and started the Chicago fire. However, it was neither a cow nor an earthquake that caused the destruction of Texas City, a busy port on the Gulf of Mexico. On April 15 a fire broke out in the hold of a French freighter loaded with over 2,300 tons of ammonium nitrate (the same explosive used in the recent bombing of the Oklahoma City federal building). At 9:15 in the morning the ship exploded without warning.

The blast triggered other explosions at Texas City chemical plants near the docks and a surge of water added to the damage. Fires burned out of control for days until the last was extinguished a week later. When it was over, 600 people were known dead and many others were missing. Every person in the town of 16,000 people was affected in some way by the explosion and fires. The city was almost completely destroyed.

One Texas paper summed it up very well: "Texas City just blew up."

Which place in the United States has the longest name? (Don't get hooked on this one.)

The longest place name in the United States is that of a lake near Webster, Massachusetts. The 2-square-mile lake is called Lake Chargoggagoggmanchauggauggagoggchaubunagungamaugg, which is a Nipmuck Indian word freely translated as "You fish on your side, I fish on my side, nobody fishes in the middle." The name has 49 letters, of which 17 are the letter *g*.

The lake is sometimes spelled as Chargoggugoggmonchaug-gagoggchaubunagungamaug. However, to make it easier for everyone, the U.S. Board on Geographic Names has shortened it to Lake Chaubunagungamaug.

The U.S. Board on Geographic Names also lists the longest place name in the world in its annals which is a hill in New Zealand. It might be difficult to say the 83-letter name in a single breath. The hill is simply called Taumatawhakatangihangakoauotamateaturipu-kakapikimaungahoronukupokaiwhenuakitanataha. It is a Maori word meaning "The brow of the hill where Tamatea who sailed all round the land played his nose flute to his lady love." Unfortunately, it doesn't have a nickname.

FACTOIDS

The Nipmuc Indians seem to be associated with water. Their name comes from the Algonquin word *nipnet*, which means "a small pond place" or "freshwater people." The name for the tribe of peoples is also spelled as Nipnet, Neepmuck, Neepnet, Neetmock, Neipnett, and Nipmug.

No Nipmuc tribe ever existed. The name simply classifies a geographical region where small bands and villages were located. These groups of peoples lived along rivers or lakes, and their ancestors occupied the area for at least 12,000 years.

The Nipmuc bands are not recognized as a tribe by the federal government although they are seeking recognition. One criterion they must follow is that of a political organization. Because the Nipmuc were a peaceful people, they never had problems that needed to be solved by a complex political body.

The Nipmuc occupied a territory of 2,500 square miles which is now part of the states of Massachusetts, Rhode Island, and Connecticut.

Before the arrival of the Europeans in the 1600s there were 3,000 Nipmuc Indians. Following King Philip's War in 1680, less than 1,000 survived and were confined to villages along with remnants of other tribes. Today there are about 1,400 descendants.

Of the estimated 100,000 Native Americans living in New England in 1614, by 1680 only 4,000 were left. Because of contact with Europeans, 96 percent of the New England Native Americans had died within the span of a normal lifetime.

DID YOU KNOW?

The term "powwow" is often associated with Native Americans. It brings to mind feasting, socializing, and trading. However, that is not how it began.

In the northeastern part of the United States, a powwow was a shaman who could cure the ill or seek advice from the spirit world. The Natick word *pauwau* is often translated as "wizard" or "magician" but that is not a good translation. A better translation is "wise speaker," such as the Narragansett word *taupowaw*.

The powwow was held in high regard by the tribe. He would cure the sick, promote success in battle, interpret dreams and visions, and give advice to the tribe and to individuals. During ceremonies, the powwows would pray, sing, dance, and beat drums. They sang to give praise to the creator and drummed to represent the heartbeat of the people.

Because tribal members participated in the powwow's ceremonies, over time the ceremony was followed by social events. Eventually powwow became the name for social celebrations.

Today all over the United States various Native American tribes hold powwows and the public is usually invited. If you should attend one, look beyond the social aspects and see if you can discover the deep spiritual meaning behind the ceremonies. It is well worth the effort.

How many political parties can be represented in a presidential election? (You could join the party of the Kingdom of Talossa.)

There is no limit to the number of political parties that can have a nominee in a presidential election. Usually, however, there are only three or four parties with nominees on ballots in all 50 states because each state has certain ballot access rules and deadlines. Therefore, some of the smaller parties are often on only one or two state ballots because they lack organization, money, or both.

The two major parties, Democratic and Republican, as well as the Libertarian Party, are always on the presidential ballot in all 50 states. Sometimes a new party, such as the Reform Party formed by Ross Perot in 1992, will also appear on all state ballots.

Here are just some of the many political parties in the United States: Democratic Party, Republican Party, American Party, American

Independent Party, American Reform Party, Conservative Party, Communist Party USA, Creator's Rights Party, Democratic Socialists of America, Grassroots Party, The Greens/Green Party USA, Labor Party, Libertarian Party, National Patriot Party, Natural Law Party, New Party, Peace and Freedom Party, Prohibition Party, Reform Party, Socialist Party USA, Socialist Equality Party, Socialist Labor Party, Socialist Worker's Party, U.S. Pacifist Party, U.S. Taxpayer's Party, Worker's World Party.

Some of these parties were founded for a specific reason that may not be relevant today. For example, the Prohibition Party was founded in 1869 to stop the sale of liquor, and the Peace and Freedom Party was founded in the 1960s to oppose the Vietnam War.

With over 30 recognized political parties in the United States, it's obvious that our country still believes very strongly in the democratic process.

FACTOIDS

In 1828 Andrew Jackson was running for president when an opponent called him a "jackass." Jackson turned the insult around by using a donkey on a campaign poster to stress his stubborn refusal to bow to big business interests. In 1840, New York cartoonist Thomas Nast began using the donkey in political cartoons and the donkey has been the symbol of the Democratic Party ever since.

The Democratic Party became the "party of the common man" in 1798. At that time it was called the Democratic Republicans.

In 1912 the Democrats feared that Republican president Theodore Roosevelt might win a third term and become a dictator like Caesar. Thomas Nast (who had created the donkey symbol for the Democratic Party) drew a cartoon showing a donkey scaring away all the other animals. One of them was an elephant, which Nast labeled "the Republican Vote." After Roosevelt lost the election, Nast drew a cartoon showing an elephant walking into a Democratic trap. Other cartoonists started using an elephant as a symbol for the Republican Party and it has been the symbol of that party ever since.

In 1876 the Republican Rutherford B. Hayes was elected president by a single electoral vote.

DID YOU KNOW?

One of the most unusual political parties is the Progressive Conservative Party of the Kingdom of Talossa, a constitutional monarchy.

The day after Christmas in 1979, a 13-year-old high school student in Milwaukee, Wisconsin, declared his bedroom to be an independent sovereign state, the Kingdom of Talossa. The kingdom has grown considerably since then and now consists of a 13-square-kilometer portion of East Milwaukee. So far, the U.S. government has not disputed Talossa's claim to this land. In 1985 the country's founder was elected king, abdicated in 1987, and became king again in 1988. The head of the Progressive Conservative Party is Michael Pope and Chris Gruber is prime minister.

Talossans claim to be descended from North African Berbers and have their own language as well as "Talossan English." The Talossan government has a foreign affairs policy and in 1980 defeated the Glib Room Empire, which surrendered and signed a peace treaty.

The Kingdom of Talossa has claimed a chunk of Antarctica (which they call Pengopats) as a colony because no other nation has ever claimed it. Part of their colony off the coast of Brittany was occupied by French troops and placed under barbed wire. Because of deficiencies in French barbed-wire technology, the Talossan prime minister at the time liberated part of the French-occupied zone and had a picnic.

If you're really interested in the Kingdom of Talossa, it offers dual citizenship. You can become a Talossan and still retain your U.S. citizenship.

It might be more fun than belonging to some of the other political parties in this country.

More questions?
Try these websites.

GOVERNMENT INFORMATION
http://lib-www.ucr.edu/govinfo.html

This site has a wealth of information about the U.S. government as well as other information. You can look through the table of contents, a list of subjects, or a list of keywords. You can also search on keywords.

AREA CODES
http://decoder.AmeriCom.com/

If you want to know the area code for a city or if you have an area code and want to find out where it is, this is the site for you.

ZIP CODES
http://www.usps.gov/ncsc/

If you know the address of a business or residence, this site will give you the proper zip code. You can also list any city in the United States and find the zip codes for that city.

SWITCHBOARD
http://www.switchboard.com/

Use this site to find businesses, people, addresses, websites, and e-mail addresses. For example, if you know a person's name but don't know where they live, you can probably find their address here.

FBI
http://www.fbi.gov/

Whether you want to know who are the 10 most-wanted criminals in the country or you want to apply for a job as an FBI agent, you'll find the information here, plus a lot more.

CIA
http://www.odci.gov/cia/

This is the official page of the Central Intelligence Agency. It even has a site for kids, facts about the little-known CIA Canine Corps, and a page that lets you try on different disguises.

KINGDOM OF TALOSSA

http://www.execpc.com/talossa/index.html

If you read the answer to the question "How many political parties can be represented in a presidential election?" you have some idea about the Kingdom of Talossa. This is the official website of the kingdom. If you want to become a citizen, just click on Acquiring Talossan Citizenship. Remember, Talossa recognizes dual citizenship so you don't have to give up your present citizenship.

ANECDOTE: A 14-YEAR SEARCH FOR A COWBOY SONG

Sometimes people have come to me as a last resort. One such desperate message was from a Jackie Whitehouse, who had been looking for a piece of music off and on for 14 years. Jackie said she had tried most conventional methods of research but hadn't come up with a clue.

Jackie explained that her 63-year-old father remembered a song that he and his family had listened to over half a century ago. Fortunately for me, Jackie did remember a few of the lyrics.

It didn't take long to find the song and the composer. It was *Ain't We Crazy*, written by Tex Fletcher, a singing cowboy who had died some years ago.

I found a gentleman in Japan who had a bluegrass songbook with all of the words to the song. I also managed to find Tex Fletcher's son, George Fletcher, who now publishes a rhythm and news magazine.

The next day, I sent the answer to the question along with the e-mail address of Tex Fletcher's son.

Jackie responded quickly, saying, "It's amazing. I've been searching for this song for 14 years and when I wrote to you, I received the answer in 24 hours!"

A year later I again wrote to Jackie. It turned out that although she had the title, lyrics, and composer, she had been unable to find the actual music. She and George Fletcher had joined forces to continue the search for the music.

I'm seriously considering joining them in the search. It could be fascinating. Even if we don't find the music, I'll certainly enjoy working with my new friends.

Weather

**What is the difference between a
hurricane and a typhoon? (It depends
which way the wind blows.)**

Actually, they're the same thing except for the name. They're both tropical storms or "cyclones." By convention, the cyclone is a hurricane if it occurs in the Atlantic Ocean or a typhoon if it occurs in the western Pacific or Indian oceans.

There is one slight difference, however, depending on which way the wind blows. Tropical storms or cyclones rotate counterclockwise in the Northern Hemisphere and clockwise in the Southern Hemisphere. This is because of the Coriolis effect.

Early in this century, an Australian weather forecaster, Clement Wragge, saw an opportunity to insult politicians he didn't like. He simply started naming devastating tropical storms after the politicians.

Naming tropical storms avoids confusion during news bulletins and warnings, especially if there is more than one storm at the same time.

During World War II, military personnel started assigning names to tropical storms to avoid confusion. They used the radio code names that were standard at the time such as Able, Baker, Charlie, and so on. Later, U.S. Air Force and Navy meteorologists monitoring and forecasting tropical storms over the Pacific named them after their wives and girlfriends.

In 1953, female names were used for tropical storms. Men were left out once again. Contrary to popular belief at the time, female names were *not* used because women were supposedly unpredictable! In 1979, male names were added to the annual lists and alternating male and female names have been used ever since. The use of French and Spanish names also dates from 1979.

FACTOIDS

The first three male names used (Bob, David, and Frederick) were retired because these storms did such great damage.

The letters *Q* and *U* are not used for naming hurricanes.

The most costly hurricanes in U.S. history were also caused by men:

- Mitch, 1998: Central America ($5 billion)

- Andrew, 1992: Florida and Louisiana ($46.5 million)

- Hugo, 1989: Georgia to Virginia ($8 million)

The hurricane that caused the greatest loss of life was hurricane Mitch in 1998. Over 11,000 people died, an estimated 11,000 to 18,000 were missing, and over 3 million people were either made homeless or severely affected by the storm.

The fastest recorded wind was in 1969 during hurricane Camille along the Mississippi-Alabama coast. Winds averaged 200 mph with gusts of 210 mph.

What is the difference between partly cloudy and partly sunny? (It probably depends on your disposition.)

There are official government rules for weather forecasting. If 40 to 70 percent of the sky is expected to be cloudy, the forecast is "partly cloudy." If the clouds are less then 40 percent, the forecast is "partly sunny." When there are no clouds in the forecast, it is called "clear," while if more than 70 percent cloud cover is expected, it is called "cloudy." Some forecasters do not use the word "partly" at all but prefer to use "mostly" because they feel it is a more accurate description.

Unfortunately, not all weather forecasters stick to the rules. Meteorologists tend to be somewhat opinionated and they all believe they can forecast the weather better than their fellow meteorologists. It has been said that if you give five weather forecasters the same data, you will get five completely different forecasts.

In actuality, there is a slim difference between "partly sunny" and "partly cloudy" so the forecast quite often depends on the disposition of the forecaster. For example, suppose the weather forecaster is in a good mood, runs into very little traffic on the way to work, and finds a good parking spot. Even though the clouds might cover half of the sky, the forecaster would issue a "partly sunny" forecast.

On the other hand, if the weather forecaster is running late for work, is in a bad mood, gets stuck in traffic, and can't find a place to park, it's more than likely that the forecast will be "partly cloudy" even if identical conditions produced a "partly sunny" forecast the day before.

FACTOIDS

If you count the chirps of a tree cricket for 15 seconds and then add 37, it will be almost exactly the true temperature in degrees Fahrenheit.

The highest wind speed recorded in the United States was 231 mph on Mount Washington in New Hampshire. The highest wind speed in a tornado was 286 mph in Wichita Falls, Texas.

Have you ever believed you could smell rain coming? It might very well be true. Many scientists believe that the moisture in impending rain makes your nose more sensitive.

In 1921 a snowstorm dropped over six feet of snow on Silver Lake, Colorado – the largest recorded snowfall in a single day. However, in 1959 a single storm that lasted 7 days dumped almost 16 feet of snow on Mount Shasta, California.

Poplar trees and both red and silver maple trees are good rain predictors. During a low pressure system before an impending rainstorm, the leaves flip up.

An average lightning bolt is only half an inch wide, has a temperature almost five times hotter than the sun, and would take only one second to travel around the equator.

DID YOU KNOW?

Of all weather systems, tornadoes can be the most fascinating, the most destructive, and the most difficult to predict. One of the most amazing tornadoes occurred in 1925 and became known as the "Tri-State Tornado" because it cut a swath through Missouri, Illinois, and Indiana.

The tornado was classified as F-5, the most violent tornado type, with winds over 261 mph. The funnel was three quarters of a mile to a mile wide moving at a speed of about 60 mph. During its 3½-hour life, the Tri-State Tornado traveled well over 200 miles.

Many witnesses said they saw no funnel but rather a black boiling cloud. Some saw an inky black sky, while others saw a strange orange color. When people finally realized it was a tornado, it was too late to find shelter.

When it was over, the entire town of Murphysboro, Illinois, was destroyed, 698 people were dead, and over 2,000 people were injured.

The Tri-State Tornado entered the record books for causing the greatest area of destruction, lasting the longest period of time, and having the longest track on the ground.

Unfortunately, it also holds the record for causing the most deaths.

What part of the world gets the most rain? (Ark building might be a good skill to have.)

The greatest average annual rainfall occurs on Mount Waialeale on the island of Kauai in the Hawaiian Islands, which receives an average of 472 inches of rain per year. Another way to look at it is that Mount Waialeale is drenched with over 40 feet of rain every year, or the equivalent in height of a 4-story building.

However, when it comes to the most rain in a single year, the record is held by Cherrapunki, India. In 1861 Cherrapunki's rainfall was 905 inches, or slightly more than 75 feet.

But neither Mount Waialeale nor Cherrapunki hold the record for the most rain in a single day. In one 24-hour period in 1911, 46 inches of rain (just under 4 feet) fell on Bauio in the Philippines.

Rain can be beneficial – in fact we couldn't live without it. It brings us water to drink, creates lakes, river, and streams, and provides needed water for trees and plants. Unfortunately, rain is not always benevolent. At times rainstorms can cause disastrous floods.

During a torrential rainstorm or continual days of steady rain, the earth cannot absorb all of the moisture and the water builds up on top of the ground. This water eventually runs off into streams and rivers. The excess water pouring into the rivers causes them to overflow their banks, flooding the surrounding area.

The most disastrous floods occur when the surrounding land is below the level of the riverbanks or when the land is flat, such as in the midwestern portion of the United States. Floodwaters in areas such as these can sweep cars and other large objects along for long distances and can rip up any object not firmly anchored to the ground. As floodwaters flow into freshwater reservoirs, the freshwater becomes polluted and unsafe for drinking. Because of this, disease can spread quickly throughout the area.

We all know the benefits of rain and its importance in growing food crops. On the other hand, in the last 15 years flood damage has cost the United States an average of more than $3 billion a year.

FACTOIDS

Arica, Chile, holds the record for the least amount of annual rainfall. It receives an average of only two one-hundredths (0.02) of an inch per year.

Devil's Lake near Minnewaukan, North Dakota, is often called "the lake that comes and goes." In periods of drought, it almost disappears, but in rainy periods it has been known to nearly double its size in two years. In 1993, after praying for rain because of a drought, residents of Minnewaukan had their prayers answered, and soon waters of the lake were lapping at the town's doorstep.

You could call 1991 the "year of the floods." The worst floods of the century in China left 10 million people homeless along the Yangtze River, the worst floods in over half a century devastated Burma, the worst floods in a century hit Iran, floods from the monsoons in southeast Asia were the worst on record, 100,000 people were left homeless after the worst June flood in history inundated Bombay, and a freak storm dumped snow and rain onto Chile's deserts, turning them into floodplains. Devastating floods also occurred in nine states along the Mississippi River.

In 1926 the Saint Francis Dam was built in Saugus, California, to hold water from Northern California before it was sent to the drier part of the state in the south. In 1928 the dam broke and waters swept through 65 miles of valley before flowing into the Pacific Ocean. The raging water destroyed everything in its path, including buildings, bridges, railroads, orchards, farms, and livestock. At its peak, the wall of water was 78 feet high. When the flood was over, 500 people were dead and part of Ventura County was lying under 70 feet of mud and debris.

DID YOU KNOW?

The South Fork Fishing and Hunting Club sounds like a quiet and exclusive vacation retreat for tired businessmen. It was that, but in 1889 it was also responsible for one of the most famous floods in U.S. history.

The club had purchased an abandoned reservoir about 14 miles from Johnstown, Pennsylvania. Its members then had the old South Fork Dam repaired and the lake level raised. They built a clubhouse and cottages along the lake's edge as a secret retreat for the rich and famous, including Andrew Carnegie and Andrew Mellon.

The city of Johnstown, Pennsylvania, and its 30,000 residents were 14 miles away from the dam and 450 feet below it.

Repairs to the dam by the Fishing and Hunting Club had been shoddy at best and on June 1, 1889, disaster struck. Residents heard a low rumble in the distance that increased to a thunderous roar as 20 million tons of water came crashing down the narrow valley toward the town. The wall of water was 60 feet high and half a mile wide, moving at 40 mph, tossing around huge chunks of debris, and destroying everything in its path.

Unsuspecting citizens were swept away to be drowned or crushed by the boiling debris. Some residents used the debris as rafts, but when the debris hit the town's Stone Bridge it started piling up until it was 40 feet high and covered 30 acres. Then it caught fire. Those who survived the flood perished in the fire.

The flood lasted only 10 minutes, but it left over 2,200 people dead.

Can it really rain frogs? (Ever hear of it raining soda cans?)

It's rare but it does happen. However, it doesn't rain just a few frogs but hundreds if not thousands of them. It has also rained fish and even soda cans in one rare event.

Scientists believe that certain types of winds, such as tornadoes or violent thunderstorms, suck up the entire contents of a small pond, carry the moisture and its frog contents some distance away, and then let them fall to earth again. Because the tiny frogs (or soda cans) all weigh about the same, they tend to drop together.

Reports of raining frogs date back to biblical times. A more recent example is described in an 1883 edition of the Decatur *Daily Republican* about an event that occurred in Cairo, Illinois: "Early yesterday morning the decks of the steamers *Success* and *Elliot* were literally covered with small green frogs about an inch in length, which came down with a drenching rain which prevailed during the night. Spars, lines, trees and fences were literally alive with the slimy things."

An 1873 issue of *Scientific American* stated, "A shower of frogs, which darkened the air and covered the ground for a long distance, is the reported result of a recent rainstorm in Kansas City, Missouri."

In 1995 a tornado swept through a midwestern bottling plant and dropped soda cans 150 miles north of the plant. One witness said, "Soda cans were falling from the sky just like raining frogs."

FACTOIDS

The golden dart frog is so poisonous that the skin of a single frog can kill up to 1,000 people.

The largest frog in the world is the Goliath from West Africa.

They can grow to be one foot long. The smallest frogs in the world are less than a half inch long when fully grown.

The bones of frogs grow a new ring every year. Scientists can count the rings to tell the frog's age in the same way they count tree rings to determine a tree's age.

A frog and a toad are not the same. A frog is moist, slimy, and jumps, while a toad is dry, warty, and walks on all fours.

Many frogs can jump up to 20 times their body length. That's the same as if a 6-foot man could jump 120 feet in a single leap.

Frogs never drink. They absorb water from their surroundings by osmosis.

When describing a group of creatures, we say "a school of fish," "a flock of seagulls," or "a herd of cattle." A group of frogs is called "an army of frogs," while a group of toads is called "a knot of toads."

Frogs live between 4 and 15 years, but one European common toad lived to be 40 years old.

DID YOU KNOW?

There are over 2,500 species of frogs and toads in the world and some scientists spend their lives studying nothing but frogs.

Not only scientists are interested in frogs. The croaking creatures made their way into literature thousands of years ago. The Greek playwright Aristophanes wrote a play entitled *The Frogs*. Native Americans have a myth called "Why Frogs Croak" and the Brothers Grimm wrote *The Frog Prince* and *The Toad Princess*. More recent is *The Wind in the Willows* by Kenneth Grahame with its famous Toad Hall, which was the inspiration for Mr. Toad's Wild Ride at Disneyland. Mark Twain's century-old story "The Celebrated Jumping Frog of Calaveras County" is not only still popular today but remembered in the annual frog jumping competition in the town of Calaveras, California.

Perhaps a fable from Aesop is the best way to end this.

A donkey carrying a heavy load of wood was fording a pond when he lost his footing and fell into the water. Because of the heavy load, he could not get up and began groaning and sighing. A nearby frog said, "Why are you making such a fuss about a mere fall into the water? What would you do if you had to live here forever as we do?"

The moral, according to Aesop: "Men often bear small grievances with much less courage than they do large misfortunes."

More questions?
Try these websites.

EXCELLENT WEATHER SITE
http://cirrus.sprl.umich.edu/wxnet/

Here you can look up current national temperatures, satellite and Doppler radar photos of your state, a 24-hour forecast for your state, storm warnings, hurricane warnings, rainfall totals, earthquake activity, and other information. It also includes links to other weather sites. Be sure to scroll because it's a long page.

WEATHER ANYWHERE IN THE COUNTRY
http://www.wunderground.com/

Just click on any state on the map to see a list of major cities within the state and the current weather.

SEE A PICTURE OF THE LOCAL WEATHER
http://cirrus.sprl.umich.edu/wxnet/wxcam.html

Simply click on a city and state to see a photograph of the current weather.

WEATHER MAPS
http://nimbo.wrh.noaa.gov/sandiego/maps.html

This page has a list of weather maps you can select.

WEATHER MAP SYMBOLS
http://www.water.ca.gov/gifs/weather.map.symbols.gif

This page explains what all those strange symbols on a weather map mean.

World

What is the oldest living thing in the world? (Animal, vegetable, or ...)

U p until the late 1970s, the oldest living thing was thought to be 5,000-year-old bristlecone pines high in the White Mountains of California and the Snake Range of eastern Nevada. However, it's now accepted that a flowering shrub called a creosote bush in California's Mojave Desert is nearly 12,000 years old.

One particular bush, named "King Clone," started from a seed. During its lifetime the last major glacial period in North America ended, the great Egyptian and Mayan pyramids were built, and the first human walked on the moon. This lonely shrub lived through it all and is still flourishing today.

An interesting attribute of the creosote plant is that it fragments as it ages and produces daughter plants that are clones of the parent. The clones form rings that expand in diameter at the rate of about one meter per 500 years.

The shrub has an interesting circular growth pattern. Each giant ring of shrubs comes from one ancestral shrub that once grew in the center of the ring. Over thousands of years, the center wood dies and rots away, leaving a barren area surrounded by a ring of shrubs. One of the oldest shrub rings is 50 feet in diameter.

FACTOIDS

When the leaves of the creosote bush fall to the ground, they poison the soil so no other plants can grow around the plant.

The creosote bush can survive up to two years without rain. Its leaves are coated with a varnish-like resin that reduces water loss by evaporation.

Leaves of the creosote bush are especially pungent after a rain, and the smell of creosote fills the desert. The bush is often called *hediondilla*, Spanish for "little stinker."

The versatile creosote bush served native peoples well:

The leaves were used as antiseptics and emetics.

The vapors of boiling leaves, when inhaled, cured respiratory problems.

Lard was mixed with the leaves to form a lotion to treat saddle sores.

Crushed leaves were used as a deodorant and disinfectant.

The resin on its branches was used as a glue to mend broken pottery and cement arrowheads.

DID YOU KNOW?

Other living wonders of our world:

Oldest living fossil: The maidenhair tree (*Ginkgo biloba*) still lives on the earth today but abundant fossil imprints of this tree's leaves have been found in sedimentary rocks 135 to 210 million years old, dating from when dinosaurs roamed the earth.

Largest living thing: A giant sequoia tree named "General Sherman" is 272 feet tall with a gigantic trunk 35 feet in diameter and 109 feet in circumference at the base. It contains enough timber to build 120 average-size houses.

Tallest tree: Another giant sequoia holds the record for the tallest tree. It is 367 feet tall, 62 feet taller than the Statue of Liberty.

Heaviest and lightest wood: The South African black ironwood tree has the heaviest wood, while the tropical American balsawood tree has the lightest wood.

Smallest fruit: The wolffia plant produces the smallest fruit. Each one-seeded fruit is about the size of a single grain of ordinary table salt. The wolffia is a tiny water plant.

Largest fruit: Records change annually, but currently a 1,061-pound pumpkin holds the title.

Smallest seed: Certain rain forest orchids produce seeds weighing only 35 millionths of an ounce, which are dispersed into the air like minute dust particles.

Largest seed: The coco-de-mer palm tree has seeds up to 12 inches long, almost 3 feet in circumference, and weighing up to 40 pounds.

What is the tallest clock in the world? (Take your time with this one.)

The tallest and most visible clock in the world is Big Ben in London, England, which is 320 feet high. A close second is the Campanile in Venice, Italy, which is 315 feet high, and the third tallest is the Sather Tower at the University of California at Berkeley, which is 307 feet high.

Big Ben, which is in a tower at the east end of the Houses of

Parliament, is noted for its accuracy and for its bell, which weighs 13 tons. When it was installed in 1859, the bell was named after the commissioner of works at the time, Sir Benjamin Hall. Eventually, the name Big Ben became synonymous with the clock rather than the bell.

The majestic Campanile in Venice was originally built as a military watchtower and lighthouse, and eventually rose to a height of 300 feet. Without warning, it collapsed in 1902. It was rebuilt to its present height in 1912. Visitors to this massive brick tower have a breathtaking view of the waterways and rooftops of Venice.

The Sather Tower at the University of California at Berkeley was patterned after the Venice Campanile. The clock faces are 17 feet in diameter and the largest in the state. The numerals are cast bronze and the hands are Sitka spruce. The clock is run by a 40-volt battery that is 20 feet long.

FACTOIDS

Big Ben has four faces, or dials, each facing in a different direction and each having 365 panes of glass, one for every day of the year. Each dial is 23 feet in diameter, the numbers are almost 2 feet high, and the minute hands are 14 feet long.

The 61 bells in the Sather Tower range in weight from 349 pounds to almost 12,000 pounds. Together, they comprise five chromatic octaves. Although the Sather Tower bells are normally played every day, they remain silent during final examinations.

After the collapse of the original Venice Campanile, the rebuilt tower was christened on April 25, 1912, exactly 1,000 years after the original structure was begun.

The original Campanile in Venice was built in the tenth century and its roof was sheathed with bronze. During the day it reflected the sun's rays and served as a beacon for sailors.

It is said that the ghost of a disgruntled student has haunted the Sather Tower since the 1930s. A legend says that students can call on the ghost for help during finals because it still holds a grudge against the university.

A light on the top of the tower housing Big Ben is lit whenever the House of Commons is in session.

Although we admire clock towers today, they were often built for reasons having nothing to do with appearance. In fact the word "campanile" means "bell tower" because bell ringing was one of the early uses for these towers.

The Venice Campanile was originally built as a military watchtower for the nearby dock. It also functioned as a lighthouse. The tower had five bells, each with a different message. The loudest bell announced the beginning of the workday, one rang the hours of the day, one called senators to the palace, one summoned judges, and the smallest bell announced the executions of prisoners held within the tower walls. This last bell was called *il Maleficio*, or "the evil one."

The Campanile has had many famous visitors, including Galileo, Goethe, and Emperor Frederick III of the Holy Roman Empire, who rode his horse up the tower. Today's visitors to the tower do not have to contend with horses. They ride a modern elevator that whisks them up to the tower's viewing platform.

When the Panama Canal was built, was it just cut through the land or did they have to build a concrete bottom and sides? (A revolutionary idea.)

The builders of the Panama Canal just cut through the land. They did not build a concrete bottom or sides. However, they did build dams to create lakes and used concrete to construct the locks.

King Charles I of Spain had proposed a canal route through the Isthmus of Panama in 1534 but nothing came of it. Then in 1881, Ferdinand de Lesseps, who had supervised the excavation of the Suez Canal, formed a company that started cutting a sea-level channel through the Isthmus of Panama. The company collapsed in 1889 because of bad planning, accusations of fraud, and most of all, disease.

Before the United States could build a canal in Panama, it had to receive permission from the Panamanian government. President Theodore Roosevelt was instrumental in inciting a successful Panamanian revolution. The revolutionary leaders had promised to give the United States control of the canal zone if the revolution succeeded.

In the past, the main obstacle to building the canal had been the prevalence of yellow fever. Americans Walter Reed and William Gorgas realized the relationship between mosquitoes and yellow fever and started a campaign to destroy the mosquitoes. As a result, they conquered the affliction of yellow fever and reduced the death rate by almost 97 percent.

In 1907 President Theodore Roosevelt selected George Goethals as the chief engineer of the canal project. The obstacles facing Goethals were not only the formidable physical tasks of completing such a large endeavor, but also housing and feeding over 30,000 workers. Seven years later the first ship passed through the canal and President Woodrow Wilson appointed George Goethals as the first governor of the Canal Zone.

FACTOIDS

The largest ship that can pass through the canal cannot be more than 965 feet long and 106 feet wide, and cannot draw more than $39\frac{1}{2}$ feet of water. Larger ships cannot pass through the locks.

Over 5,600 men died while building the Panama Canal. Today it takes 8,000 workers to run and maintain the canal.

In 1979 control of the Panama Canal passed from the United States to a joint agency of the United States and Panama. On January 1, 2000, Panama will have complete and independent control of the canal.

A palindrome is a word or sentence that reads the same forward or backward. The following summary of the Panama Canal is a palindrome: "A man, a plan, a canal, Panama!" It reads the same in either direction.

The canal locks raise and lower ships a total of 85 feet.

It takes a ship an average of 33 hours to travel the length of the canal but it can cut thousands of nautical miles off the routes ships had to take before the canal was built.

DID YOU KNOW?

The Panama Canal is just one of the world's famous canals. The Suez Canal, which links the Red Sea to the Mediterranean Sea, is the world's largest and is just over 100 miles long. Over 120,000 workers died during its construction. There are also the famous canals of Venice, Italy, and those in the city of Amsterdam in the Netherlands.

Not many people know that ancient China's Grand Canal was 1,107 miles long. Started in 540 B.C., it took over 1,800 years to complete. The canal linked the city of Hangchou in Chekiang province to Peking.

A lesser known but fascinating canal system was the one built in Venice, California, in the early part of this century. Gondolas moved slowly past stately homes as they glided quietly along the two-mile canal system.

However, in the late 1920s the "Age of Progress" began and the growing city needed more roads. Officials decided to fill in the canals. As the first loads of dirt were dumped into a drained canal, hundreds of angry citizens jumped in and started shoveling the dirt out as fast as it was coming in, but to no avail. By the end of 1929 all of the canals had been filled in and paved over with asphalt.

Perhaps there is some kind of lesson here. Is it possible for ordinary citizens to shovel back the tide of technical progress or must they surrender to its inevitable onslaught?

What are the seven natural wonders of the world? (Will wonders never cease?)

There are many sources that list the seven natural wonders of the world and each list is different. However, the wonders that occur on most of these lists are:

1. The Grand Canyon (Arizona)

2. Yosemite Valley (California)

3. Mount Everest (Nepal)

4. Nile River (North Africa)

5. Niagara Falls (United States/Canada)

6. Victoria Falls (Zimbabwe, Africa)

7. Harbor of Rio de Janeiro (Brazil)

Four other likely candidates are:

1. Great Barrier Reef (Australia)

2. Caves in France and Spain

3. Paricutin (volcano in Mexico)

4. Rainbow Bridge National Monument (Utah)

When the Empire State Building was completed in 1931, a new list called the "Seven Wonders of the Modern World" included:

1. Pyramids (Egypt)

2. Leaning tower of Pisa (Italy)

3. Church of Hagia Sophia (Turkey)

4. Taj Mahal (India)

5. Washington Monument (Washington, D.C.)

6. Eiffel Tower (France)

7. Empire State Building (New York)

Among the many "wonders of the world" lists is a compilation of the world's wonders that the United Nations plans to protect and preserve. Qualifying sites must have outstanding global value and be either a "natural" wonder, such as Australia's Great Barrier Reef, or a "cultural" wonder, such as the Chartres Cathedral in France. The Statue of Liberty is one of the hundreds of sites listed.

FACTOIDS

The Tibetan and Nepali names for Mount Everest both mean "Goddess Mother of the World."

From 1921 to 1952 there were 10 attempts to reach the summit of Mount Everest. They all failed. Finally, in 1953 Sir Edmund Hillary of New Zealand and Tenzing Norgay of Nepal reached the summit.

The tightrope walker Blondin crossed the 1,100-foot span across Niagara Falls on a tightrope 160 feet above the water. He did this a number of times: blindfolded, in a sack, pushing a wheelbarrow, on stilts, and carrying a man on his back (we don't know the name of his fearless passenger).

Before the arrival of the Spaniards in our country, the Paiute Indians called the Grand Canyon "Mountain Lying Down." The Spaniards who first saw the canyon named it "Gran Canon," which is how it is still known today.

A courageous one-armed army veteran, Major John Wesley Powell, and nine companions were the first men to navigate the Colorado River 1,000 miles through the Grand Canyon. They had flimsy boats, few rations, and endured many hardships. Three men died on the journey.

DID YOU KNOW?

Each of the seven wonders of the natural world has its own legends. Stories of courage, tragedy, deprivation, and even humor. But perhaps one of the most interesting stories is that of the Niagara Falls daredevils who were willing to risk their lives for a moment of fame. They went over the falls in a barrel.

The first person to go over the falls in a barrel and survive was Annie Taylor, who performed the amazing feat in 1901. She wore a special harness inside a wooden barrel that was towed into the mainstream of the river and cut loose. After going down the falls and slamming into numerous rocks, she was pulled from the barrel 17 minutes later. Upon emerging, the slightly dazed Annie said, "No one ought ever do that again!"

The day she went over the falls Annie claimed she was just 43 years old. However, historical records proved that she was actually 63 years old at the time.

An Englishman, Bobby Leach, was another survivor of the falls. Although he had used a steel barrel, he still spent six months in the hospital recovering from numerous fractures and injuries. At age 67 he went on a tour of Australia. While walking on a New Zealand street he slipped on an orange peel and fell. Complications led to the amputation of his leg. Unfortunately, he got gangrene poisoning and died. A plunge from Niagara Falls could not kill him but a simple orange peel did.

Why is the Tower of Pisa leaning and will anyone ever straighten it?

A bell tower was built in the town of Pisa, Italy, in 1174 near a church in Cathedral Square. It was the final structure in the city's cathedral complex and was made of white marble. It was supposed to be eight stories (185 feet) high. However, after the third floor was completed, the building started to sink because of the marshy, unstable soil. As they continued construction, workers tried to compensate for the lean by making the new stories slightly taller on the short side. However, the extra construction material made it sink even more. Since that time, the tower has leaned a little bit more each year. Today the 185-foot tower leans at a 10-degree angle and is now about 17 feet out of perpendicular.

This 800-year-old tower looks as if it defies the laws of gravity and is an extremely popular tourist attraction. More than 700,000 tourists climbed to the top in 1989, but no visitors have been allowed to climb the structure since then. Although this resulted in the city of Pisa losing millions of dollars in tourist revenue each year, it was deemed necessary for safety reasons. Tourists were banned because a similar bell tower had collapsed without warning in 1989.

Today an international commission of experts has agreed to save the famous Tower of Pisa. Eight years of effort to correct the tilt have only changed it one inch. A plan to dismantle the tower stone by stone and then rebuild it on more solid ground has also been rejected. Current plans are to correct the tilt to about 5 degrees.

FACTOIDS

Because the tower tilted in different directions during the first stages of construction, it has become curved like a banana and can never be truly upright.

Various wars took away money slated for the tower's construction, which was halted a number of times. It actually took 200 years before the tower was finished.

The tower walls are 13 feet wide, and you must climb 300 steps to reach the top.

It is often said that Galileo dropped a cannonball and a wooden ball of the same size from the top of the tower to prove that balls of different weights fall at the same rate. However, this story has been proven to be untrue.

The first bells were added when the third floor was completed, probably because it was designed as a bell tower and because builders were unsure if they could continue construction because of the leaning.

There are seven bells in the tower tuned to a musical scale. The largest bell weighs $3\frac{1}{2}$ tons. The oldest bell is named Pasquarreccia.

In a war with Florence, Pisans lost a major sea battle because they were betrayed by their own count, Count Ugolino della Gherardesca. Citizens locked the count and his family in the tower of Gualandi and then threw the key into the Arno River. The count and his family died of starvation in the tower.

DID YOU KNOW?

Pisa became a Roman colony around 180 B.C. yet survived the collapse of the Roman Empire to remain a principal urban center and flourishing center of commerce. Because of its participation in the Crusades, it gained valuable contacts with Syrian traders and eventually rivaled Genoa and Venice.

Later defeated by the Genoese fleet, Pisa still became a busy center of woolen manufacturing and was also the chief port of Tuscany.

The Tower of Pisa was originally designed to show the entire world how wealthy the city of Pisa was. The city's fortunes eventually turned and the entire town was sold to the city of Florence.

Although the town never managed to regain its former wealth, the citizens of this small city in Italy are still showing off their tower.

What is the largest museum in the world? (From the Spirit of Saint Louis to The Star-Spangled Banner.)

If we talk about museums in the most general sense, then it is the Smithsonian Institution in Washington, D.C. It has well over 160 million items and a staff of 6,000. The Smithsonian is actually a complex of 16 different museums, including the National Museum of Natural History, the National Air and Space Museum, the National Gallery of Art, and the National Museum of History and Technology.

However, if we talk about single museums, then the largest in the world is the American Museum of Natural History in New York

City, which houses over 30 million artifacts and has more than 3 million visitors a year.

The Louvre in Paris, France, is one of the largest art museums in the world and houses over 400,000 works of art. Not only does it have an unsurpassed collection of fifteenth-to nineteenth-century French paintings, it also houses the antiquities that Napoleon brought from Egypt.

The Russian State Hermitage Museum in Saint Petersburg, which sometimes claims to have the largest museum collection in the world, houses a rich assortment of European paintings and extensive collections of Asian art.

The Smithsonian was founded in 1846 when James Smithson, an English scientist, bequeathed funds to the United States. This money is held in trust "for the increase and diffusion of knowledge."

Among its many exhibits, the Smithsonian has the Wright brothers' 1903 airplane, Lindbergh's *Spirit of Saint Louis*, Chuck Yeager's *Bell X-1* rocket plane, the *Apollo 11* command module, and a moon rock. It also houses Benjamin Franklin's printing press, Alexander Graham Bell's experimental telephone, and the American flag that inspired Francis Scott Key to write our national anthem, *The Star-Spangled Banner*. The flag is currently being meticulously restored.

FACTOIDS

Although people tend to think of museums as cultural sites exhibiting great works of art and historical artifacts, our country is full of unique private museums.

The American Police Hall of Fame and Museum in Miami, Florida, has a bloody guillotine, an electric chair, skulls showing entry wounds, and bricks from the Chicago garage where the Saint Valentine's Day massacre occurred on February 14, 1929.

The Gourd Museum in Angier, North Carolina, displays a Last Supper picture made out of gourd seeds, a gourd xylophone, and gourd lamps.

Medical monstrosities are housed in the Philadelphia College of Physicians' Mutter Museum. Interested physicians can see not only a display of numerous objects swallowed and surgically removed but also the soap woman, who died in 1792 and was buried in soil containing chemicals that turned her into soap.

Specialty museums include Frederick's Bra Museum in Hollywood, California; the Museum of Whiskey History in Bardstown, Kentucky; the Wheels Museum in Woodhull, Illinois, where you can see a collection of spark plugs and gearshift knobs; and the Museum of Questionable Medical Devices in Minneapolis, Minnesota, which boasts a prostate warmer, an abdominal brain, and an ultraviolet comb.

DID YOU KNOW?

Historically, museums are not very old. During the Renaissance, wealthy individuals kept private collections of art and artifacts as a symbol of prestige. However, the first recorded case of a collection being turned over to a public body did not occur until 1523 when two Venetian brothers bequeathed their private collection to the Venetian republic.

Oxford University's Ashmolean Museum opened in 1683. This was the first time a building was constructed for the sole purpose of housing a collection of art and artifacts. This museum has the honor of being the oldest museum in the world still in use today.

The British Museum, the Louvre, and the Vatican City's Capitoline Museum all opened in the eighteenth century. After that, museums started cropping up all over the world.

We often forget about the treasures housed in a museum. If you want to do something different for diversion, visit a public museum. You might find it both educational and fun.

More questions?
Try these websites.

WORLD ALMANAC

http://cirrus.sprl.umich.edu/wxnet/

This is an Internet world almanac covering everything from architecture to disasters to a chronology of historical events.

Exploring the Internet

Many websites allow you to find information on the Internet by searching on keywords. I know of over 50 such sites, but rather than list them all, I'll just give you 5 that I've found to be most helpful.

ALTAVISTA
http://www.altavista.com/

HOT BOT
http://www.hotbot.com/

YAHOO
http://www.yahoo.com/

INFOSEEK
http://www.infoseek.com/

LYCOS
http://www.lycos.com/

To use a search tool effectively, you must try to be as precise as possible. For example, let's say you want to find a recipe for chocolate fudge cake.

If you search on "cake" you'll get a list of over half a million links (540,830 to be exact). If you are a little more specific and enter "chocolate cake" you'll see a list of over 13,000 links. If you next try "chocolate cake recipe" you've narrowed the list down to 222 links but that's still too many to look through. If you enter "chocolate fudge cake recipe" you'll see only 4 links. Of these, 2 simply have references to the cake while the other 2 are recipes.

If you run into trouble when looking for an item, try synonyms or related words. For instance, if you are looking for the "origin" of something and having difficulty finding what you want, try using the words "history," "beginning," and "start."

The search tools have explanations or tips on how to use them effectively. Be sure to read them carefully. For instance, when you use AltaVista you must put a sign between the words.

If you search on "chocolate+fudge+cake+recipe" you will find only 4 links. However, if you search on "chocolate fudge cake recipe," the search tool will find every site that has the word "chocolate," every site that has the word "fudge," and so on. You'll end up with 656,740 links.

Finally, don't be surprised when you see what the search tool finds. When I was answering a question relating to jelly and jam, I searched on the word "jam." In addition to the food, I discovered that rock groups share that name. There were many links to "Space Jam" and "Pearl Jam." There may be times when you search on a simple word and end up finding a rock group, a book, or a pornographic site. If that happens, refine your search and try again.

Index